SACRED JOURNEY

SACRED JOURNEY

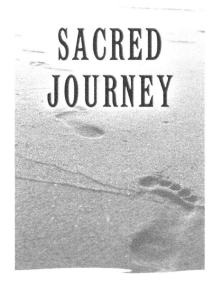

Edgar Cayce, the Bible,
and the Path to
Enlightenment

M.K. Welsch

A.R.E. Press • Virginia Beach • Virginia

A.R.E. Press
215 67th Street
Virginia Beach, VA 23451-2061

ISBN 13: 978-0-87604-862-7

The Holy Bible. Authorized King James Version. New York: Oxford University Press, 1947.

A Note to the Reader

Edgar Cayce's readings are numbered to provide confidentiality. The first set of numbers refers to the individual or group for whom the reading was given. The second set of numbers refers to the number in the series from which the reading was taken. For example, 254-8 identifies the eighth reading that was given to the subject who was assigned #254. All Cayce quotes in this book are given as Gladys Davis typed them with the exception of words originally typed in all caps. Those have been written in italics using both upper and lower case letters as appropriate. When curly brackets appear around a word(s) in italics, they represent what the author has added to the quote for clarity. It is important to remember that the readings were given for individuals even though they carry a universality of content.

Cover design by Christine Fulcher

Contents

The power of the word is limitless. It takes the stuff of your heart and gives it life, filling it with the timeless breath of heaven.
MKW

Acknowledgments

This book could not have been written without the legacy of 14,306 readings bequeathed to us by Edgar Cayce and now archived at the Association for Research and Enlightenment (A.R.E.) in Virginia Beach, VA under the auspices of the Edgar Cayce Foundation. The truths found in those readings have been my beacons, lighting the way along the winding path of a long spiritual journey.

My most sincere and humble thanks to all the members, friends, and supporters of the A.R.E., including those dedicated, loving people who have served on its Board of Trustees, for tending the flame so that the wisdom found in the Edgar Cayce material will keep shining across the ages.

Thanks, too, to the many devoted teachers who have passed through the A.R.E.'s doors, giving of their time and talents to help the rest of us better understand life's purpose: to manifest the love of God and man. I will mention a few in particular who over the years have opened a window to new perspectives and helped deepen my own understanding: Charles Thomas Cayce, Mark Thurston, Kevin Todeschi, and John Van Auken.

I could not have traveled the protracted and sometimes bumpy road as an author without the support of my cherished family and friends. These wonderful traveling companions on life's journey include my "soul sisters" Karen Shwedo and Patricia Abrams and "spiritual brother" Francis "Doc" Moreau, as well as many more good friends such as Teresa Farquhar, Sally and Bill Meadows, Melita DeBellis, and Richard Abrams, who also kindly lent me his publishing expertise. Additional thanks belong to the members of the Saturday Goldsmith Group for their constant, loving support: Shirley and the late Dick Guy, Claudia Donaldson Selby, Beth Hampton, Linda and Danny St. John, and Steve Krawczyk.

My sincerest appreciation also extends to the staff and Governing Council of The Wilderness Society who comprised my work family for so many years and whose idealism continues to inspire me to this day. These courageous wilderness stewards have kept the dream alive, never losing sight of the fact that everyone deserves an opportunity to find peace and renewal in the spiritual cathedrals of the natural world.

Needless to say, I am enormously indebted to the countless authors who have come before me, especially to those whose efforts to promote and explain the truths found in the Cayce material laid the groundwork for the range of topics handled in this book. My thanks in particular to Glenn Sanderfur for his seminal work, *Lives of the Master* and *Edgar Cayce on Jesus and His Church* by Anne Read under the editorship of Hugh Lynn Cayce.

Equally important to note is an unpublished manuscript by the late Janet Highland who in the 1970s handed me a draft chapter on Jesus from a book she hoped to write but was never able to finish. I had hung onto a faded copy of that document all these years, knowing that her beautiful prose and the ideas we had discussed were important, but until now had lacked the opportunity to bring them to light in any meaningful way. The theories promulgated through those long-ago conversations together with ideas advanced in the Edgar Cayce readings were the catalysts which started to raise the curtain on the unique role the Master Jesus had played for the world. Portions of several chapters draw from her groundbreaking approach to the subject.

I will forever be grateful to the gracious and talented professionals at the A.R.E. Press who from the beginning believed in my book and skillfully led me through the twists and turns of the publishing process while making it all look easy. Special thanks belong to my editor Stephanie Pope whose generosity of spirit, insight, and steady hand helped turn an imperfect manuscript into an actual book; Director of Production, Cassie McQuagge, who led the team and kept everything on track; and our gifted Graphic Designer and Typesetter, Cathy Merchand. A special thanks also goes to Linda Caputi of the A.R.E. Library who helped with some of the research in this book.

Finally, these acknowledgments would not be complete without my thanking the army of teachers now in the earth or living on the "the other side" who, through the centuries, have helped transform human consciousness by means of the spiritual legacies they left behind. Among those in the Cayce pantheon are Gladys Davis Turner, who recorded, organized, and protected the original readings, and Hugh Lynn Cayce, who exposed the material to the larger world. Other selfless mentors whose wisdom has informed my work include Joel Goldsmith, Mary Baker Eddy, Eckhart Tolle, and many others—as well as all of the unseen forces which surrounded and guided me as I wrote. This humble scribe could not have written a word without them.

Preface

Every story has a beginning—the precipitating event that kick-starts the action into motion. This book is no exception. It began many years ago when I stumbled across the name Edgar Cayce and read about his life and extraordinary psychic readings during a time when I was searching for more meaning in my life. At first I was leery. Was this some kind of cult or religious scam perpetrated by a skillful con artist out to fool gullible people? I promised myself then that if I ever discovered anything in the work attributed to Cayce or the organization he founded—the Association for Research and Enlightenment—which didn't ring true or deviated from my highest and best sense of what was right, I would run away as fast as possible. I never did.

By the end of his lifetime, the renowned seer Edgar Cayce (1877–1945) had given more than 14,000 psychic readings on subjects ranging from the mundane to the mystical. A humble man with only an eighth-grade education, Cayce hailed from the small town of Hopkinsville in Christian County, Kentucky. Ever since he was a young child, this simple tobacco-country farm boy had demonstrated remarkable psychic abilities. Luckily for young Edgar he was brought up in a loving family surrounded by people who accepted his prodigious gifts. Cayce always believed his unusual talents to be God-given and decided early on to make it his life's purpose to use those powers for the greater good of humankind.

That decision eventually led him to give psychic readings for thousands of individuals suffering from dis-ease of body, mind, and spirit. They had heard about his remarkable abilities, at first mostly by word of mouth, and approached him in person or by letter, asking for help. Even as the numbers of requests for readings increased and his reputation grew to the point where celebrities and highly placed public officials were seeking out his advice, Cayce made no claims to being someone the world should set apart as special. In fact, he believed that by holding onto the right ideal and making a sincere effort to develop their own gifts, everyone had the innate capacity to do what he did.

It is difficult to imagine the deep faith and personal commitment to service it must have required for Edgar Cayce to set aside the immediate circumstances of his life every day, twice a day, and to lie down on the couch in his office in order to give readings. (And near the end of his life, he was giving multiple readings per day to try to fill the thousands of requests for help from people with loved ones embroiled in the conflict of World War II. Overtaxing his body in this way would take a huge toll on his health, which eventually led to his death.) After lying down and putting aside his conscious mind, Cayce would enter into a semiconscious state, totally unaware of his physical surroundings and the people around him or the words he might utter in answer to their questions. This outgoing but gentle man had to trust that those present in the room conducting and transcribing the reading had his best interests at heart. He also had to hold fast to the conviction that whatever emerged from his unconscious state would do no harm but bless those individuals who needed it most.

Remarkable information came through this sleeping prophet during those daily sessions, including medical prescriptions and advice, information about the history of the human race since the beginning of time, and material on astrology, dreams, world events, planetary sojourns, previous lifetimes, religion, and philosophy to name several. In addition to some of the amazing events that transpired during the time Cayce was actually asleep, such as his proclivity for describing in detail the state of health of people located thousands of miles away, what has always struck me about his body of work is its astonishing breadth and consistency. Taken together the 14,306 readings Edgar Cayce left behind present a formidable record of important but heretofore unknown information. Many decades after his death we have only begun to plumb its depths.

Edgar Cayce was a deeply religious man who read the entire Bible once for every year of his life and attended church regularly, yet many of the ideas articulated in his readings veer away sharply from mainstream religious beliefs. It's easy to overlook the fact that in the 1920s, '30s, and '40s, during the period when Cayce was most productive, topics such as reincarnation, meditation, and astrology were not widely acknowledged or discussed as they might be today. The taproot of the philosophy outlined in the readings is the Christian tradition as defined by the ideal of the Christ, but its branches spread across cultures, traditions, centuries, and the world. The readings paint a picture of history as the story of the movement of consciousness through space and time as human beings seek to fulfill the soul's deep longing to return to its Source, to God.

In the years since Edgar Cayce's passing, numbers of outstanding books and articles have been written expounding on the wealth of information compiled in the readings. And more than a few have served as guideposts on my own spiritual quest. My aim in adding to that library was to try to explain in laymen's terms Cayce's story of the soul and its passage through the earth as viewed through the lens of one particular soul: Jesus of Nazareth. In general, the mystical thread running through the Cayce material begins with Spirit, manifests in the multitudinous religious philosophies the world has embraced throughout history, reaches its apex with the appearance of the second Adam, Jesus, and will culminate one day in the expression of the risen Christ in each and every incarnated soul.

The approach this book takes is to synthesize information scattered among a cross section of the readings with select passages from the Bible, especially the New Testament, in order to highlight the congruity of the two messages. The significance of the Christ sits front and center in the Cayce philosophy, but it is difficult for most people to get their arms around the somewhat presumptuous notion that the man called Jesus really did lay out a pattern others could follow in order to do what he did—a pattern detailed in the most practical way by Edgar Cayce who interpreted the Master's message for people living in the twentieth century and beyond. Despite the challenges posed in trying to decipher some of the convoluted syntax found in many of his readings, Edgar Cayce generally did not speak in platitudes. He was direct, solved real problems, and presented seekers with a clear plan of action for making spiritual progress.

My aim in integrating Jesus' parables and teachings with the wisdom culled from Edgar Cayce's unconscious mind was to merge the two records into a more cohesive whole. Seeing the ideas laid out side by side might help fill in some of the missing pieces of the puzzle about why the Prince of Peace came to earth and what he did while he was here. The Cayce information changes the picture of the Christ from an "idol" to be worshipped from afar into an ideal and presence within, and the Master soul, Jesus, to our elder brother and teacher who came to show us that we, too, have the ability to advance to the same level of spiritual understanding and expression he had achieved. My secondary objective was to try to unravel some of the symbolism coloring the Old and New Testaments, which supports this more inclusive description of Jesus' words and work. Hopefully the result will allow others, perhaps for the first time, to catch a glimpse of the greater purpose for humanity's sojourn in the earth and begin to understand its meaning to the destiny of the soul.

Since Edgar Cayce never attributed any of his achievements to himself, when I employ phrases such as "Cayce says" or "according to Cayce," I am referring to the words that came through him as he slept while tapping into the universal mind. I have placed quotation marks around those passages lifted directly from the readings as well as selections from the King James Version of the Bible. In other cases I paraphrase Cayce's words to try to help clarify their meaning while attempting as far as humanly possible to stay true to the original intent of the reading. The specific readings that appear in the book and references for segments quoted from the Bible remain with the text; citations drawn from secondary sources are listed in the footnotes.

I hope, dear reader, you will join me in fearlessly venturing into the uncharted territory of this sacred journey to find the God within.

M.K. Welsch
August 2015

Know Thyself

Introduction

Let the gates of heaven open on earth—
for here is where we experience our
God. MKW

There is a God whom we can know consciously. Deep within the recesses of every human heart is a divine spark—a candle flame of love—available to safely guide us through this sojourn on earth. And with every breath we take, we have the opportunity to fan this spark into a glowing flame, spreading enough light and warmth to illuminate and comfort the entire world. This book is one of those small flames. And when it merges with the light dwelling at the center of your own being, together we can ignite the alchemical fire that will transform the base metal of pain and suffering into gold.

The story of humanity's journey on earth began millions of years ago, when the morning stars sang together as the Source of the created universe sought to express itself. Mystical traditions refer to this impulse as the Creator seeking companionship. Boundless spirit, desiring to mirror itself in an infinite variety of thought-forms, began to create; and as individual expressions of the totality were spun off, living souls emerged. All too soon, however, these souls would choose to distance themselves from their Creator and in the process forget who they really were.

Look closely at the words of the Master and listen well within. The message of Christ, the *Christos* or anointed one, reflects a simple yet profound truth. We are children of the Most High. Our bodies are formed of the dust of earth but animated by the very breath of the Godhead itself. And no greater triumph exists for the human race than to recognize life as the outpouring of Spirit into form and collectively manifest that reality.

Disclosing the presence of the good news of Immanuel or God-with-us was the central mission and earth-shattering achievement of the man called Jesus whose destiny was to lead the lost souls wandering the earth back to an awareness of their supernatural origins and identity. His journey through this plane, lifetime after lifetime, resulted in the demonstration of an astounding reality: God and man are one. And the feat of achieving complete, *conscious* union with the divinity he had realized within himself ordained him a Christ. Therein lies our purpose too.

Human beings are on a spiritual journey spanning multiple lifetimes and sacred in its intent—a story retold with every birth. If the route we are traveling feels familiar, it is, for it follows the footprints left behind during many previous incarnations of soul work on this planet. Earth is the platform by which we will be able to remember our divine heritage and shine the sacred light of our God-selves into the dim recesses of a third-dimensional world. Today presents us with the opportunity to rediscover our Source, He-who-has-no-name as described by the Hebrew scriptures, and receive the great key to life—the secret words whispered to Moses when he ventured up to the top of Mount Sinai: "I am that I am."

Twenty-one centuries ago an unparalleled spiritual teacher promised that the same state of divine awareness he had achieved was attainable by everyone. Yet soon after the three brief years of his public ministry ended, spiritual amnesia set in and new, mind-based interpretations of the Christ-idea this savior preached were transformed into the belief that time spent on this planet was no more than an exhausting climb toward the "next" life, punctuated by moments of joy and pain.

While most of us no longer worship idols like the golden calf the Israelites molded in the desert, we steadfastly cling to the notion of a God fashioned in the image and likeness of ourselves. Rigid and remote, this deity demands strict obedience and constant invocations before it will deign to heal or offer us respite and salvation. Like tired, scared children stumbling around in the dark, we keep looking outside of ourselves for help, begging this Supreme Being to intercede on our behalf. But help seldom seems to arrive. Hope is the final victim of our man-made God.

It does not have to be this way.

Scattered before us are the seeds of ancient wisdom sown by holy teachers since the dawn of time and ripe for harvest once we are ready to digest the fruits of their work. The route home has always been lit by the inner radiance of those who walked the straight and narrow way, by the few who discovered sacredness in the only place it ever existed—in themselves.

Sacred Journey is the tale of humanity's journey in consciousness back to paradise. "Let there be light!" was the command of Genesis. And now is the moment to dispel the shadows in our thinking and reignite the holy fire that will burn away the dross of outmoded ideas and attitudes and will lead to a higher level of understanding. Today presents us with the opportunity to know God aright by basking in loving contact with the great "I am."

This book is one tiny light illuminating the path back to our Source. You are the next one.

Chapter 1
The Long Road Home

For a man is a little lower than the angels,
yet was made that he might become
the companion of the Creative Forces;
and thus was given—in the breath of
life—the individual soul, the stamp
of approval as it were of the Creator;
with the ability to know itself to be itself, and to make itself, as one with the
Creative Forces—*irrespective* of other
influences.   1456-1

Every moment spent on earth has profound meaning. We are here to
allow "the divine purpose of the universe to unfold."[1] Human history
is a tale told through countless iterations of the soul's journey back to

[1]Eckhart Tolle, *The Power of Now* (Novato, CA: New World Library, 1999), 109.

God awareness—a record of the human race and its pilgrimage through the earth on a quest to find the Holy Grail of its God-self again. The time has come to remember who we really are. Consciousness is expanding, and each of us plays a vital role in its universal evolution.

Masters throughout the ages have pointed out the way back to the Godhead—the wellspring of our existence and true abode. The great teachers that were Shankara, Buddha, Lao Tze—and every other awakened individual able to directly experience the presence of God on this plane—have helped map out the route for this spiritual adventure, which began so long ago. So, too, did the work of a twentieth-century psychic and mystic named Edgar Cayce shed new light on the soul's tenure on earth by offering a more expansive and multifaceted view of humankind and its passage through time and space in the search for God. His legacy of more than 14,000 readings focused extensively on the journey of one particular soul, which more than any other, had discovered the way back to a state of paradisiacal harmony with its Creator and then chose to serve as the transparency by which others might experience that reality here and now. By fully reuniting with the central principle of the universe, this soul established the pattern for salvation and in the process literally became the law: Jesus of Nazareth.

For Christians especially, the movement back to God consciousness was demonstrated most powerfully by this one man whose life story has mesmerized and inspired billions of people around the globe. Jesus' unsurpassed mastery over sin and the downward pull of materiality had ordained him a *Christos* or Christ, the anointed one. And for twenty-one centuries his followers have venerated him as God itself. But the belief that he alone was divine corrupted the core truth this deliverer had come to reveal. God-with-us was the message the Son of Man had disclosed to the masses and proven with the miracles attributed to his ministry. Yet ever since his death and resurrection those who dreaded the impact this truth might have on the status quo have tried mightily to suppress his astounding revelation, burying it under the weight of thousands of years of theological constructs, religious iconography, and fear. But the good news Jesus preached has refused to die. The evidence of its vitality lies in the remarkable staying power of his words.

The New Testament narrative about an historical figure named Jesus of Nazareth is the tale of a soul who had reached the pinnacle of divine awareness and entered into a state of being beyond the scope of mortal limitation and law. As such his extraordinary achievement and benediction speak to souls everywhere by calling on them to wake up and embrace their heritage as the sons and daughters of Spirit traversing this planet on a sacred journey homeward. Our elder brother became a Savior when he successfully completed his soul's mission of unveiling the truth of Immanuel to the human race. But the job had taken eons to complete. It would be a protracted struggle to attain the heights of a Christ able to release the lost souls estranged from their Maker from ignorance and the viselike grip of a material world. The effort had begun millions of years ago.

Evolution of a Soul

In the first cause, or principle, all is perfect. In the creation of soul, we find the portion may become a living soul and equal with the Creator. To reach that position, when separated, must pass through all stages of development, that it may be one with the Creator.   900-10

The soul that became Jesus had trod the globe during many lifetimes under different guises before its final incarnation as the Nazarene rabbi. Like the rest of us, Jesus had stood center stage during these previous appearances in the earth, playing the starring role in his soul's evolution through time and space. His earliest incarnation is reported to have been as Amilius, a being who abided in spirit form in a place called Atlantis more than ten million years ago. Edgar Cayce explains: " . . . Individuals in the beginning were more of thought-forms than individual entities with personalities as seen in the present . . . " (364-10) Known as the first begotten of God, Amilius was also the first soul to become aware that the original divine plan for creation had somehow gone awry.

Before time as we count it now and the human body as it appears today, souls—unique aspects of the divine—manifested solely in spirit form. Fashioned to be companions with the Creator, these beings were the mirrors which allowed Spirit to reflect back to itself. But things began to diverge from the primordial plan and veer off track when the wayward mind entered the picture and an "involution" of spirit into the material realm occurred. Souls originally spun off from the Godhead in spirit form slowed down their vibrational frequencies and began to play with matter, using thought and free will to create new worlds for themselves. It did not take long for these rookie "creators" to become enamored with their own formations and start yearning to experience material sensations. The desire to feel various sense impressions kept growing stronger until it led to a startling mistake. These nonmaterial beings of light, which until then had been completely unencumbered and free to move about the universe, pushed themselves into matter.

At first the situation appeared temporary and for a while spirits were able to enter and depart the physical realm as they pleased. Eventually, however, captivated by this new dimension and seeking greater and greater sensual pleasures, they became completely encased in physicality and no longer were able to leave at will to reside among the higher celestial vibrations. Souls were trapped. Worse, tantalized by the fascinating exercise of generating new creations in the province of lower and slower vibrations, they turned away from the light and grew increasingly distant from the transcendental force out of which they had emanated. As time passed, souls would completely forget their spiritual origins and begin to see themselves as totally separate beings confined by the boundaries of a physical form. And with that sense of limitation, selfishness entered the picture. Incorporeal souls whose true home was the boundless cosmos were stuck—spellbound—in the third dimension, cut off from the light by the inventions of their own minds. Such was the fall from grace of which so many spiritual traditions speak.

Earthbound
ॐ

Myths from around the world recount the remnants of this prehuman era. Some of the mesmerized spirits were so intrigued with matter that they entered and occupied plants and animals, taking on the characteristics of those species. Strange creatures projecting tree limbs and leaves or possessing animal legs, hooves, fish scales, and furry skin now inhabited material form. Edgar Cayce indicates that universal legends about mermaids, centaurs, satyrs and other exotic beings are the vestiges of this far distant past. The Bible also describes one group of entities intensely enmeshed in materiality as the sons and daughters of men or "Sons of Belial" who assumed a variety of forms, including as the Nephilim (giants) portrayed in the Old Testament. The readings refer to this particular group of souls as " . . . those that sought more the gratifying, the satisfying, the use of material things for self, *without* thought or consideration as to . . . the hardships in the experiences of others. Or, in other words, as we would term it today, they were without a standard of morality." (877-26)

All was not lost however, for the Father–Mother God desired to prepare a way out for the souls that had gone astray. " . . . For He hath not willed that any soul should perish, but hath prepared a way of escape," (262-84) assert the Cayce readings. Recognizing the dilemma the entangled spirits faced, the first begotten of the divine, Amilius, was moved to action. He and a group of souls not yet hopelessly locked into physicality determined they would provide a way to free other souls from their entrapment in matter. The law of limitation and self-aggrandizement characterized the Sons of Belial and their activities, but the souls Amilius led were different and offered a sharp contrast to the "fallen angels." His group comprised those who understood and followed the Law of One because they still could remember their spiritual origins and intimate relationship with the divine. Together Amilius and his cohorts made the decision to act as guides to help the wayward children reestablish a relationship with their Source. They would lead them back to the presence of God.

The task was not without peril, however. Even Amilius, whose original purpose in entering the earth plane was to help other souls remember their innate divinity, eventually succumbed to the attractions of a material world. According to Edgar Cayce, Amilius " . . . allowed himself to be led in the ways of selfishness . . . " (364-8) When all was said and done, this self-proclaimed leader and principal representative of the Law of One was going to have to find his way out too. Fortunately for the human race its prospective savior never strayed so far afield that he was not able to extricate himself. Despite myriad temptations to abandon the Herculean task, the first begotten of God continued working lifetime after lifetime—advancing in most but occasionally losing ground—to construct the pattern by which the soul would finally be released from its imprisonment in matter and return to God awareness.

In His Image
ক্লেন্ড

Hence, every form of life that man sees in a material world is an essence or manifestation of the Creator; not the Creator, but a manifestation of a first cause . . .   5753-1

Meanwhile it had become painfully evident to the Sons of God that their success was predicated upon creating a new type of bodily structure. The animal-like bodies with which the lost souls were intertwined were not adequate for their long-term habitation nor the arduous task of reigniting the divine spark—raising up the individuated spirit—and liberating it. Clearly souls enshrouded in matter needed access to a different type of vehicle—a more spiritualized and perfect physical form—in order to be able to break free. A new body would allow them to experience the third dimensional world yet still maintain a connection to higher awareness and their true nature.

The key was to design a way for souls enmeshed in a physical world to recognize their estrangement from the divine while at the same time reawakening in them the conscious desire to return to companionship with their Creator. This redesigned body became the first of what is called a human being or Homo sapiens: " . . . man's indwelling as man in the form of flesh in this material world . . . "(364-5) as described in the Edgar Cayce readings. Hundreds of thousands of years after spirit became ensnared by matter, a more advanced form of physicality emerged. And the soul, which had first entered the earth plane as Amilius and later would return as Jesus of Nazareth, was the soul which would inhabit the earliest prototypical human form.

A glorious period dawned as Amilius and the other Sons of God prepared the way for the entry of a physical *human* into the earth. The Cayce information reports that the morning stars sang together in the glory of the coming of the Lord as divinity was reflected in flesh; " . . . when the Sons of God came together to announce to Matter a way being opened for the souls of men, the souls of God's creation, to come again to the awareness of their error." (2156-2) The offspring of divinity, fallen away in consciousness from their Source, now had access to the most effective vehicle by which to rise up to those celestial heights again. Souls would have the pathway to freedom embodied in the very forms they carried around with them. Hope abounded. But it would be a long and difficult journey home.

Adam

> ... He, our Lord was the first among those that put on mortality that there might be the opportunity for those forces that had erred in spiritual things ...   5749-5

The presence in the biblical account of not one but two creation stories culminating in the appearance of a human being on earth is an enigma which has intrigued biblical scholars for centuries. According to Edgar Cayce, the first version of the story found in Genesis refers to the original formation of the soul and describes a being made in the image and likeness of God who, by virtue of its emanation from a divine source, had dominion over the rest of creation. The second rendition pertains to the creation of the physical body of man fashioned from the dust of the earth. After the materialization of this outer form occurs, God breathes the breath of the life force into its nostrils and a living being emerges: Adam. The readings describe the appearance of Adam this way—

> When there was in the beginning a man's advent into the plane known as earth, and it became a living soul, amendable to the laws that govern the plane itself as presented, the Son of man entered the earth as the first man. Hence the Son of man, the Son of God, the Son of the first Cause, making manifest in a material body. This was not the first spiritual influence, spiritual body, spiritual manifestation in the earth, but the first man—flesh and blood; the first carnal house, the first amenable body to the laws of the plane in its position in the universe.   5749-3

Further, the emergence of human beings in this new material "home" for the soul built according to a divine blueprint was not an isolated incident. The readings indicate that souls in humanoid form entered in five different places at the same time, and the form called Adam resided in just one of them. Other Sons of God assisted in the job of leading spirit's entrance into these newly formed earth–bodies with each entry representing a different race: red, yellow, white, black, and brown. The locations were Eden, Atlantis, the Andes, western America, and India, although the continents and oceans were not in the same configurations as they are today. Interestingly Islamic tradition also states that Adam was created from red, white, and black clay. And the Jewish Talmud notes that dust was gathered throughout the whole earth to create Adam's body, which resulted in the homogeneity of the multicolored human race.[2] The Adam soul, however, remained the leader of the Sons of God and set the pattern for those who had entered in the other four areas, serving as the primary interface between God and all the souls trapped in matter. The Cayce information also ascribes to Adam the establishment of the " . . . altars upon which the sacrifices of the field and forest . . . "(364-4) were made as religious tributes to the divine.

While a literal reading of the Old Testament and most recognized biblical scholarship give no shrift to the kind of prehistory recounted in the Cayce material, other ancient sources of wisdom paint a slightly different picture. Gnostic Mandaean literature mentions a mystic or secret Adam who preceded the human Adam by countless years and the Hermeticists apparently held similar beliefs. The Kabbalist Zohar discusses two Adams as well. The first was "a divine being" who stepped forth "from the highest original darkness, creating the second, or earthly, Adam in His own image."[3] Likewise, ancient Jewish mystics claimed that "God first created the Heavenly Man, the Archetype, who filled the universe and served as the pattern on which it was made."[4]

---

[2] *Encyclopedia Judaica*, (16 volumes) (Jerusalem: Keter Publishing House, 1972), II:241.

[3] Manly P. Hall, *An Encyclopedic Outline of Masonic, Hermetic, Quabbalistic and Roscicrucian Symbolical Philosophy* (Los Angeles: Philosophical Research Society, Inc., 1957), CXXVI.

[4] Hugh Schonfield, ed., *The Authentic New Testament* (New York: New American Library, 1958), n. 59, 309.

In the Garden
⁂

The mystical passage of the human race through the earth experience begins in the first book of the Bible with the Garden of Eden and the baffling story of Adam and his helpmeet Eve whose choices lead to a paradise lost. Here is where the record of the soul's movement through the material dimension sets sail. It is worth noting that the Cayce material describes the Bible, as a whole, as the history of humanity's spiritual development and search for God. The readings regard it as an account of the soul's supernatural origins, its memory lapse and fall, and the long and fitful progression upward to reach a state of divine awareness again. Occasionally the story shows the children of God taking huge leaps forward with the help of some of the highly evolved patriarchs and prophets populating the Old Testament. Yet more often than not, the climb appears daunting and painfully slow. The epic does not reach its apotheosis until one soul attains a state of being never before achieved in the material realm: the full flowering of the Christ spirit in the earth through one man's conscious union with God. The advent of the newly structured Adam–body is what sets this sacred journey into motion.

Helpmeet
⁂

The second chapter of Genesis conveys an interesting moment in the biography of Adam, who dwells in a magnificent garden flourishing with everything he could possibly want or need. But the man is lonely. Realizing the problem, God proceeds to address it by setting aside Adam's conscious mind and causing a deep sleep to come over him. Then the unseen Creative Forces remove one of Adam's ribs and from that bone fashion a separate being—a woman called Eve. Out of the blue and from the innermost depths of Adam's own being, a separate spirit emerges—something born of his deeper, unconscious self. And a new energy, which until that moment had been hidden from human awareness, is released to take form in the world.

This dramatic scene in the creation narrative harks back to the soul's original, formless condition within the cosmos when the very first soul made "in our image, after *our* likeness" emerged from the Godhead. (Gen. 1:26) The biblical allusion to "our" likeness refers to the fact that from the outset souls were created male *and* female. Since the very first soul came into being and began roaming the universe in spirit form, entering the earth plane as an entity named Amilius, it and every other soul had incorporated both polarities. As explained in the Cayce information, only much later did the actual physical separation into the two sexes occur as a means to help souls advance.

The developments in Eden speak to the fact that the male spirit (Adam) and its female counterpart (Eve) were actually two halves of one whole. They were twin souls—coequal reflections of a unique aspect of divinity spun off at the moment of creation. And now the pair would occupy the planet in visible form as material representations of the masculine and feminine polarities. Interestingly, the Old Testament allegory confirms the unity and native equality of the two by describing Eve as an element of Adam taken from his side. Edgar Cayce elaborates further on Eve's purpose for coming into being—

> . . . this as a being came as the companion; and when there was that turning to the within, through the sources of creation, as to make for the helpmeet . . . *then*—from out of self—was brought that as was to be the helpmeet, *not* just a companion of the body . . .
>
> 364-7

More than a bodily companion, Adam's helpmeet Eve is a symbol of that which issues forth from the soul itself to assist humankind along the path back to divine awareness. A previously overlooked aspect of the soul has come into expression in order to aid in its spiritual development.

As with most of the Bible, layer upon layer of meaning infuses the relatively simple story of the glorious garden that once was our home. Running through this tale of a paradise lost are the intertwining elements of the plot which mask profound spiritual truths. First, only by laying aside the mind, putting the outer self to sleep so to speak, can the unseen Creative Forces hidden deep inside us enter into this world. Second, each "half" of the now-split soul, its male and female counterparts, has an individual destiny and specific role to play in the spiritual upliftment of the human race. In that same vein, the Edgar Cayce readings reveal an as yet unrecognized but astonishing fact about Adam's "twin soul," his consort Eve. She will enter the earth again for another significant lifetime at a pivotal moment in human history. It is during the period when the first begotten of God or Adam soul makes its climactic appearance on earth as the Messiah. In that future incarnation the soul known as Eve will return to assist the deliverer in his holy mission by taking on the role of Mary, the mother of Jesus.

The Serpent Beguiled Me

In paradise—humanity's original "perfect" condition—Adam and Eve live in peaceful coexistence and companionship with their God enjoying dominion over every cell of the created universe. The readings state that " . . . in the first was given man and mind [to] subdue the earth in every element . . . all manner of animal in the earth, in the air, under the sea, has been tamed of man . . . "(900–31) As a pot is comprised of and no different from the clay out of which it is shaped, the man and woman embodied the stuff of divinity and as such experienced a state of uninterrupted harmony and bliss. Their Edenic utopia might have continued unabated had the serpent not entered the picture. While it is intriguing and perhaps somewhat comforting to believe a literal talking snake was Eve's tempter, that notion is far too simplistic. The human adventure on this planet was launched by the same forces still at work today: the temptation to misuse the sacred knowledge we possess for self-gratification—Selfishness.

The lamentable events that occurred in the Garden of Eden at the dawn of time actually are a record of the downward movement of human consciousness. Long ago when souls could still perceive their Oneness with the divine and the totality of creation, they chose instead to put their faith in a counterfeit reality: dualism. Understood from its mystical standpoint, the snake in the Bible is the life force found inside each individual—what Eastern mystical teachings refer to as kundalini energy (the serpent). And because every human being is endowed with free will, he or she chooses where to direct this creative spark, deciding either to use these soul forces for the good of the whole or to enhance oneself. Genesis is a fable about how the human race turned away from its divine source and misused its sacred energy as well as a potent reminder about the need to stay alert to the misguided antics of the restless mind. The mistake Adam and Eve made stands as a warning never to pervert the spiritual power to which our souls have access for selfish ends. If we do, it may be to our eternal detriment.

The female (Eve), representing the unconscious, veiled aspect of the human being, becomes aware of a frisson of energy inside her—the serpent. In close touch with this inner life force she soon becomes entranced with the possibility of wielding such a power and, unbeknownst to the outer male aspect (Adam), engages the notion with her mind. But the snake, which is both subtle and cunning, quickly tempts Eve to ignore her innermost guidance and stray outside the boundaries of divine law by seeking to aggrandize herself. It persuades her to ingest the knowledge of good and evil with the promise that she will become as a God. Eve has allowed her mind to grab hold of an idea and convince herself it is true: "I need something more than what I am right now in order to be divine." With her decision to reach for the forbidden fruit and try to add "more" to what she already is, Eve has accepted the principle of duality. She perceives herself as separate and apart from the whole, from God. And the game begins.

Adam and Eve already existed in the midst of perfection as far as the eye could see, but after becoming cognizant of the kundalini energy within, living in attunement with divine order no longer was enough for them. Something mind-made, external to Eve's inner recognition of an uninterrupted state of Oneness, becomes the apple of her eye. She then proceeds to involve Adam in the sorry drama. Thus will the more hidden aspect of ourselves (female) flirt with using the sacred life energy (the serpent) to convince the outer consciousness (male) that we must know more, have more, be more, in order to be whole. " . . . For, it is knowledge misapplied that was the fall—or the confusion—in Eve" (281-63), states the Cayce reading. The irony is that Eve's soul was constituted of divine stuff, and by its very nature encompassed everything she could possibly need or desire, including any knowledge that for the moment appeared to be lacking. Infinity resided within her. But with that singular act of disobedience to her highest sense of awareness,

Eve gave in to the desire for separation from her divine source over attunement with that source. The yen for matter and material form had bewitched the soul again.

Worse, Eve's companion, Adam, follows suit, then accuses his partner of leading him astray. Adam's charge is the earliest known example of the all-too-human tendency to align one's thinking with the thinking of others until together—through the sheer force of the collective mind and will—problems emerge. Thousands of years later, when the same Adam soul incarnates for the last time in Galilee, Jesus of Nazareth will offer a more enlightened perspective on the power of like-mindedness in his teaching about the enormous good that results from two or more gathered together with the ideal of the Christ in mind.

Fig Leaves

According to the Genesis story line, immediately following their rebellious act Adam and Eve suddenly became aware of their physical bodies and sewed fig leaves together to hide their nakedness. Feeling exposed by their blatant disregard of divine law and burgeoning sense of an ego self—a "self" separate and apart from the whole—they make a feeble attempt to keep the naked truth under wraps by covering up their flesh. The two have accepted a universe comprised of good and evil and now perceive creation in a new light. Up to this moment the soul had experienced itself solely in relationship to the divine—as an integral thread bound up in the fabric of the whole. But once a sense of defiant self-consciousness emerges, these same souls begin to view themselves as isolated fragments with a separate existence laid bare for scrutiny by their detachment from the rest of creation. Estranged from their Creator, which literally had placed the universe at their feet, Adam and Eve are ashamed.

Before long the two hear the voice of God who is said to be walking in the garden during the cool of the day, seeking his companions. The deity wonders where Adam and Eve have gone only to find them secreted away. Adam admits that he and his helpmeet had hidden, fearful of coming forward, because they realized they were naked. God bluntly responds by asking Adam, "Who told thee that thou wast naked? Hast thou eaten of the tree, whereof I commanded thee that thou shouldest not eat?" (Gen. 3:11) Neither the man nor the woman has a ready answer and soon the jig is up. It is evident to the Creator his beloved progeny have ingested the fruit of the forbidden tree and now know the "two-ness" of separation—a transgression whose penalty is far-reaching and inescapable.

The gates of paradise will be forever closed to Adam and Eve and to every human being who believes in an existence apart from the divine totality—anyone who accepts the deception of duality instead of the truth of the Law of One. And the serpent or divine energy animating the created world will continue to crawl on its belly, eating the dust of the lower vibrations of matter until these heirs to heaven choose to raise it up again. Further, in navigating the fallen, intensely material, and dualistic circumstances to which the soul had descended, human beings are destined to experience enduring hardship where childbirth is painful and man must till the soil.

Unbridled Hope
ᏜᏁ

Q. When did the knowledge come to Jesus that he was to be the Savior of the world?
A. When he fell in Eden.   2067-7

Adam and Eve's impatience with the original divine plan of eternal attunement with their Creator results in a fall in consciousness from an effortless state of at-One-ment into the chaos of a mortal world subject to the laws of cause and effect. Once they had crossed the border into the wilderness of duality and self-centered thinking—believing this is good, this is bad; I want this, I don't want that—the reality of divine perfection, though still ever-present, was largely forgotten. Yet all was not lost. Luckily the fateful decision by the two to defy the divine command to remain innocent also becomes the doorway for hope to enter the scene. Their disobedience is what places the children of God on a path to individuation.

The Cayce philosophy asserts that the soul's fall from grace and subsequent ascent in consciousness toward realization of its true identity defines man's purpose on earth. To " . . . become aware of yourself *being* yourself yet one with Him," (1992-1) is how the readings define it. And yet it was the heartbreaking loss of Eden that presented humanity with the opportunity to grow into that awareness. Banishment allowed the fallen children to move beyond the limited confines of the garden walls, which hemmed in paradise and restricted the soul to knowing its Creator solely through the eyes of a naïve child. Now during the steep climb upward through a material world, these same divine offspring will have the autonomy to act as mature, self-directed entities—beings with the ability to deliberately *choose* to return to that original, higher state of consciousness, that paradise, and dwell anew with their God.

In the end, humanity's chastisement and expulsion from the child-like conditions of Eden gave the soul the chance to become fully itself—consciously. But the human race was going to pay a stiff price for the opportunity. Finding the way back in consciousness to God through a mind-created universe—overcoming the world—would prove to be a lengthy and difficult process. The demand to lift up the serpent or divine life force wallowing in the mud of the earth and elevate it to the heights of perfection once more was an undertaking that ultimately would require eons of time, space, and patience to achieve. In the meantime, during the countless days and years spent between the bookends of birth and death, human beings would be subject to the complex set of laws governing a material existence. In addition, an eternal injunction was put in place. The exiled souls could not scale the walls, sneak through the gates, or force their way back into paradise because mighty cherubim, members of an unseen army of Spirit, continuously guard the entryway back into the heavenly estate. And these divine messengers allow admittance only when a soul is ready—only when it has overcome the desire to misuse its celestial fire for self-gratification and no longer places material ways and means above the Law of One. "Do not gain knowledge only to thine undoing," Edgar Cayce cautioned. "Remember Adam." (5753-2)

The story of Adam and Eve in the Garden of Eden stands as a timeless allegory about a lost opportunity to choose at-One-ment over duality. And the Tree of Life reaching skyward at the center of the garden of paradise, crudely mirrored in the body's own nervous system, represents the divine energy coursing through every man, woman, and child. Countless centuries after the fall in the garden, this same arche-type will reappear at another critical moment in the human drama. In a powerful expression of synchronicity, the symbolic Tree of Life first depicted in Genesis will be transformed into the universal symbol for the soul's sacred journey upward through time and space: when the cross is raised over Golgotha.

Chapter 2
Enduring Soul

> ...The entity—as an entity—influenced
> either directly or indirectly all those
> forms of philosophy or religious thought
> that taught God was One.　　364-9

After the fall in Eden, it would take many thousands of years for a soul to regain conscious awareness of its supernatural identity, rise out of its entombment in matter, and reach the pinnacle of God awareness or Christhood on this plane. Interestingly, the Cayce readings provide additional insight into the lengthy process of spiritual evolution in commenting that "perfection is not possible in a material body until you have at least entered some thirty times . . . " (2982-2) The first soul to accomplish this task, correctly identified as the second Adam, was Jesus of Nazareth. His soul had spent multiple incarnations in both spirit form and in the flesh working to perfect itself until it was ready to serve as the flawless transparency through which divinity might be reflected in the earth.

Knowledge is gained or lost every time a soul agrees to incarnate, and advancing on the path toward complete realization of and unconditional surrender to the will of the divine was as challenging for the Adam soul as it was for every other soul deeply entrenched in the material realm. Edgar Cayce discloses a host of previously unknown details about the history and evolution of this soul, which eventually became the Messiah. It starts with its incarnation as the entity Amilius present on earth in spirit form prior to its appearance as the flesh and blood Adam and then adds several subsequent lifetimes to the list. "First, in the beginning, of course; and then as Enoch, Melchizedek, in the perfection. Then in the earth of Joseph, Joshua, Jeshua, Jesus," (5749-14) explain the readings.

Moreover, the Cayce material indicates that since the beginning of time the first begotten Son or soul has served as the primary entity responsible for carrying the light of God to humanity: " . . . Christ in all ages, Jesus in one, Joshua in another, Melchizedek in another; *these* be that led Judaism! These be they that came as that Child of Promise, as to the Children of Promise . . . " (991-1) The New Testament gospels, which relate the story of a young Jewish rabbi who wandered the Judean countryside teaching more than 2,100 years ago, are merely the concluding chapters in a prolonged epic spanning hundreds of thousands of years. The Amilius/Adam/Jesus soul had been at work for a very long time.

Melchizedek

According to Edgar Cayce after the first begotten soul departs its flesh-and-blood body and Adam passes away, it makes a second appearance in the earth plane by incarnating as the mysterious entity named Melchizedek. The Bible mentions this shadowy figure only a handful of times. We learn about Melchizedek from a few brief paragraphs in Genesis, a single line in Psalm 110, and several references in a couple of the Epistles. Similar to this same soul's much later appearance as Jesus whom the gospels reveal was immaculately conceived, Melchizedek is said to have entered the earth without any link to a material impulse or cause. " . . . Without father, without mother, without descent, having neither beginning of days nor end of life, but made like unto the Son of God," states the holy text. (Heb. 7:3) One epistle refers to Melchizedek as "made not after the law of carnal commandment but after the power of an endless life." (Heb. 7: 16) In this case the first begotten soul, descending from the higher vibrational realms to interact with the human race, passes into the material plane unencumbered by a corporeal body. Amazingly, the readings also assert that Melchizedek was the entity who wrote the book of Job. "...*Who* recorded same? The Son of man! Melchizedek wrote Job!" (262-55) states Cayce.

The biblical narrative describes Melchizedek as the king of Salem and a being without days or years. Called holy, harmless, undefiled, separate from sinners, and made higher than the heavens, this strange, otherworldly teacher emerges as the first representation of the Christ or spirit of God visible to mortal sight. Centuries later we will see the same soul once again serve as a teacher committed to demonstrating the pattern for living to his fellow souls. After experiencing a corporeal birth through the body of Mary and living in the flesh for thirty-three years, the Adam/Melchizedek/Jesus soul will lift itself out of its encasement in matter and prove for all time that material law and a physical form cannot confine the infinity of Spirit. The divine in man is bound to rise again to become one with the universal Creative Forces.

Despite the scant amount of information on Melchizedek recorded in the scriptures, the Bible credits him with having established the order of the priesthood, which became a symbol of the sacred community of individuals willing to help close the circuit between God and man. During the relatively brief span of time this enigmatic figure is present to human awareness, he is also the one chosen to place the stamp of approval on Abram's (Abraham's) evolving consciousness. The holy messenger Melchizedek who had arrived on earth full-blown from the celestial spheres will bestow a divine blessing on the forerunner of the Jewish people, the man celebrated throughout history as the first human being capable of grasping the concept of God as one. "And he blessed him, and said, Blessed be Abram of the most high God, possessor of heaven and earth." (Gen. 14:19)

It is Abram's willingness to listen to the inner voice of divine wisdom and worship a single God—a construct still foreign to the rest of the human race—which conveys upon him the power of heaven and earth. Further, in the not-too-distant future the invisible deity the man Abram venerates will establish an enduring covenant with his servant and in the process give him a new name. "Neither shall thy name any more be called Abram, but thy name shall be Abraham . . . " (Gen. 17:5) relates the biblical account. The heavenly promise is that Abraham will become the father of many nations and his descendants as numberless as the stars.

Arguably the capstone of Melchizedek's fleeting appearance in the material plane is the unusual act he performs immediately prior to bestowing his blessing on Abram. As stated in a single cryptic verse recorded in the Book of Genesis this enigmatic being, the first "priest," is said to have placed a unique oblation on the altar before his God—not the blood of a slain animal but an offering of bread and wine. The sacred chronicle reports that " . . . Melchizedek king of Salem brought forth bread and wine: and he was the priest of the most high God." (Gen. 14:18) Thus does the Amilius/Adam/Melchizedek soul foreshadow its own future incarnation as the Master Jesus who will use these same two ancient symbols during the Last Supper to represent the soul fed by ingesting Christ-truth.

Enoch

The Cayce readings describe Noah's great-grandfather, Enoch, as another one of the significant incarnations of the Amilius/Adam/Jesus soul. Although he was a man, Enoch is said to have fulfilled the office of God's messenger to the angels. There is lingering controversy over the origin and authorship of the actual Book of Enoch, but the volume includes several clear parallels to passages found in the New Testament. Moreover, the historian Tertullian claims Enoch's great-grandson, Noah, may have preserved his ancestor's book in the ark or miraculously reproduced it through the inspiration of the Holy Spirit. The Book of Enoch forms a literary bridge between the kind of prehistory found in the Bible and information from the Edgar Cayce readings, which discuss the presence on earth of Amilius in a non-corporeal form. In addition, Enoch's writings relate a story very similar to the Genesis account of the fallen angels who interact with human beings and produce Nephilim or giants as offspring.

What is evident from the material attributed to Enoch are the clues left behind about a coming Messiah as well as certain portions of the text which closely resemble the philosophy and sayings of the Master. Among other highlights, the Book of Enoch weaves together threads of several of the same ideas and uses language similar to that recorded in the four gospels and the Book of Revelation. Interestingly the Genesis narrative describes Enoch as not only faithful to his God but also as someone who never actually dies. "And all the days of Enoch were three hundred sixty and five years: And Enoch walked with God: and he was not; for God took him." (Gen. 5:23–24) While much of what is known or believed about the character of Enoch remains cloaked in mystery, this extraordinary soul nonetheless left a lasting imprint on the skein of time and spiritual evolution of humanity. His teachings and legacy lay one more brick in the foundation for the history–bending lifetime of Jesus the Christ, which will follow many generations later.

Joseph

. . . The greater meaning of the word Israel—those called of God for a service before the fellow man.   587-6

Evidence of a spiritual "bloodline" tying the Adam soul to Jesus grows stronger with its incarnation as one of the twelve sons in the family of Jacob, later called Israel. In this instance the first begotten of God lived in the earth plane in the person of Joseph, the biblical character renowned for wearing a coat of many colors. (In an intriguing sidebar to the history of the Adam soul's sacred lineage, the Bible notes that after Joseph's mother Rachel dies, she is buried near Bethlehem—the place where the same soul one day will reenter the earth as the infant Jesus.)

The Joseph story actually begins to gel decades prior to his mother Rachel giving birth to her first child. The roots of this particular lifetime for the Adam soul were germinated in the history of his father Jacob whose biblical exploits reveal a man slowly but steadily growing in spiritual awareness. Early on Jacob is known for having played a trick on his twin brother Esau in order to steal the birthright of his more earthbound sibling, which in turn forces Jacob to become a spiritual wanderer. That is until the night he dreams about a ladder reaching up to heaven, full of angels ascending and descending on its rungs. During the course of this extraordinary visionary experience in which he sees the "Lord God O Abraham," Jacob receives divine assurance that his God is with him. "And, behold, the Lord stood above it, and said, I am the Lord God of Abraham thy father, and the God of Isaac: the land whereon thou liest, to thee will I give it, and to thy seed." (Gen. 28:13) Jacob's heightened awareness has broken new ground and this enlightened state of being is the place he and his spiritual descendants will inhabit from that day forward.

As it was with Abraham, the God of Jacob reveals that one day the seeds of his spiritual understanding will cover the whole earth, blessing every nation. "And thy seed shall be as the dust of the earth, and thou shalt spread abroad to the west, and to the east, and to the north, and to the south: and in thee and in thy seed shall all the families of the earth be blessed." (Gen. 28:14) The divine impartation continues by assuring Jacob that wherever he goes, his God will accompany his footsteps. "And, behold, I am with thee, and will keep thee in all places whither thou goest, and will bring thee again into this land; for I will not leave thee, until I have done that which I have spoken to thee of." (Gen. 28:15) When Jacob awakens from his sleep and realizes the significance of what has just occurred, he declares, "Surely the Lord is in this place; and I knew it not." (Gen. 28: 16)

Years later during a similar nighttime episode when he once more finds himself alone, Jacob will meet a mysterious stranger who suddenly sets upon him, wrestling with him until the dawn. His unearthly opponent ends up wounding Jacob's thigh, but the injured man continues to hold on, refusing to let his adversary go until the stranger, a force he neither recognizes nor understands, blesses him. Once he has overcome his rival and won the struggle, Jacob, like the ever-loyal Abraham, also receives a new name. "And he said, Thy name shall be called no more Jacob, but Israel: for as a prince hast thou power with God and with men, and hast prevailed." (Gen. 32:28) It must have been Jacob's sincerity and dogged persistence in seeking to be blessed that created the vibrations, which eventually would attract the Adam soul to the earth again as a member of his immediate family. This time the first begotten soul will enter the planet as the cherished son of the patriarch Israel who had wrestled with his lower nature and come away victorious—a man so devoted to his God he establishes a nation of God-seekers in the earth.

Into Egypt

See, I have set thee over all the land of Egypt. Gen. 41:41

Over the course of many years Jacob has a dozen sons, but Joseph, the second-to-last born of his beloved wife Rachel, is his favorite—treasured more than all of his other offspring. The Joseph narrative takes a tragic turn one day, however, when Jacob's ten older sons, jealous of their younger sibling whom they mockingly refer to as the dreamer, plot to get rid of him and end up throwing Joseph into a desert pit without any water. The eldest son, Rueben, who had convinced his brothers not to kill the boy, has every intention of coming back to retrieve him. But before he is able to save his little brother, a passing group of merchants removes Joseph from the pit and sells him into slavery for twenty pieces of silver to a band of Ishmeelites bound for Egypt. Forced to return home without their sibling, the ten sons lie to Jacob by showing him animal blood they had smeared on Josephs' cloak and claiming a wild creature had killed the child. The distraught father believes their tale and is heartsick grieving the loss of the precious son he will never see again. (Gen. 37)

But God appears to have great plans for the young captive. Despite the dire straits he finds himself in, the Bible indicates the Lord was with Joseph and caused him to prosper. It turns out to be true when through a series of remarkable twists and turns the lowly slave rises to unforeseen heights in a country wholly foreign to him. An officer named Potiphar, captain of Pharaoh's guard, makes Joseph a servant in his home and soon after, recognizing the young man's unusual aptitude and innate wisdom, promotes him to oversee the entire household. As the spiritual drama progresses, Potiphar's wife begins to cast her eye on the handsome young overseer and soon makes a move to try to get him into her bed. But Joseph will not betray his master Potiphar in such a manner and spurns her overtures. Angry at his rejection, the woman subsequently accuses Joseph of making unwanted advances and, although he is innocent of the charges, causes him to be thrown into another pit. Yet God resides in that dungeon too and has prepared a way out for his servant. The divine plan is to use Joseph's skill as the "dreamer" his brothers had ridiculed to raise him up to greatness a second time.

Pharaoh's Court
⌒⌒

As it so happened during this period, Pharaoh had experienced a series of disturbing dreams, which neither the priests nor the magicians of the court were able to interpret. After exhausting every possible avenue to try to solve the nighttime mystery, Pharaoh appears to be out of options until his chief butler tells him about Joseph who had successfully explained a dream for him and another prisoner, a baker, when the three of them were incarcerated together. Pharaoh proceeds to call Joseph before him to get his help. "And Pharaoh said unto Joseph, I have dreamed a dream, and there is none that can interpret it: and I have heard say of thee, that thou canst understand a dream to interpret it. And Joseph answered Pharaoh, saying, [It is] not in me: God shall give Pharaoh an answer of peace." (Gen. 41:15-16) Joseph successfully deciphers the meaning of Pharaoh's nightmares by recognizing them as omens signifying seven years of bountiful harvests followed by seven years of drought. But he takes no credit for himself. Impressed by his prisoner's demeanor and interpretation of the prophetic imagery, Pharaoh asks, "Can we find such a one as this is, a man in whom the Spirit of God is?" (Gen. 41:38) He ends up making Joseph second-in-command to himself and placing the Hebrew in charge of Egypt's preparations for the foretold periods of plenty and lack.

The history of Joseph's estrangement from his own people concludes when the same ten brothers whose vengeful decision years earlier had caused him to be sold into slavery arrive in Egypt to purchase the only food available during those lean years. Joseph immediately recognizes his siblings but only after a series of tricks and complications does he finally reveal his true identity to them. His father eventually also learns that the boy taken from him so long ago, his beloved son

Joseph, is still alive and rejoices. The saga comes to an auspicious end when the patriarch Israel along with all of his wives, children, and other members of his extended family travel to Egypt to take up residence there. The people of the one God will continue to reside in the land of the Pharaohs until the days recorded in the Book of Exodus when Moses will lead the Hebrews out of that country to their freedom in the Promised Land.

Soul of a Deliverer

In an interesting sidebar pairing the events surrounding Joseph in the court of ancient Egypt with the future incarnation of this same soul as Jesus, the Old Testament text states that Joseph was " . . . thirty years old when he stood before Pharaoh King of Egypt" (Gen. 41:46) and made a ruler over all the land. The age of thirty was the point at which both Joseph and Jesus step forward to begin their life's missions. Unbeknownst to Joseph at that moment standing in front of Pharaoh as the newly appointed overseer of the entire kingdom, he is destined to become a savior to his people. Joseph ends up serving as the mediator and vehicle by which the Israelites—the followers of the one God—will gain access to the bread they need to stay alive during the grinding famine, just as Jesus the Christ will become the bread of life, feeding spiritually starving souls held captive in the arid landscape of a material world.

Other bits and pieces woven into the rich tapestry of the history of Joseph, whose ultimate destiny is to one day rise to the heights of a Christ, provide additional clues about this soul's seminal role in fulfilling the promise of deliverance. The coat of many colors Joseph wears as a boy suggests the sign of the rainbow that Noah saw after the biblical flood receded, sealing the eternal covenant between God and man. And the statement made by Joseph in revealing his true identity to his kinsmen as the brother they had cast off before he was sold into slavery might well have been spoken by Jesus who will also be sold into captivity for a bagful of silver. "Now therefore be not grieved, nor angry with yourselves, that ye sold me hither: for God did send me before you to preserve life," states Joseph. (Gen. 45:5) The first begotten soul is assuring his siblings that it was the spirit of God working through those awful events which had raised up their deliverer.

Joseph's tale represents the archetypal story of the beloved son lost to his father and held in bondage but whose deep rapport with the divine raises him up to unimaginable heights. And in the process becomes the catalyst for transformation and freedom. "So now it was not you that sent me hither, but God: and he hath made me a father to Pharaoh, and lord of all his house, and a ruler throughout all the land of Egypt," (Gen. 45:8) the overlord Joseph declares. So, too, will the crown of Christhood allow Jesus to rule over the furthest reaches of the material realm. Many other words spoken by Joseph in Egypt centuries before the advent of the Messiah take on a fresh and more profound meaning when contemplated in light of this particular soul's intimate connection with the Master. "But as for you, ye thought evil against me; but God meant it unto good, to bring to pass, as it is this day, to save much people alive. Now therefore fear ye not: I will nourish you, and your little ones. And he comforted them, and spake kindly unto them." (Gen. 50:20–21)

Joshua

But as for me and my house, we will serve the Lord. Josh. 24:15

The Israelites had been enslaved in Egypt for generations when the Adam soul makes its next appearance by donning the mantle of another notable figure in Jewish history. But this time the gains made in helping humanity attain new levels of awareness and understanding are tempered by the spiritual ground lost through the brutal subjugation of others. The first begotten of God incarnates as the illustrious warrior named Joshua—he of Exodus fame who served as Moses' closest aide and man-of-arms. Identified by Edgar Cayce as " . . . the prophet, the mystic, the leader, the incarnation of the Prince of Peace," (362-1) Joshua hails from the tribe of Ephraim, who was one of Joseph's sons, and is famous for leading the Israelites into the Promised Land.

Not surprisingly, this exceptional individual is the only one of the Israelites allowed to accompany Moses to the top of Mount Sinai for forty days and forty nights after God has summoned the Jewish leader there. "And the Lord said unto Moses, Come up to me into the mount, and be there: and I will give thee tables of stone, and a law, and commandments which I have written; that thou mayest teach them. And Moses rose up, and his minister Joshua: and Moses went up into the mount of God." (Exod. 24:12–13) Edgar Cayce remarks that prior to the two ascending the mountain, the Hebrews had " . . . seen the Lord Jehovah descend into the mount . . . {and} seen the mount so electrified by the presence of the God of the people . . . that no living thing could remain {there} . . . save those two [Moses and Joshua] who had been cleansed by their pouring out of themselves to God, in the cleansing of their bodies, in the cleansing of their minds . . . " (440-16) It is Joshua who stands nearby on that holy ground supporting the liberator Moses as he receives divine instruction to build an Ark of the Covenant and hears the word of God expressed as the principles of the Ten Commandments, which will be carved onto stone tablets and carried down the mountainside to the people below. The readings recognize Joshua as the medium through which Moses obtains the law, calling him " . . . the interpreter through whom the message was given to Israel." (3645-1)

The Bible provides several additional clues about the depth of the man Joshua's devotion to his God and his soul's unique mission in that particular lifetime. "And the Lord spake to Moses face to face, as a man speaketh unto his friend. And he turned again into the camp: but his servant, Joshua, the son of Nun, a young man, departed not out of the tabernacle," states the Book of Exodus, (Exod. 33:11) explaining how Joshua chose to tarry for a while in that consecrated space communing with the divine presence. Sometime later God will choose Joshua as the next leader of his people and direct Moses to enhance the authority of his aide by honoring him before the priest and entire congregation—a sign of the very special role this soul is going to play in the divine plan. Near the end of his life Moses will call Joshua before the community a second time to reaffirm his successor's sacred charge. "Be strong and of a good courage: for thou must go with this people unto the land which the Lord hath sworn unto their fathers to give them; and thou shalt cause them to inherit it." (Deut. 31: 7) Upon completion of the Israelites' escape from Egypt after wandering through the desert for forty years, it is Joshua who will open the way for the Hebrews to secure their inheritance of the Promised Land, a land for which they did not labor.

The Lord Will Do Wonders
⋘∾

Other details sprinkled throughout the Book of Joshua portray a man associated with a host of phenomena deemed miraculous. "Sanctify yourselves: for to morrow the Lord will do wonders among you," (Josh. 3:5) the Jewish warrior tells his people in words prefiguring his soul's later incarnation as the Master Jesus who also lived from the standpoint of a divine presence that never would forsake or fail him. The Old Testament even describes a moment when Joshua purportedly spoke an order which halted the orbit of the sun and the moon. "Sun stand thou still upon Gibeon; and thou, Moon, in the valley of Ajalon," (Josh. 10:12) he commands. The Old Testament account reports that with these words the sun stopped moving and the moon stayed in its place in the midst of the heavens until the Hebrews had avenged themselves upon their enemies. "And there was no day like that before it or after it, that the Lord hearkened unto the voice of a man," (Josh. 10:14) attests the biblical author in an extraordinary moment of understatement.

It was this same unyielding certitude about the presence and power of his God that caused Joshua to send forth the Ark of the Covenant to conquer Jericho. Carried among the armed troops and surrounded by an assembly of priests blowing on rams' horns, the Ark circles the city seven times—until the people shout and its walls fall down, allowing the Israelites to take that stronghold. (Josh. 6:1-20) Repeatedly the biblical account describes Joshua's army winning the day, vanquishing even the most formidable foes as the Hebrews capture city and field in an all-consuming quest to take their "rightful" place in the land pledged to the people of God.

And under Joshua's extraordinary leadership—shaped and guided by his intimate relationship with the divine—the ragtag group of former slaves is ultimately triumphant. But there is a catch. The unmitigated violence by which the victory is won becomes a karmic debt demanding recompense someday—a squaring of the cosmic accounts in order to help the soul awaken to its error of violating the Law of One. It is only with the advent of the Master who institutes a new covenant in the earth—the Law of Endless Mercy—that karma will lose its grip on humanity. Still, generations later in a final act of willingness to live out the consequences of what he had sown, the Adam/Joshua/Jesus soul will accept personal responsibility for indulging in such cruelty by choosing to experience a savage crucifixion.

Additional links in the metaphysical chain tying the Joshua soul to Jesus appear in the Cayce information. One reading indicates that a study of the life of the ever-patient Joshua will help us interpret the meaning of the life of Jesus. It mentions the pair were much alike in their earthly activities, not in terms of the combative soldier's warlike behavior but " . . . in spirit and in purpose, in ideals, these were one." (3409-1) In an intriguing parallel, the general area Jesus traverses over the course of his public ministry includes many of the old Canaanite cities Joshua had conquered during his career. The Master will heal and minister to people residing in some of the same places he had vanquished as a man-of-arms whose bloody assaults destroyed untold lives.

Ordained to fulfill the divine plan, Joshua completes his soul mission as the Israelites enter the Promised Land. Similarly, Jesus of Nazareth's purpose was to lead the children of God to occupy a new place in consciousness—the original, celestial state of being promised to souls since the dawn of creation. But unlike the warrior Joshua whose ruthless battles expropriated actual physical soil, Jesus' work involved the conquest of an internal terrain. And conquer he did, providing the pattern for human beings to follow if and when they choose to break free of their enslavement to selfishness and enter into the "land of milk and honey." One can almost imagine Jesus speaking the selfsame words Joshua used to instruct the tribes of Israel centuries before the birth of the Messiah: "But take diligent heed to do the commandment and the law, which Moses the servant of the Lord charged you, to love the Lord your God and to walk in all his ways, and to keep his commandments, and to cleave unto him, and to serve him with all your heart and all your soul." (Josh. 22:5)

Jeshua

Jesus answered and said unto them, "Destroy this temple, and in three days I will raise it up." John 2:19

Generally less well known but equally significant is the lifetime the Master-soul spent as the Old Testament figure Jeshua, listed among the Jewish exiles who returned to Jerusalem following their captivity in Babylon. Identified by the name Jeshua, meaning "Yahweh is deliverance" in the books of Ezra and Nehemiah, this same individual is referred to as Joshua in the writings of Haggai and Zechariah. The high priest Jeshua is known to be a descendant of another religious figure noteworthy in his own right. His grandfather Seraiah was the last high priest of the Old Temple in Jerusalem before the Babylonians destroyed it when they sacked the city.

Around 538 BC, after Cyrus of Persia had issued his edict permitting the Jews to return to their homeland and proclaimed he would use funds from the royal treasury to help rebuild a temple there, Jeshua and a provincial governor named Zerubbabel took responsibility for organizing the Israelites' return to Zion. Shortly after their homecoming the two men began the process of reviving some of the religious practices sacred to the Jews by presiding over the building of an altar, very likely constructed on the same spot where Solomon's original temple had once stood. "Then stood up Jeshua . . . and his brethren the priests, and Zerubbabel . . . and built the altar of the God of Israel, to offer burnt offerings thereon, as it is written in the law of Moses the man of God." (Ezra 3:2) Naturally the high priest Jeshua would inaugurate the resettlement of the Jewish remnant in the Promised Land by erecting an altar since it was impossible to offer sacrifices without one. Given that the primary mission of the Adam soul was to lead other souls back to an awareness of the divine, it is no surprise that Jeshua served as the chief architect in reestablishing the act of worship for the people of the one God.

Approximately two years after the Israelites were restored to their homeland Jeshua and Zerubbabel appoint the Levites to begin rebuilding the actual temple. In an interesting twist to the story some Samaritans, considered "foreigners" even during that early period long before the appearance of the Christ in the earth, approach the leaders to inquire if they might assist with the construction. Apparently because the Jewish elders did not trust the group's sincerity and possibly regarded their offer to join the project as a veiled attempt to undermine its progress, they decline the help, intimating that the Jews must rebuild the structure themselves. The Israelites' instincts turn out to be correct for according to the book of Ezra, the Samaritans "weakened the hands of the people of Judah, and troubled them in building" by hiring counselors to "frustrate their purpose." (Ezra 4: 4–5) Soon, due to continued, strong opposition by the Samaritans as well as pushback from other groups, temple construction grinds to a halt. The biblical account reports that the work stagnated for a very long time, but finally, spurred on by the prophets who had urged the community to finish, rebuilding gets underway again. It continues until the second temple is completed more than two decades after the Israelites' repatriation.

Edgar Cayce amplifies what we know about the Old Testament figure Jeshua adding several new details to the story. The process of repatriation he led must have posed significant challenges because in referencing the Adam soul in that lifetime, the readings mention that " . . . this is the same soul–entity who reasoned with those who returned from captivity . . . " (5023–2) Another individual who had requested help from Cayce was told he had been an associate in the household of Jeshua in a previous life and in that capacity had interacted with those not of "the entity's own group or faith," which apparently had created within him a desire to learn how to associate with many different types of people. (2905–3)

Overall, the Cayce information ascribes momentous meaning and purpose to the appearance of the entity Jeshua in the earth, claiming that besides reinstituting the act of worship of the one God, he was the scribe who " . . . translated the rest of the books written up to that time . . . " (5023–2) Jeshua is literally credited with having rewritten or translated the spiritual record of humanity compiled over generations and recorded in the books of the Bible. In a reading for someone described as having worked as one of Jeshua's closest aides, Cayce again noted the high priest's remarkable legacy as a scribe in " . . . interpreting of the law to the language of the peoples of that period." (2498–1) In other words the same soul, which many generations later will incarnate as the great Teacher of teachers elucidating the Father's message to his children, is sowing the seeds for that future lifetime living as Jeshua, recognized for making the word of God more accessible to all.

Perhaps the most the most striking example of the congruity between the ancient high priest and the Master Jesus is this soul's clear–cut mission to rebuild the temple. In Jeshua's case the enterprise involved the construction of an actual physical building with four solid walls and a roof. When Jesus comes to earth, he assumes responsibility for revealing the temple within—an edifice not made with hands but fabricated out of finer stuff which was the spirit of God in man. During the course of his ministry, the Master will refer to his flesh-and-blood body as the temple, leading one of his accusers during the sham trial prior to his Crucifixion to charge, "We heard him say, I will destroy this temple that is made with hands, and within three days I will build another made without hands." (Mark 14:58) In this instance destruction of the temple did not entail marauding Babylonians plundering the city of Jerusalem, but the death of the man Jesus who will raise up his body—rebuild the temple—after spending three days in a tomb.

Many Lifetimes

In all those periods that the basic principle was the Oneness of the
Father, He has walked with men.   364-8

In addition to the sequence of appearances stretching from Amilius to Jeshua, the Edgar Cayce information also ascribes an incarnation of the Adam/Jesus soul to Zend [San/Zan], the father of the first Zoroaster, spiritual leader, and author of the *Zend Avesta*, the sacred writings of the Persians. (Report 262-36) The readings subsequently highlight an equally notable incarnation of this soul as the multi-talented biblical character named Asaph, whose name in Hebrew means "God has gathered or sustained." Appointed chief musician to the courts of King David and Solomon and charged with playing before the Ark of the Covenant, Asaph is credited with composing twelve of the psalms recorded in the Old Testament (Psalms 50; 73–83).

The mysterious character the Greeks refer to as Hermes Trismegistus (meaning "thrice great") and known to native Egyptians as Thoth, or Thoth-Hermes, is pinpointed by the Cayce readings as potentially one additional lifetime of the Master's. While the Cayce material never directly states that Hermes was an incarnation of the Adam soul, it places that soul in the earth at the same time as Hermes and includes other interesting references that make a good case for Jesus having previously lived as this extraordinary figure from the past. The ancient Egyptians, who regarded Thoth-Hermes as a being self-begotten and self-produced, deified him as the god of wisdom. Recognized as the "scribe of the gods," Thoth is associated not only with developing a system of writing but is also equated with the disciplines of science and magic. Befitting the spiritual vision and purpose of the Master-soul, Thoth-Hermes was also revered as the arbitrator or mediating power between good and evil.

Cayce ups the ante even further by attributing an astonishing achievement to the figure Thoth-Hermes. The readings claim that in approximately 10,500 BC, in concert with a priest by the name of Ra or Ra-Ta, this entity was responsible for the construction of the Great Pyramid at Giza. They refer to Hermes as the "guide, or the actual (as would be termed in the present) constructing or construction architect" of the pyramid. (294-151) Elsewhere the Cayce material provides a brief discourse on the underlying purpose for creating this dazzling monument. "Then, with Hermes and Ra . . . there began the building of that now called Gizeh, with which those prophecies that had been in the Temple of Records and the Temple Beautiful were builded, in the building of this that was to be the hall of the initiates of that sometimes referred to as the White Brotherhood." (5748-5) The reverberations from both of these statements by Cayce are amplified when considered from the angle of the readings' interpretation of the story of Jesus. The information reveals that as a young man Jesus travelled to Egypt and was tested in the Great Pyramid as part of his initiation before becoming a master. One reason Edgar Cayce may not have specifically linked Hermes to the Adam soul could be a preference for using the biblical name Enoch. There is an intriguing theory associated with several religious traditions that Hermes and Enoch may, in fact, have been one and the same person.

It is conceivable the Adam soul may have had many more incarnations as well, which the readings never bother to mention. Not specifically featured in the Cayce information but open to speculation is the possibility that this same soul had entered the earth as Akhenaton—the maverick pharaoh of ancient Egypt who turned that country's polytheistic tradition on its head by demanding worship of a single God named Aton. Despite a comprehensive campaign following Akhenaton's death to wipe out all references to the heretical pharaoh and his capital city of Amarna, the world seemed destined to learn about this extraordinary soul and its unique perspective on the divine. The way was opened with the discovery of what is possibly the most famous Egyptian pharaoh in all of history. Akhenaton not only was the husband of the beautiful Queen Nefertiti, but the father of the legendary boy-king, Tutankhamun, known far and wide as King Tut.

Life on earth is both a soul adventure and a school. The lessons the Adam soul learned lifetime after lifetime during untold sojourns within this dimension provided the means for its continuing evolution until it was able to break completely free of the limitations of mortality. Through the ages the first begotten of God would climb higher and higher out of the darkness toward the light until it reached the climactic summit by achieving the level of a Christ, thus completing the mission it had undertaken at the dawn of creation. For the first time in history a soul dwelling in a human body *consciously* would realize its own divinity and be capable of fully manifesting that state of being in the earth. People everywhere eventually would come to recognize the fruits of the Adam soul's labor and find their own salvation as they acquainted themselves with the record of this soul, which had succeeded in overcoming the limitations of the form-based world, by studying the life of a man called Jesus.

Chapter 3
Christ Awakening:
The Story of Jesus

A Pattern Written on the Soul . . .

> . . . The *power* then is in the Christ. The
> *pattern* is in Jesus.   2533-7

The Cayce readings reiterate the true purpose of life as contained in one simple yet elegant phrase: To know our selves to be ourselves—yet one with God. (254-114) This is the motivational force behind humanity's journey through the earth and the mystical heart of the story of a man, who in the relatively short span of thirty-three years, fully revealed his divine nature. His story is our story too. The Bible is a record of the history of humanity's long journey homeward back to the Godhead with all of its adventures and massive challenges, incremental successes, petty squabbles, courageous steps forward, and tragic pitfalls. And the apotheosis of that saga is the appearance of a Christed one—a "savior" named Jesus of Nazareth born more than 2,100 years ago.

He was not always known by that name, nor did this soul appear on the human scene only once and in a single place. According to the Edgar Cayce information, since its debut in material form at the beginning of time, the Adam soul had descended from the higher realms to our planet on any number of occasions inhabiting various fleshly bodies and different areas of the globe. By preparing and working lifetime after lifetime the first soul had evolved in consciousness to the point that during its final incarnation as Jesus it would become the penultimate pattern for the human race. The firstborn Son of God would blaze a trail for his brothers and sisters hopelessly lost in a wilderness of their own making, guiding them on the arduous trek upward through the third dimension by helping them remember their long-forgotten past and innate divinity. Driven by this singular mission, he had arrived on earth to teach every "fallen" soul how to free itself from the irresistible pull and confines of matter.

The entrance of the Adam soul back into physicality in Judea twenty-one centuries ago was the apex of a Herculean, centuries-long process, which at its climax would alter the course of human history. This soul's incarnation as Mary and Joseph's son Jesus marked the juncture at which the first begotten of God, living as a man on earth, would flawlessly mirror in the outer world the divinity residing within the innermost recesses of the human heart. Through his efforts, men and women would be able to see firsthand how a single soul encased in a material body might use that vehicle as the tool to regain the awareness of itself as a limitless, unfettered being of light. The perceived barrier between spirit and flesh, God and man, had ceased to exist in the personhood of Jesus who became a Christ. His life and work confronted human beings with an inescapable truth: these two seemingly disparate aspects of themselves were never really separate. They were and are one.

The man from Galilee was able to succeed in his mission because consciousness had risen high enough on this plane so that a sufficient number of people were now able to grasp the message he imparted. Our destiny is to follow in the footsteps left behind by this master, the consummate spiritual teacher, and joyfully return to our Father's house to dwell in a state of divine awareness just as he did. It was no fluke that this savior appeared in the remote corner of the Roman Empire that the Jewish people inhabited during this particular period in history. Those from around the known world in tune with the universal forces had been anticipating such a momentous occasion and laying the groundwork for his coming for a very long time.

Preparing the Way:
The Essenes

Before that we find the entity was in what is now known as the Promised Land, during those periods when there were the preparations for the coming of the teacher, the lowly one, yet the Great I *Am* into the experience of flesh—that man might again have an advocate with the divine that had grown so far away to the hearts of those that were lost in the toils of the day.   1463-2

The Edgar Cayce readings describe the Essenes as a group of Jews who had come together to dedicate their minds and bodies to becoming the channels through which the body of the Messiah or " . . . chosen vessel might enter—through choice—into materiality." (5749-7) The community was committed to preparing for the time when " . . . there might come that beloved Son, who would make the paths straight, who would bring then *man out* of darkness into light . . . " (587-6) Cayce also refers to the unusual sect as " . . . sincere in their purpose, and yet not orthodox as to the rabbis of that particular period . . . "(2067-11), having separated themselves in body, mind, and spirit to accommodate the foretold deliverer and upcoming spiritual awakening. Expectancy was their watchword and the possibility of fulfilling the messianic promise by " . . . offering themselves as channels through which there might come the new or divine origin . . . " (254-109) formed the context for every aspect of their daily lives, even the most mundane activities. Members of the Essenes were devoted to creating the most auspicious setting for the entrance of that consciousness we know as the Son of Man.

The Essenes' belief, fervent hope, and ideal was that through a stricter adherence to both the letter and the spirit of the law they might so purify themselves that it would be possible, through them, for the Promised One to come into the earth. And according to Edgar Cayce, this consecration of thought and activity led to the fulfillment of the law of like begetting like.

> . . . Did the darkness bring the light? Did the wandering away from
> the thought of such bring the Christ into the earth? Is this idea not
> rather refuting the common law that is present in spirit, mind and
> body that "Like begets like?" As was asked oft, 'Can any good thing
> come out of Nazareth?' . . .   262-61

While scholarly disagreements and heated debate continue over the significance and historic role of the Essene community, this pious sect was the group to which Jesus' family belonged. Linked to the ruins found at Qumran and the Dead Sea Scrolls, which comprised the sect's spiritual literature and informed its social precepts, the Essenes never rose to great prominence in the ancient world. But it was within the context of the religious and cultural climate they engendered that John the Baptist conducted his mission and Jesus initially was reared.

Looked upon as rebels and radicals, especially by the Sadducees and Pharisees who held to a strict interpretation of the law of the prophets, members of the Essene community were considered outcasts at the time of Christ. While they sincerely held to the tenets of the Mosaic law, a separate set of rules, beliefs, and unusual rituals set them apart from Orthodox Jewish life. Adherents made use of astrology, numerology, and phrenology and also believed in reincarnation. In general, the community followed its own agenda, which put them in direct conflict with many of the wealthier aristocratic families, high priests, and temple officials vehemently opposed to their heretical ideas.

Central to the Essene philosophy was the conviction that it was possible to receive revelation and guidance directly from the Divine, not just through the prophets of old. The Cayce readings state that the Essenes " . . . taught the mysteries of man and his relationship to those forces as might be manifested from within and without." (2520–1) The community also kept detailed records of those occasions when individuals in their midst had been visited by supernatural beings or had reported extraordinary experiences coming in dreams, visions, and voices. As diligent students of the universal forces, the Essenes taught the mysteries of man and regarded such revelations as valid promises to humanity.

The sect occupied several areas—one of which was a community on Mount Carmel built on the original site of the school of the prophets established during the time of Elijah. According to the Cayce readings, Mount Carmel was the main headquarters of the Essene temple and its most important branch in terms of preparing for the arrival of the Messiah. Members from that location had studied the records of the early Egyptian period including the activities of the Temple Beautiful and Temple of Sacrifice and had incorporated those findings into their temple services. Cayce also reports that many Essenes or the " . . . near adherents of same . . . "(1602–4) were not part of the rigid, monastic order living in semi-seclusion in formal communities such as the ones established at Mount Carmel or near the Dead Sea. While holding to the sect's beliefs and cooperating with the brotherhood's stated purposes and objectives, this loose network of believers remained scattered throughout the countryside, maintaining private homes in various villages and towns.

Interestingly it was not just the Essenes who were engaged in special preparations for the entrance of the Messiah. In every land where man sought to understand and know his relationship with the Creative Forces there were " . . . those who looked for the day, the hour, when that *great purpose*, that event, was to be in the earth a literal experience," (1908–1) reports one reading. Through astrology and numerology the Essenes along with other clairvoyants hailing from the far corners of the world and advanced in the interpretation of signs and symbols kept watch, trying to ascertain the time when the great changes were to take place.

The Cayce information also mentions an extensive level of cooperation among groups from many lands who embodied the same high spiritual ideals and purposes as the Essenes. Not surprisingly, interactions among the different circles also involved an exchange of information. Members of the Essene community seeking knowledge about the promised events were able to study material handed over to them by other communities as well as to review the research generated by their own sect. Seers all over the world at that time had come to recognize the onset of the Piscean Age, which marked the start of another cycle, and understood the dawning of this new era portended a major transformation of the old order.

Unfortunately, though, for the majority who realized change was imminent and a new order at hand, including many inside the Essene community itself, the wait was still for a deliverer who might free the Israelites from their physical bondage by either setting up a separate government or creating an entirely new nation. The Jewish people, Essenes included, were under the thumb of Rome and paying heavy taxes to a hated conqueror. In addition, a corrupt and oppressive priest-hood constantly demanded devotion and tribute. Cayce depicts these spiritual leaders as gormandizing themselves and their own interests through the sale of privileges associated with temple activities, which were steeped in the letter of the law without its spirit.

Choosing Mary
ॐ

> . . . the entity was in that now known as or called the Promised Land, during those periods when there were the preparations of the channels through which the Essenes looked for choice to be made of one, from those who had been consecrated for the service of being the channel, through which He, the Prince of Peace, might come.   1981-1

Through choice, the soul that would become the Son of Man was going to enter into materiality again. Preparing for that moment eventually led the Essenes to hand-pick twelve young maidens for special religious training. The hope was that with very strict discipline and concentrated effort this carefully selected sorority would be the group from which the mother of the Messiah might be chosen. Edgar Cayce's rendition of the birth-of-Jesus story begins at this point with the description of a gathering on Mount Carmel when all the parents of young girls who were perfect in both body and mind—and wanted to dedicate their children for this unusual service—brought them to the temple school overseen by the Essene priests. The leaders eventually culled a dozen girls from the larger group of children brought forward because those twelve were regarded as the most fit to consecrate their minds and bodies in preparation for serving as the sacred vessel and becoming—

> . . . the channel through which there might come that beloved Son . . .

> that there must be . . . through the very expression of that Being
> in the earth—the understanding that the law was written in the
> hearts of men, rather than on tables of stone; that the temple, the
> holy of holies was to be within . . .   587-6

The readings say the Essene priests chose according to the selection indicated by Spirit. Among the assembly was a child of four, Mary, the daughter of Elizabeth, an unmarried woman who alleged her daughter had been immaculately conceived. While the Cayce information asserts it was true, many in the community doubted Elizabeth's claim and questions about Mary's parentage caused divisions among the sect's leadership. Some thought it was improper for the child to be among those set apart to potentially fulfill such a holy purpose. Others felt that because of her perfection in body and mind, Spirit had directed her inclusion within the group and should not be refused. In the end Mary and eleven other maidens were singled out " . . . each as a representative of the twelve in the various phases that had been or that had made up Israel—or man." (5749-8) Their training and preparation by the priests (similar in many ways to that of present-day novices in some Roman Catholic religious orders) began immediately and continued for several years until Mary reached the age of twelve or thirteen.

All the happenings at Mount Carmel are said to have drawn the first visits of the Wise Men of the East who hailed from Persia, India, and Egypt and who, according to the Edgar Cayce readings, visited the Holy Land on more than one occasion to better understand what was about to come to pass. The temple at Mount Carmel was widely considered a sacred place by those in tune with the impending spiritual transformation. So it is not too difficult to understand why this consecrated ground became the site where the mother of the Messiah was chosen from the initial group of twelve Essene girls. Edgar Cayce describes the scene this way—

> The temple steps, or those that led to the altar—these were called the
> temple steps. These were those upon which the sun shone as it arose
> of a morning when there were the first periods of the chosen maidens
> going to the altar for prayer, as well as for the burning of the incense.
>   On this day, as they mounted the steps, all were bathed in the

morning sun, which made a beautiful picture, clothing all as in
purple and gold. As Mary reached the top step, then there were the
thunder and lightning, and the angel led the way, taking the child
by the hand before the altar. This was the manner of choice; this
was the showing of the way; for she led the others on *this* particular
day.   5749-8

After the selection of Mary to become the channel through which the
Messiah would enter the earth, she was separated from the other girls
and associated more closely with those in the community responsible
for her further training and preparation, which lasted approximately
four years.

Teacher in Training:
Judy
꞊ꞩꞤ

During this period, a woman named Judy headed up the Essene
community. Her appointment as its leader had been fraught with controversy too. Born approximately twenty-five years before the birth
of Jesus, Judy had entered the world to fulfill a critical soul mission.
Before her birth an angel had appeared at separate times to her parents,
Hannah and Elkanah, to reveal the ministry and glorious work their
child would perform. Due to the significance of the child's future role
in the life of the Messiah, everyone in the community had assumed
Hannah's baby would be a boy. When a girl was born, her gender
" . . . brought some disturbance, some confusion in the minds of many,"
(1472-3) reports Cayce.

Holding onto their faith in the angelic messages and the promises
they had received concerning their only child, Hannah and Elkanah
dedicated Judy's life to study. Cayce explains she learned about " . . .
those things that had been handed down as part of the *experiences* of
those who had received visitation from the unseen, the unknown—or
that worshipped as the Divine Spirit moving into the activities of man."
(1472-3) Judy is also credited with having the experience of hearing
voices and much of her training was in disciplines the Essenes considered conducive to the development of psychic or prophetic abilities.

In addition to the in–depth studies of the prophecies and traditions of her own people, she explored all the teachings of the East, including the traditions of India, Egypt, and " . . . the conditions and traditions from many of the Persian lands and many of the borders about same . . . " (1472-3) Impressed by the fact that numerous teachings and experiences related to her by these distant groups were handed down orally rather than through the written word, Judy made it a priority to devote a portion of her studies and time to the work of recording these oral traditions and discovering the best methods for preserving the information for future generations.

The Cayce material describes Judy as becoming not only a prophet and healer but also serving as a teacher and recorder, which boded well for her future work as one of Jesus' primary instructors. After her appointment as head of the Essenes, she actively pushed to collect all the information concerning the advent of the promised Redeemer from groups in other lands and then compiled it with the records held by the Essenes. Select members of the Brotherhood were assigned to go gather this data from disparate gurus and communities by tapping " . . . the teachings of those groups in Persia, India, Egypt, and even of the Hebrews and the activities in Olympus and the isles of the sea." (2520-1) There were also individuals from far-flung regions of the world who traveled to Mount Carmel to consult with the Essenes and brought with them information received through their own research and study.

Conceiving the Christ

Then when the days were come that the prophecy might be fulfilled that had been given by Isaiah, Malachi, Joel and those of old, she, Mary, espoused to Joseph—a chosen vessel for the office among those of the priests, the sect or group who had separated and dedicated themselves in body, in mind, in spirit for this coming—became with child.   5749-7

The story in the New Testament about a man named Jesus begins with the tale of a young girl who is told by an angel, a messenger of the universal Creative Forces, that she will bear a son. The Cayce readings comport with the biblical account in confirming the angel Gabriel appeared to Mary in the home of Elizabeth. Upon the appearance of this supernatural intermediary Mary is made aware of the presence of the Spirit within her. Similar to Abraham's wife Sarah in the Old Testament who thought she was too old to bear a child, Mary finds the angel's pronouncement hard to believe for she is still a virgin who has never been with a man. The divine emissary responds by remarking that nothing is impossible with God. "The Holy Ghost shall come upon thee, and the power of the Highest shall overshadow thee: therefore also that holy thing which shall be born of thee shall be called the Son of God," (Luke 1:35) recounts the Gospel of Luke. The life force spontaneously quickening within Mary had done so without any connection to a human father or material cause. That which was conceived within her had been implanted by the unseen forces and the holiest of spirits. Its origins were of God.

The debate over the Immaculate Conception has raged for centuries and likely will continue far into the future. But the Cayce readings say it was true and go even further to reveal that this event was in compliance with natural law. The conception of Jesus is a manifestation of the law underlying the projection of mind into matter—the very same process that marked humanity's entrance into the earth plane at the beginning of time. The soul's separation from its source and subsequent involvement in matter, which now encased it in a physical or bodily form, had started the journey through this dimension. And because this encasement had a beginning, "there must be an end" to it—a time when the powerful yoke binding man to materiality would be broken. Such was the process, says Cayce, which began during this particular period of human history. (5749-8)

When asked to explain the Immaculate Conception or the virgin birth of Jesus, the readings suggest the reason it was called forth was for the " . . . manifestation in the earth of the holy influence necessary for the sustaining of a backsliding world . . . " (5749-3), because "flesh is the activity of the mental being (or spiritual self and mental being) pushing itself into matter, and as spirit—as He {Jesus} gave—is neither male nor female, they are then both—or one." (5749-7) Thus " . . . the immaculate conception is the physical and mental so attuned to spirit as to be quickened by same." (5749-7) This is how the spirit or soul of the Master was brought into being: " . . . through the accord of the

Mother in materiality that ye know in the earth as conception." (5749-7) Elsewhere Cayce refers to the virgin birth as " . . . the living influence of the Spirit through the body that became the child Jesus . . . ," adding that " . . . the manifestation of the spirit of the oneness of the Father became a manifestation of the Christ Spirit in material surroundings." (5749-3)

Cayce's account also adds new details to the generally accepted historical record, stating that several years before the conception of the holy child, the Essenes had chosen from the sect a man named Joseph to become Mary's husband. Yet when informed by the leaders of the sect that he was to be espoused to her, Joseph was not very happy about the plan. He was twenty years older than his prospective partner and Mary's unconventional background put her at odds with a normal betrothal. Because her mother was unmarried, she was not considered a member of a credible Jewish family. But a dream and direct celestial voice finally convinced Joseph that these plans were the will of the divine, which allows him to accept the situation. New doubts and concerns arise, however, when after three or four years he goes to claim his bride only to find her already with child. Although his brethren assure him the unborn baby is of a divine origin, it was only the appearance of Gabriel—an experience recorded in the Gospel of Matthew—which ultimately reconciles Joseph to the idea of Mary's pregnancy and convinces him to accept her as his wife.[5]

When their wedding finally occurs, it was pulled together somewhat hastily due to the Essenes' wariness about the political turmoil then embroiling various sectors of the Jewish community. Part of the uproar was a byproduct of the issues surrounding the birth of Jesus' cousin John (later called the Baptist) to Mary's cousin Elizabeth who was also an Essene. Since Elizabeth's husband, Zacharias, was an orthodox priest, he had kept his pregnant wife in the hills of Galilee for her own safety. But following an announcement in the orthodox temple about the birth of his son, Zacharias related experiences and visions he had had prior to the birth of baby John and subsequently proclaimed his own newfound belief in and adherence to the teachings of the Essene community. Sometime later, according to the biblical

---

[5] Anne Read, *Edgar Cayce on Jesus and His Church*, ed. Hugh Lynn Cayce (New York: Warner Books, Inc., 1970), 38.

narrative, Zacharias was slain in the holy temple with his hands upon
the horns of the altar. The Cayce readings explain that " . . . those of
his own school . . . " (5749–8) had instigated his murder, which likely
was carried out at the behest of the Pharisees. Jesus will call out this
same group during his ministry for shedding "the blood of Zacharias,
son of Barachias, whom ye slew between the temple and the altar."
(Matt. 23:35)

Understandably, the horrific death of Zacharias in the temple causes
the Essenes to fear for the life of Mary and other members of their community, especially if word got out that the child she carried was deemed
to be of divine origin. Cayce states that Mary also spent a portion of
her pregnancy in the hill country of Judea, and based on the record in
Luke, it was likely with Elizabeth. (5749–8; Luke 1:39–40) When all was
said and done, concerns about the safety of the Holy Family during
those turbulent times would end up coloring the way the history of
the nativity unfolded.

The Birth of Jesus
చ్‌

. . . He gave up heaven and entered physical being that ye might
have access to the Father . . .   5081-1

From the biblical accounts of the nativity story, it appears Mary was
living with Joseph in Nazareth after their marriage as the couple left
from that town to go register in their ancestral city for the polling Rome
had decreed necessary for tax purposes. Thus Joseph and Mary, who
by that time was heavy with child, began the long journey to the city
of David or Bethlehem—the cradle of their lineage and a critical element in the prophetic record about the coming Messiah. Any number
of prophecies had identified Bethlehem with the arrival of the savior
centuries before the couple began their journey south.

Crowds of other travelers also heading back to their ancestral environs jammed the small city, which was only a "Sabbath-day's journey"
from Jerusalem. It is easy to imagine the apprehension filtering through
the Essene community considering the dangers inherent in such explo-
sive circumstances: a young woman in a weakened state almost ready

to give birth, hordes of strangers, and the possibility that this vulnerable couple—like everyone who belonged to the Essene sect—would be questioned not only by government officials but also by the religious authorities in the area. Luckily, Joseph and Mary were not alone on the road. Members of Joseph's household along with many of his carpenters' helpers accompanied them as did workers from the fields around Nazareth, shepherds, husbandmen, and others. Locally based Essenes no doubt also kept their eyes out for this special group of travelers as it approached the city. Delayed somewhat by Mary's condition, husband and wife appear at the inn where they had hoped to stay at twilight long after the place must have already been filled for the evening. Met with more than a little laughter and the jeers of the rabble at the sight of a much older man and his very pregnant younger wife, the answer they received according to Edgar Cayce was, " . . . 'No room at the inn', especially for such an occasion . . . " (5749-15)

The biblical account of the innkeeper turning Mary and Joseph away in spite of their desperate need deviates considerably from what the Cayce readings report actually happened. The innkeeper, Apsafar, was either a member of the Essene community or at least sympathetic to them, but kept his religious convictions secret in order to act as a go-between among those with authority in the " . . . religious influences in the Roman and Jewish faith . . . "(1196-2) He also happened to be serving as a counselor for people hoping to overcome political and religious oppression. The intolerance of the Pharisees and Sadducees toward any religious teachings other than their own was widely known and feared. These powerful religious leaders vehemently opposed sects such as the Essenes as well as all the other beliefs gradually being introduced by outside groups such as the Greeks, who were Apsafar's own people. The fact that he was so closely associated with such "revolutionaries" placed Apsafar in a very dangerous position. He could not afford to become involved in any situation that might call any attention to himself and his unorthodox activities. (1196-2)

Yet because he held to the basic Essene beliefs, had experienced a vision, and had seen the star in the East, Apsafar had made every provision possible in keeping with what was foretold in order to care for the chosen ones when they finally arrived. In addition, his daughter named Sarapha, who herself was an Essene, had been keeping him apprised of everything that was supposed to occur. She had gone to great lengths to ready the quarters the new parents would be using with whatever they might need. Cayce commented that " . . . the entity aided, so that all was in readiness . . . " (1152-3) In the end, however, for Mary and Joseph's safety and especially to shield them from the prying eyes of the authorities, Apsafar turns them away from his inn. "Disappointment was written on the face of Joseph," states Cayce as well as on the face of Sarapha and the others who understood who they were. (5749-15) The Essenes who had heard the stories whispered among their community about Mary's selection by the angel and what had happened during the visit to her cousin Elizabeth were gravely concerned the couple did not have a room and began looking for a place to shelter the family. Necessity demanded a site be found quickly and it was—" . . . under the hill, in the stable above which the shepherds were gathering their flocks into the fold." (5749-15)

The readings paint a picture of the glorious scene that day: " . . . When in the evening—just before the sun in all its glory of the Palestine hills gave forth almost into the voice of nature, proclaiming the heralding of a new hope, a new birth to the earth, and the glorifying of man's hope in God—the spectre of His Star in the evening sky brought awe and wonder to all that beheld." (1152-3) The Child was born at midnight states Cayce—the one " . . . who through the will and the life he manifested became the savior of the world . . . " (5749-15) The readings target this date as " . . . not as counted from the Roman time, nor that declared to Moses by God, not that same time which was in common usage in that land, but what would *now* represent January sixth." (5749-15) Interestingly today we celebrate the sixth of January as the Epiphany, which means "manifestation" or "showing." The birth of Mary's child was indeed the revelation to human consciousness of the divine in man and as man.

The readings remind us not to become confused by considering just the physical birth of the baby Jesus. " . . . While to you it may seem to be the first Christmas, if it were the first then there would be a last, and you would not worship nor hold to that which passes. Time never was when there was not a Christ, and not a Christ mass," (262-103) they maintain. The Cayce material goes on to eloquently describe the extraordinary phenomena accompanying that fateful night when a new creation took hold. "All were in awe as the brightness of His star appeared and shone, as the music of the spheres brought that joyful choir, '*Peace on earth! Good will to men of good faith.*' All felt the vibrations and saw a great light—not only the shepherds above that stable, but those in the Inn as well." (5749-15) It is said the innkeeper's daughter, Sarapha " . . . felt a new light, a new vision, a new experience was *being born* in every atom of {*her*} being." (1152-3)

As with most mystery laden, high-vibrational incidents observed by those not yet ready for or receptive to the spiritual impulse, doubters later would dispel their experiences that night by declaring they had been " . . . overcome with wine or what not." (5749-15) Cayce elaborates—

> And the hour approaches when nature is to be fulfilled in the natural courses in the experience of the Mother, and His Star has appeared—and the angels' choir, and the voices of those that give the *great message!* Who heard these, my children? Those that were seeking for the satisfying of their own desires or for the laudation of their own personality? Rather those close to *nature*, to the hours of meditation and prayer, and those that had given expression, "No room in the Inn!" For no inn, no room, could contain that as was being given in a manifested form! . . . Only then to those that sought could such a message come, or could there be heard the songs of the angels, or that music of the spheres that sang, "*Peace on earth—Good will to men!*"   262-103

Three Gifts
⚮

Many others in the immediate area were deeply touched by what had transpired and, sensing the truth and significance of the event, began to spread the word about what they had experienced. Their listeners in turn carried the news back home to the cities and towns from which they had originally traveled. The following day the Wise Men arrived " . . . with their ladened beasts or camels . . . " (1152-3) The readings explain that during those times there were men throughout the world who sought a closer understanding of the deeper mysteries and

universal Creative Forces—individuals who had subdued the earthly
influences within themselves. Holy in body and mind and wholly at
one with the divine purpose, this priestly caste was known as the Wise
Men. These seekers after truth also were recognized for counseling
others " . . . using the mathematical activities of the ages old, as well as
the teachings of the Persians from the days of Zend and Og and Uhjltd,
bringing for those people a better interpretation of the astrological as
well as the natural laws." (1908-1)

The gifts these sages carried into the lowly stable (symbol of Spirit
encircled by the physical or animal form) represented the triune phases
of man's experience in this dimension: gold, the material; frankincense,
the ethereal; and myrrh, the healing force—or body, mind, and soul.
Along with the metaphysical meaning they carried, their offerings
also brought " . . . encouragement for the mother and those who had
nourished, who had cherished this event in the experience of man-
kind." (5749-7) The three sages worshipped the holy baby and praised
everyone " . . . who had kept the faith, in making and preserving, in
keeping and helping those that were in need, that were alone—yet *God*
with them!" (1152-3) The Cayce information also reports that although
Sarapha was impressed by the glories of the exotic Magi and the precious things of the earth they had arrayed at the newborn's feet, she
was deeply touched that the lowly shepherds, who had come down
into the cave from watching their flocks with nothing more than love
to present, were just as acceptable to the child. " . . . There was no respecter of persons in the face or heart of that Babe . . . ," remark the
readings. (1152-3)

Circumcision
&

The Gospel of Luke reports that after eight days the infant was circumcised and given the name Jesus (Jeshua) as revealed by the angel
before his conception. While central to the traditions and tenets his
parents held sacred, the circumcision of the holy child unquestionably
carries added significance when viewed through the filter of the messianic story. Passing references to circumcision scattered throughout the
Bible belie its enormous significance in the spiritual history of human-

kind. Steeped in mystery and regarded as one of the bedrock rituals of Judaism and other religious traditions, the practice of circumcision was instituted during the period of Abraham as a sign of his covenant with God. "This is my covenant, which ye shall keep, between me and you and thy seed after thee; Every man child among you shall be circumcised," (Gen. 17:10) recounts the Book of Genesis. The removal of a precious piece of flesh intimately connected with the male sex organ eight days after the birth of a baby boy (the male signifying the outward expression of spirit in matter) is a rite religious believers and nonbelievers alike have continued to perform generation after generation. Yet few have understood its deeper esoteric meaning.

The ancient rite of circumcision, established by a sacred directive as interpreted through the enlightened mind of Abraham, the father of the Israelites, represents an unbroken link between a people and their God. At some point during the primordial epoch when he walked the earth, Abraham's consciousness had evolved to the level where he was able to grasp the idea of one God—a single force embodying all the power of heaven and earth. The patriarch's highly developed understanding of the Spirit he venerated moved him to introduce a custom that would forever identify his offspring as belonging to this unseen deity. Set apart from other nations by their belief in the one God, the Hebrews would bear the mark of circumcision, which for generations has compelled the descendants of Abraham to remember they are a people wholly pledged to the same mysterious being their ancestor worshipped and as such comprise more than mere flesh and bone. Their heritage is divine.

The act of cutting off the foreskin of an infant is the mystical equivalent of announcing that man's regard for the material dimension must diminish in order that he may pay homage to the omnipotent Spirit that created him—an invisible force which depends on nothing in the exterior realm for its existence. "Do not glorify matter over Spirit" is the message communicated through the rite of circumcision, for just as this piece of bodily tissue is discarded so, too, will all material form be cast off someday. Centuries after Abraham establishes his compact with heaven, a Jewish infant by the name of Jesus will be presented in the temple and marked with the sign of circumcision. But after growing into manhood and taking up his life's work, this same child will annul every known religious doctrine and mandate, including the need for corporeal circumcision, by heralding a new covenant: God and man as one.

Chapter 4
Becoming a Master

For this, then, is in *every* birth—the
possibilities, the glories, the actuating of
that influence of that entrance again of
god-man into the earth that man might
know the way.   262-103

Even as the Holy Family was busy fulfilling its religious obligations, an emotional storm was brewing, which would soon alter their original plans. The problem started with a decision made months prior to Jesus' birth. According to Edgar Cayce, psychic forces had set the three Wise Men on their original course and directed them to " . . . the place 'where the child was . . . '" (5749-7) The readings also parallel the biblical account in mentioning that the trio had stopped along the way to tell Herod the Great, the regional Jewish tetrarch under the jurisdiction of Rome, about their search for the long-awaited child. (Matt. 2:1-2)

Apparently prior to their journey, the Essene leader Judy had dis-

cussed with the Magi the possibility of informing Herod about the baby's impending birth and together the group had decided it was worth
doing for a number of reasons. Judy realized that the announcement
" . . . would arouse in the heart and mind of this debased ruler—that
only sought for the aggrandizement of self—such reactions as to bring
to him, this despot, turmoils with those then in authority." (1472-3)
Herod was only second or third in authority in the region, and Cayce
clarifies the fact that there was no " . . . proclamation by the Wise Men,
neither by Judy nor the Essenes that this new king was to replace Rome!
It was to replace the Jewish authority in the land!" (1472-3) Following
the Magi's visit the damage was done. Herod's fear of a new ruler sup-
planting his sovereignty set in motion a tragic turn of events.

The slaughter of the innocents reported in the Gospel of Matthew
is a heart-wrenching moment in the saga of the infant Jesus. Enraged
by the duplicity of the Magi who never returned to tell him where the
newborn king resided, Herod proceeds to order the death of every
child from six months to two years old living in Bethlehem and the
surrounding environs. (Matt. 2:16) Cayce describes this as the period
" . . . when many in the land about Nazareth and Bethany and Capernaum suffered from the edict of the ruler that only ruled with a reflected
power or Herod, the Great." (578-2) Fortunately before the hated ruler's
edict was officially announced, Joseph's inner guidance had warned
him in a dream that he needed to take Mary and the baby and flee into
Egypt to protect the child from certain death. The couple was of one
mind about the necessity of leaving their home and promptly fled.

The Cayce readings note that the Essene Brotherhood already had
begun making preparations in anticipation of the need for a possible
flight and had selected individuals to act as handmaids for Mary, Jesus,
and Joseph during transit. In addition, small supportive groups preceded and followed the family to provide extra protection. The readings
suggest that their journey into Egypt did not go unnoticed by the locals
living along the route and in fact later became part of the oral traditions
of those communities. "Through that period there were many of the
stories that have come down as legends, even of those people in some
portions of Egypt and of Arabia, as to the happenings along the way,
as to how there were the unusual happenings—indicating not only the
divinity of the Child but that purpose later recorded, 'And she kept all

of these and pondered them in her heart.'" (5749-16)

Surrendered Innocence
ରେ

To this day Herod's treachery after the birth of Jesus endures in the collective psyche as one of the most horrifying episodes recorded in the New Testament. Ironically after the entrance into the earth of a holy child destined to deliver freedom to the people of God, their deliverer barely escapes death at the hands of one of his own—a Jewish monarch determined to sacrifice guiltless babies at the shrine of his anger and vanity.

The story of Herod's twisted claim to power, which resulted in the massacre of the innocents, holds profound significance as an allegory. It presents a warning about the dangers posed by sinister forces vehemently arrayed against the coming of the light and describes what can happen when a single unrestrained ego aligned with these energies unleashes them in the earth. The blind opposition of a Herod, self-absorbed and fearful of the establishment of a more spiritually advanced order, is both deep-seated and raw. Intent on destroying what they cannot understand, the legions of darkness will stop at nothing in their quest to blot out the Christ spirit newborn into the earth. But hope cannot die when highly developed souls such as Joseph stay alert to the still small voice of wisdom within and follow its guidance. These are the guardians of the light who will keep the holy child, the Christ in man, safe and alive, allowing it to develop until it gains enough strength to illuminate the world.

Seen from a more conventional angle, biblical scholars have interpreted Herod's callous bout of infanticide as a preordained event designed to ensure that ancient prophecy was fulfilled. Old Testament references to Rachel mourning for her children and the statement "out of Egypt have I called my son" (Matt. 2:15) are cited as part of a body of evidence predicting the coming of a savior, Herod's murderous decision following his birth, and the flight of the Holy Family. The recurring theme and deeper metaphorical meaning of the death of the sinless child takes on added significance when viewed not merely as an isolated incident from the first century AD but against the sweeping backdrop of the entire Bible. The story's roots lie deep in the remote past, extending as far back as some of the first books of the Old Testament. In many ways the dramatic image of the infant Jesus whisked away to elude the jaws of death bears a striking resemblance to a moment much earlier in Jewish history when another deliverer comes out of Egypt to liberate the people of God.

Moses
⨪

The series of events surrounding the birth of Moses depicted in vivid detail in the book of Exodus most closely foreshadows the catastrophic events that will transpire in the area around the tiny town of Bethlehem during the reign of Herod the Great. Here, too, a miraculous chain of circumstances occurs after Pharaoh orders the death of all the newborn sons of the Hebrew slaves. Determined to save her baby, Moses' mother, Jochebed, places him in a tiny ark made of bulrushes which she floats on the Nile River. Then something unexpected happens. The child is plucked from the water by Pharaoh's sister and ends up not only eluding death but also becoming a member of the monarch's own family. Little Moses grows up in the rarified atmosphere of the royal household and eventually is elevated to great heights of temporal glory.

But like Jesus many centuries later, Moses' destiny is not to wear the crown of an earthly king. Forced by extreme circumstances, including a murder, to leave behind his wealth and material-minded ways, this former son of a Pharaoh ends up enslaved for a short period of time and then is thrown out of Egypt to wander alone in the wilderness. Amazingly, the destitute outcast stumbling through the desert is able to preternaturally evade death a second time and eventually comes to embrace a new way of life as a shepherd—a job which induces him to turn within. After spending months in quiet contemplation, Moses raises his consciousness to such a high level that he is able to experience direct awareness of the divine and recognizes God as the spirit within him, present right where he stands—on holy ground. "I am that I am" are the words he hears. Moses' conscious realization of this divinity— his enlightenment—is what will support him throughout the rest of his lifetime and, against all odds, will allow a lowly shepherd to rescue the Hebrews from their captivity.

Once Moses returns to Egypt following his religious experience, he pushes Pharaoh hard to release the Jewish slaves. But Pharaoh taunts him, asking "Who *is* the Lord, that I should obey his voice to let Israel go?" (Exod. 5:2) A series of devastating plagues ensues until the Egyptian ruler leads Moses to believe he has relented and finally will allow the Israelites to leave. Yet before they are permitted to depart, the sacrifice of the guiltless child enters the picture again. The Old Testament account states that after many false promises Pharaoh hardened his heart one last time causing a tenth and final plague to settle on the land. On the eve of what will turn out to be the exodus of the Israelites from their bondage, the firstborn of every household dies—except for the sons and daughters in homes where the blood of the innocent lamb is painted on the lintels and door posts as a sacred sign that death should pass over. The surrender of the firstborn is the event that precipitates freedom for the people of God.

Beloved Son
∾

> Thus is He the only begotten, the firstborn, the first to know flesh,
> the first to purify it.   1158-5

Allusions to the loss of the firstborn or favored son appear again and again throughout the holy text beginning with Abraham in Genesis and culminating in the story of Jesus, thirty-three years after Herod's slaughter of the innocents when the first-begotten of God, the Adam soul, will be slain on a cross at Calvary. Closer examination of the theme of the sacrifice of the child reveals a thread tying together the horrific events in Bethlehem in the weeks following the infant Jesus' birth to several of his former lifetimes as well as the place of the Messiah in spiritual history.

Thousands of years before Mary's baby appeared on the scene, the patriarch Abraham's wife Sarah, a woman long past child-bearing age, miraculously becomes pregnant and gives birth to a son named Isaac. The story related in Genesis indicates that the homage the God of Abraham sought from his servant was the unconditional alignment of

Abraham's will with the will of the divine. And the indisputable evidence of the man's deference to the Almighty would be his obedience to the divine command to offer his only son on the altar of sacrifice. That which was created and loved most in the material realm by the man Abraham belonged to God and must be given back to the same unseen force from which it had emanated. But in the end, due to the patriarch's undeviating resolve to surrender all personal desire in order to fulfill a greater holy purpose, this unnamed deity does not require him to surrender his child. The sacred impartation Abraham receives at the moment of dispensation thunders down through history: "Lay not thine hand upon the lad, neither do thou any thing unto him: for now I know that thou fearest God, seeing thou hast not withheld thy son, thine only *son* from me." (Gen. 22:12)

Spirit requires of man only humble submission to his innermost sense of knowing. And due to Abraham's willingness to listen and obey—his unwavering fidelity to the highest ideal—God promises his descendants shall be as numberless as the stars and his seed a blessing to all the nations of the earth. Abraham and Sarah's beloved son Isaac grows up to father Jacob, who will wrestle with the angel, earn the name Israel, and have twelve sons of his own.

Out of Egypt

It was Jacob's eleventh son, Joseph, a previous incarnation of the Master who was thrown into slavery in Egypt (symbol of the material world) that sets the stage for the Moses narrative generations later. A divine hand raises up this soul to greatness, empowering Joseph with the authority and opportunity to provide sustenance to the Israelites and literally keep that nation alive. The child lost to his father and believed dead ends up becoming the fulfillment of the divine promise originally made to Abraham: to forever preserve the people of the one God. So, too, will the first begotten son, the Adam soul, lost to the heavenly realms at the beginning of time, be raised up to glory and become a savior. But first, he has to prepare for the role.

Jesus as Student

Did the Father prepare the Master, or did the Master prepare
Himself for the Father's purpose?   2067-7

As detailed in the Edgar Cayce readings, following their flight from
Judea the Holy Family stayed in Egypt approximately two-and-a-half
years. They may have been gone from their homeland for as long as
four or five years, however, counting the length of time it took in those
days to travel back and forth on slow-moving animals over rugged
terrain. Most of their stay was spent " . . . dwelling by the brooks or the
portions where there were wells in the upper portion of the Egyptian
land to which they fled," close to what was then Alexandria, which
already was a great center of learning. (1010–12) Mary, Joseph, and the
members of their household were said to have taken advantage of the
opportunity for study during their visit. According to the Cayce material, they reviewed some of the same records and prophecies the Wise
Men had researched concerning the advent of the Messiah and some
of the experiences that were going to occur in his life. "Those same records from which the men of the East said and gave, 'By those records
we have seen his star.' These pertained, then, to what you would call
today astrological forecasts, as well as those records which had been
compiled and gathered by all of those of that period pertaining to the
coming of the Messiah . . . " (1010–17) In addition, the information included references to the forerunner of the deliverer, John the Baptist, as
well as the " . . . nature of work of the parents . . . " and " . . . their places
of sojourn . . . " along with those qualities concerning the nature and
character of the people who would be " . . . coming in contact with the
young Child . . . " (1010–17)

Upon their departure from Egypt, Joseph decides against returning
to the place where they had previously lived and instead chooses to
settle in Galilee at Capernaum primarily for political reasons. "Then
there was the return to Judea and to Capernaum, where dwelt many
of those who were later the closer companions of the Master," (5749–7)
explains Cayce. The area in general was quieter and provided a more
secure location for his family. It also offered greater proximity to the
activities and teachings of the Essene Brotherhood overseen by Judy.

For the most part there is a paucity of information about Jesus' childhood in the biblical accounts of those early years. Luke's gospel reports that the young boy grew and waxed strong and increased in "wisdom and stature, and in favour with God and man." (Luke 2:51-52) Jesus was said to have had the grace of God upon him. The Cayce readings fill in several blanks in the information concerning this special child, mentioning his unusual interactions with the community and singular presence in the world. One interesting fact we learn about Jesus is that he was already healing at a very young age—

> ... garments worn by the child would heal children. For the body, being perfect, radiated that which was health, life itself. Just as today individuals may radiate by their spiritual selves health, life, that vibration which is destructive to dis-ease in any form in bodies ...   1010-17

In commenting further on this activity, Cayce goes on to explain that his apparel " . . . brought more and more the influence which today would be called a lucky charm, or a lucky chance . . . " (2067-7) Although present within him and plainly evident to others on more than one occasion, apparently the healing capacity was not yet a conscious awareness in the child.

Lest we begin to believe this little boy was completely different from all the other children brought up in that day and age according to the Oriental customs of Egypt and Galilee, we learn from the readings that Jesus was " . . . in every manner a normal, developed body, ready for those activities of children of that particular period." (1010-17) " . . . Remember and keep in mind, He was normal, He developed normally . . . " states Cayce in the same reading. It is said those around him saw the same characteristics that might belong to anyone who wholly places his or her trust in God. Mary watched her son closely and having studied the prophecies and records while preparing for her own role in the divine adventure, must have started to put a few more of pieces of the puzzle together. But as Luke had reported, at the time of Jesus' birth she quietly kept "all of these things and pondered *them* in her heart." (Luke 2:19)

The family had some additional help in the person of a woman named Josie who had been among the group of twelve maidens on the stairs when Mary was chosen as the one who would give birth to the savior. Josie also had accompanied the Holy Family to Egypt—a journey which Cayce described as "... no mean distance for a very young child, and a very young mother—during such delicate conditions." (1010-12) She is said to have been "... active in all educational activities as well as the care of the body and the attending to the household duties with every developing child." (1010-17) In terms of Jesus' educational activities as a youngster, his studies were "... in keeping with the tenets of the Brotherhood {*the activities and beliefs of the Essenes*}; as well as that training in the law—which was the Jewish or Mosaic law in that period." (1010-17)

The Bible picks up the story again around the time Jesus reaches the age of twelve when on a trip to Jerusalem he becomes separated from his parents who finally discover him in the temple conversing with a group of learned rabbis. The Cayce readings say a mix-up is what caused the child to be left behind. (1010-17) Mary and Joseph believed he was elsewhere in their caravan in the care of Josie, and Josie must have thought he was with his parents. "And it came to pass, that after three days they found him in the temple, sitting in the midst of the doctors, both hearing them, and asking them questions. And all that heard him were astonished at his understanding and answers. And when they saw him, they were amazed: and his mother said unto him, Son, why hast thou thus dealt with us? behold, thy father and I have sought thee sorrowing. And he said unto them, How is it that ye sought me? wist ye not that I must be about my Father's business?" (Luke 2:46-49) Interestingly the episode in the temple actually is the first time Jesus begins to comprehend his powers and abilities. This understanding was "... not as a consciousness ..." in his boyhood according to Edgar Cayce. The awareness really starts to dawn on him during the more formal preparations for his ministry, the first step of which was his great thirst for knowledge about spiritual subjects: "... Thus the seeking for the study through the associations with the teachers of that period." (2067-7)

Mastery
ঙ্ক

. . . in first India, then Persia, then Egypt: for "My son shall be
called from Egypt."   5749-2

Grounded in a thorough knowledge of Jewish law via the instruction
he had received at home before his twelfth birthday, Jesus leaves the
household of Joseph and Mary and is placed in the care and ministry
of the priests and leaders of the Brotherhood. From the age of twelve
to about fifteen or sixteen, Judy taught him the prophecies in her home
at Mount Carmel. But at a certain point the young man had gleaned
what he could from his Essene teachers and began his education
abroad—first in Egypt for a short period, then in India for three years
followed by studies in the area later called Persia. (Approximately one
year was spent in travel and another year spent studying with various
masters in Persia.) Cayce says it was from Persia that Jesus was called
back to Judea at the death of Joseph. (5749-7) The culmination of all
of this schooling was a second stint in Egypt a few years later, which
marked the final step in his development as a teacher.

In all of his studies he was registered under the name Jeshua. This
name and its variant, Joshua, of which the Greek form is Jesus, are
contractions of Jehoshua, which means "Help of Jehova," or "Savior."
His lessons overall were broad-ranging and demanded enormous
amounts of personal discipline. In India he explored "those cleansings
of the body as related to preparations for strength in the physical as
well as the mental man . . . " and in Persia " . . . the union of forces
as related to those teaching of Zu and Ra . . . " (5749-2) Egypt was the
capstone however. There he delved into all the teachings that had been
part of the ancient Temple of Sacrifice and Temple Beautiful and the
" . . . after actions of the crucifying of self in relationships to ideals that
made for the abilities of carrying on that called to be done." (5749-2)
In other words, he learned how to set an ideal and overcome self. The
Bible alludes to the fact that Jesus was called "Rabbi" or teacher, a title
accurately describing his educational achievements. The readings also
comment that "hence in all ways of the teachers (Jesus) was trained."
(5749-7) They go on to explain that he became distinguished for learn-

ing and was an authoritative teacher of the law as well as a Master of the teachings of the East.

Jesus' cousin, the messenger John, was with him during a portion of the time he spent in Egypt, although John was in one class and Jesus in another. It was while Jesus was in India that John, at the age of seventeen, had first gone to Egypt for his own dedication and preparation. Jesus and John studied together in Heliopolis, which had schools of astronomy and philosophy, and was located about six miles northeast of what is now modern Cairo—not far from the Great Pyramid. His second sojourn in Egypt represented the period when Jesus would attain the final degree needed to complete his formal training before publicly launching his soul mission and work.

According to Edgar Cayce, scholars in Egypt during that era had gathered together and unified the teachings of many lands. Egypt was the center from which there was to be a " . . . radial activity of influence in the earth—as indicated by the first establishing of those tests, or the recording of time as it has been, was and is to be—until the new cycle is begun." (2067-7) Jesus and his cousin were there " . . . for the periods of attaining to the priesthood, or the taking of examinations . . . passing the tests there . . . through which one attained to that place of being accepted or rejected by the influence of the mystics as well as of the various groups or schools in other lands . . . " (2067-7) The most important and decisive trials were conducted inside the Great Pyramid.

Great Pyramid

In this same pyramid did the Great Initiate, the Master, take those last of the Brotherhood degrees with John, the forerunner of Him, at that place . . .

5748-5

Contrary to popular theories held by most archeological scholars today, the Great Pyramid was not originally built as a tomb but " . . . to be the hall of initiates of that sometimes referred to as the White Brotherhood." (5748-5) The readings talk about the era of its construction at the time of Ra-Ta and describe its mystical purpose as a symbol in stone of humanity's " . . . passage through that to which each soul is to attain in its development . . . "(2067-7) Astonishing in its size and enveloped by a sense of the occult, Egypt's Great Pyramid still speaks to souls everywhere, silently calling them to contemplate the deeper mysteries of life and what will be unveiled within the human heart once we awaken to who we truly are. The readings say the inner chamber of the Great Pyramid was the site where the great Initiate, the Master, took " . . . those last of the Brotherhood degrees with John, the forerunner of him at that place . . . " (5748-5) It was inside the Great Pyramid that Jesus came face to face with the meaning of death and saw through it.

The climb up through the Great Pyramid is a long and somewhat challenging trek ending in the King's Chamber where an empty sarcophagus cut from a single piece of rock sits with its lid open. Curiously, Edgar Cayce states that all of the changes in religious thought in the history of the world are recorded in the pyramid's structure through the variations in the stone as one passes from its base to the top or " . . . to the open tomb *and* the top . . . " (5748-5) These changes are signified by both the layer and color of the stone and by whatever direction turns are made while moving through the pyramid's interior. The readings elaborate on the symbolism of Jesus' initiation and the breaking open of the tomb to release the soul from its entrapment in a material world—

> . . . that through which each entity, each soul, as an initiate must pass for the attaining to the releasing of same—as indicated by the empty tomb, which has *never* been filled, see? Only Jesus was able to break same, as it became that which indicated His fulfillment.
>
> 2067-7

Jesus had embarked on his preparatory studies first by gaining a better understanding of the foundations of Jewish law. His life as a student concluded with him reaching the pinnacle of mysticism or God awareness. Out of the law this Great Initiate would bring grace as " . . . love, mercy, peace that there may be the fulfilling wholly of that purpose to which, of which, He was called," states Edgar Cayce. (5749-2) Now it was time for his ministry to begin. But before that work could commence, he would have to retreat into the wilderness to meet " . . . that which had been his undoing in the beginning." (2067-7)

Sign of the Dove

Once Herod the Great had passed on, the Essenes had more freedom of movement and activity and no longer felt the need to keep their operations so secret. And after returning from his own studies in Egypt, Jesus' cousin John assumed a larger role in the sect. Renouncing the orthodox priesthood (John was the lineal descendent of the priest Zacharias), he was appointed leader of the sect and began preaching in the backcountry and baptizing followers in the Jordan River, becoming a rather notorious outcast from the more traditional Jewish community in the process. "Repent ye: for the kingdom of heaven is at hand" (Matt. 3:2) was his message and mantra. During this period Andrew, who would later become one of the Master's apostles, became John's first adherent or disciple, serving as his aide until Jesus entered the picture.

Jesus' formal ministry is set into motion when he arrives at the shore of the Jordan River where John is working. Standing together, the two cousins exemplify the juxtaposition of the new and old world orders. John had come forth wild from the desert where he lived apart from other men. And though he indeed was the harbinger of the coming of the Christ to the sensate world, John still hewed to the tactics of the old way: hard-nosed, bombastic, and convinced God could be found through harsh disciplines of the body. "Unkempt, unshaven, and clad in the skins of animals, he had burst like a specter on the scene of the time," the specter of a bygone age.[6] John was a prophet of old, railing against sinners who transgressed the law and heaping disdain on anyone who did not adhere to fixed rules and boundaries or see the error of his ways. Yet this prophet also understood that his moment in the sun was fading and told his followers that he baptized merely with water. The one who would follow him, whose shoes he was not worthy to unlatch, would baptize them with the Holy Ghost and fire—the inner purification of Spirit raised up in matter. John freely admitted his ideas and methods must decrease so that Jesus and his doctrine might increase in the world.

---

[6] Janet Highland, "New Testament" (unpublished manuscript, 1979).

Baptism

Similar to the arrival of the angel announcing the impending birth of the savior to his mother Mary, the baptism of Jesus in the River Jordan represents an enormous spiritual turning point for the human race. The baptismal rite remains a solemn part of the liturgy of many religious traditions but one whose ancient origins for the most part have been lost to history. The ritual harks back to the floodwaters of the Old Testament that had enveloped the earth at the time of Noah. Just as new life took root and sprang forth after the cleansing waters of the Great Flood had receded, the individual surfacing from the waters of baptism emerges into a different kind of life—washed clean of former ways and conditions.

The Master knew that John's revelations about him being the Messiah were true and that the end of the old order was imminent. So, in a nod to the time-honored ceremony of baptism, he humbly assents to letting his cousin immerse him in the river, saying "Suffer it to be so now: for thus it becometh us to fulfil all righteousness." (Matt. 3:15) He used the baptismal ritual to indicate a washing away of the past before he emerged from the waters ready to take up the mantle of spiritual teacher and deliverer. Jesus would be the one to help humanity reestablish itself on earth in a different way, and his baptism signaled the unveiling of this new covenant. A new order of love and mercy was at hand.

Jesus' teachings would model an approach to living in the material world in which spirit was primary. Setting aside the destructive weapons, prejudices, and tactics of old, an outlook held by those who believed "might makes right," he would promote a more evolved way of thinking and acting built on the pillars of balance, wisdom, nurturing, and healing. For thirty years the Master had prepared for this moment, and now, standing next to his cousin in the river, he was given a sign that the time for his ministry to begin had arrived. It was the same sign the patriarch Noah had seen when the old world, deteriorated to the point of ruin and submerged by the deluge, was ready to be regenerated.[7]

---

[7] Janet Highland, "New Testament" (unpublished manuscript, 1979).

And again Noah "sent forth the dove out of the ark; And the dove came in to him in the evening; and, lo, in her mouth was an olive leaf pluckt off: so Noah knew that the waters were abated from off the earth. And he stayed yet other seven days; and sent forth the dove; which returned not again unto him any more."

Gen. 8:10-12

Seeing the sign of the dove, Noah understood it was time to leave the ark and begin building anew. Well versed in the stories of the Old Testament, Jesus also understood as he rose from the river waters and saw the Spirit of God descending upon him "like a dove," that he, too, was about to commence his work. Spirit had found a place "for the sole of her foot" (Gen. 8:9)—for the establishment of a radically different order for the world. And he was the ground upon which it would be built. Yet even with such a sign, he had no certainty anyone would listen to him. With few credentials to support his unconventional ideas and the backing of only a small, splinter group of Jews, what proof could he give that he spoke the truth?[8] The answer ultimately would come from within him, but only after he had grappled with the same issue which had tested Adam and Eve in the garden. Left unresolved, it might spell his downfall just as it had for the souls cast out of the heavenly estate in the beginning: to use one's spiritual light for oneself.

Wilderness Experience
⚬❧⚬

> . . . He passed from that activity into the wilderness to meet that which had been His undoing in the beginning.   2067-7

Led by the unseen divine forces, Jesus withdrew into the wilderness—a physical venue symbolizing the shadowy, untamed recesses of his own inner being—for an extended period of solitude. Here in this uncharted territory he would face and overcome three formidable temptations by meeting that which originally had caused his downfall. The Gospel of Luke places Jesus in the wilderness for forty days and

---

[8] Janet Highland, "New Testament" (unpublished manuscript, 1979).

says he ate nothing during the entire period. The devil or Satan, a word meaning "adversary" or "one who resists,"[9] soon arrives to tempt him. This was the moment when Jesus was perhaps the most vulnerable because, being filled with the Holy Spirit, he was now fully cognizant of the divinity dwelling inside him. Feeling hungry, the devil or self-serving aspect of his humanhood tempts him to use the divine energy he possesses to create a loaf of bread. But Jesus resists. He understands that the God force he carries inside him is not to be employed to indulge material appetites. Reaffirming the primacy of spirit, he reminds himself that man does not live by physical bread alone but by the inner presence and voice of God.

Having successfully overcome his physical appetites, Jesus must wrestle with the longing for earthly power by subjugating the desire to use the divine energy entrusted to him to attain political glory and the riches of a mighty king. All he has to do is bow down and worship the earth-bound compulsion to see himself as separate and apart from the whole—to act in an ego-driven and selfish manner. He dismisses this second temptation with the words "Get thee behind me, Satan!" (Luke 4:8) asserting that the only thing man should revere (and serve) is Spirit—the God who is one.

The fascination with earthly modes and means is not dispelled so easily however, and inner resistance to the ways of the Spirit seduces Jesus once more when he fancies the idea of testing God. Perhaps he should demonstrate to the world in one grand show-stopping gesture that he knows what he is talking about. He quickly and summarily avoids this trap, too, with an unequivocal statement: "Thou shalt not tempt the Lord thy God." (Luke 4:12) Divinity does not depend upon man manipulating material substances or employing magic tricks so human beings can judge whether or not a thing is divine. No man-made "test" will ever accede to the material dimension the right to determine who, or what, is of God.[10]

Jesus' days in the wilderness were the proving ground where he struggled with doubt and the tendency to determine his own divinity by the yardstick of the mechanical mind. The thought must have kept

---

[9]http://www.biblestudytools.com/dictionary/satan/
[10]Janet Highland, "New Testament" (unpublished manuscript, 1979).

coming to him that if he really were divine, the world would recognize him as its Lord. If he really had God within him, he could use that power "to turn rocks into bread or sail safely through mid-air."[11] Yet for forty days he refused to accept the limited judgment of the senses and adhered solely to the knowledge imparted from a divine source. In faith he stayed focused on the single truth that God is—and that is all we ever need to know. And when his internal battles were resolved this Master left his wilderness to return to Galilee and begin his work, living "in the power of the spirit." (Luke 4:14)

The sole credentials Jesus held comprised an understanding of the new order, which would bind up old wounds and serve the world rather than egoistic interests. He would demonstrate to the few individuals then capable of understanding his message that proof of the presence of divinity had nothing to do with the ability to control material resources and power. As an Eastern master he had learned how to manipulate the physical realm but that type of dominion did not make him a Christ. The true sign of Godliness was the ability to love and do the constructive work of Spirit. The Edgar Cayce readings sum up his retreat into the wilderness and victory over Satan in this way. Jesus was tempted in all ways like we are: in that of self-indulgence, of self-gratification, of self-glorification—" . . . yet without sin . . . " (262-82)

---

[11]Janet Highland, "New Testament" (unpublished manuscript, 1979).

Chapter 5
The Kingdom of
Heaven Is at Hand

Come, ye blessed of my Father, inherit
the kingdom prepared for you from the
foundation of the world. Matt. 25:34

Time and again during his three-year public ministry, Jesus will
reinforce the message that Spirit/God is primary and everything
else secondary. Spirit is the generative force out of which all life emanates—the reality sitting behind everything we see and the essence of
who we are. The Gospel of John takes a giant leap in illuminating this
truth when it uses the analogy of the word in its opening statement:
"And the Word was made flesh and dwelt among us." (John 1:14) Easily
recognized as a physical manifestation of the movement of thought, the
written or spoken word attests to the creativity and power of nonmaterial realms.[12] So, too, will the life of Jesus of Nazareth give credence

---

[12]Janet Highland, "New Testament" (unpublished manuscript, 1979).

to the place that unseen dimensions hold in what is perceived as life on earth.

The story of the Master's conception via nonphysical means had set the stage for the ideas he would eventually preach and what his time among the people of the "Promised Land" would conclusively prove: the unperceived presence of divinity here and now. The entrance of God or the Christ into human experience is always the end product of a process that begins in Spirit, is channeled through the mind, and then blossoms forth into materiality.[13] Thus does the triune nature of the human being (soul, mind, body) reach the pinnacle of its expression in the earth.

Jesus' revolutionary message is ultimately going to transform the world. At the same time, just as he had predicted, his words would pit brother against brother because the principles the Master preached represented a fundamentally different way of interacting within this earthly domain. His precursor, John the Baptist, "had railed against the establishment, verbally attacking its political, social, and religious leaders. Naming names, seeking the downfall of factions, alerting people to the sins of those in high places,"[14] John hoped to motivate his listeners to throw off the oppressive yokes of religious and political authority. His way was the same process by which established orders always had been toppled—by reformers as well as those grabbing at personal power. Its method of operation was to step in, using harsh, coercive tactics to alter the situation and thereby institute a new regime. But merely changing the outer symptoms of a problem never worked for long because the inner state of mind from which the problem originated remained the same. Get rid of one corrupt system and another one equally corrupt inevitably gained power. The cycle was never-ending.[15]

The way of the Christ followed a different path. Despite what many of his closest followers as well as the religious zealots and political rebels of the first century may have wished, Jesus' mission was not to overthrow the Roman government, eliminate Jewish authority, or replace the existing social structure with an equally onerous set of political,

---

[13] Janet Highland, "New Testament" (unpublished manuscript, 1979).
[14] Ibid.
[15] Ibid.

social, or religious powers and taboos. He was going to take an ax to the root of the tree. The Master knew the process of releasing humanity from its enslavement to a materially focused existence dictated a fundamental reorientation of thought. The new Adam understood all too well that true, lasting change—change which finally would free souls trapped in a toxic world—could only be built from the inside out with patience, humility, and loving service to the whole.

The Ministry Begins

Now after that John was put in prison, Jesus came into Galilee, preaching the gospel of the kingdom of God and saying, The time is fulfilled, and the kingdom of God is at hand: repent ye, and believe the gospel. Mark 1:14-15

After recounting Jesus' sojourn in the wilderness, the Gospel of Matthew quickly moves the story along and describes the Master finding his first disciples, two fishermen—symbols of the Piscean Age—trained to cast their nets and haul in a harvest from the sea. Jesus proceeds to ask Simon (Peter) and Andrew to follow him and become "fishers of men" by helping gather up souls from the sea of humanity ready to receive his message. Soon after the brothers join the Master, he asks two more fishermen to commit themselves to this new way of thinking and being. And the sons of Zebedee, James and John, immediately leave their father's ship to follow the obscure rabbi. Matthew then reports that Jesus "went about all Galilee, teaching in their synagogues, and preaching the gospel of the kingdom, and healing all manner of sickness and all manner of disease among the people." (Matt. 4:23)

The moment for the Master to begin revealing his message to the larger world had arrived. And for the next three years he would explain points from the ancient scriptures, relate parables, answer questions, confront the religious authorities of the time, and, like a gypsy, move from place to place among the people of Judea to awaken those who had "ears to hear" (Mark 4:9) to the truths he taught. The recurring theme this extraordinary teacher kept hammering home to his students was to look beyond finite forms and recognize the divinity dwelling behind the material shell. God is with us.

Anointed One
⸻

> . . . Jesus was the man—the activity, the mind, the relationships
> that He bore to others. Yea, He was mindful of friends, He was
> sociable, He was loving, He was kind, He was gentle. He grew
> faint, He grew weak—and yet gained that strength that He has
> promised, in becoming the Christ, by fulfilling and overcoming the
> world! . . .   2533-7

Armed with the certitude that he and the Father—the creative principle of life—were one, Jesus announced his work to the community
by speaking in the synagogue where learned Jews regularly gathered.
Cayce notes that on the first Sabbath following his return to Capernaum
to reside with his own people, he had gone into the local synagogue
and was shown the deference due a rabbi in Israel—until the tenor of
his teaching and the authority with which he taught began to evoke
not just astonishment but outright dismay.

He spoke with the authority imparted by other-dimensional
realms—an authority at which people marveled. And just as he had
expected, many listeners became upset by his words, wondering how
someone they knew only as Joseph's son thought he had any right to
say such things. The Master was planting the first seeds of a revolutionary message. We are God's own children—born of Spirit. And he was
giving people a choice where no choice had existed before. They now
had the opportunity to understand that their human identity as children of the flesh was merely one facet of a tripartite heritage of body,
mind, and spirit. From the beginning his message about man's innate
divinity—God with us—was greeted with joy by some and rage by others. Sadly, even many, who at first were receptive to his teachings, later
would oppose the truths he spoke.[16]

Reading from the scriptures, Jesus confirmed that the Spirit of the
Lord was upon him, " . . . because he hath anointed me to preach the
gospel to the poor; he hath sent me to heal the brokenhearted, to
preach deliverance to the captives, and recovering of sight to the blind,

---

[16]Janet Highland, "New Testament" (unpublished manuscript, 1979).

to set at liberty them that are bruised, To preach the acceptable year of the Lord." (Luke 4:18–19) Edgar Cayce also reports that the Master's sister, Ruth, was present in the synagogue that morning and " . . . for the first time heard in the synagogue His first utterances as to the prophecies of Isaiah, Jeremiah, and the teachings of the lesser prophets, and as to how they applied in the experiences of that day." (1158-4)

Wedding at Cana

With his fame slowly growing, stories about the unusual rabbi and his extraordinary presence and powerful words were voiced from one to another. Soon those stories would include the remarkable events that occurred at Cana—an account in the Bible representing one of the only instances where Jesus performed a miracle among his own people. It happened unexpectedly at a wedding. The young bride was a daughter of one of Mary's close cousins, and Mary had been helping the family during their preparations for the celebration. Cayce's description of the gathering in 5749-15 states that the families of Mary were present, as well as those of the groom. And when the Master arrived, " . . . return-ing with those who were hangers–on, {he} naturally sought to speak with His mother. Learning of this happening {the wedding} He, too, with his followers, were bid to remain at the feast." Apparently the family of Zebedee was part of the upper class, " . . . Thence, the reason why Mary served or prepared for her relative the feast."

As was the custom at the time, the guests drank a great deal of wine during the course of the festivities so much so the supply began to run low. "The day had been fine; the evening was fair; the moon was full," states Cayce. "This then brought the activities with the imbibing more and more of wine, more hilarity, and the dance—which was in the form of the circles that were a part of the customs, not only of that land then but that are in your own land now and then being revived. With those activities, as indicated, the wine ran low . . . " (5749-15)

According to the account given in the readings, based on every-thing his mother personally had witnessed, Mary was certain her son could solve the problem and avoid potential embarrassment for the hosts. Cayce reveals that "from those happenings that had been a portion of her experience upon their return from Egypt—as to how the increase had come in the food, when they had been turned aside as they journeyed back towards the Promised Land—Mary felt, knew, was convinced within herself that here again there might be such an experience, with her son returning as a man starting upon his mission . . . " (5749-15) Hearsay also was being bandied about that a mere ten days ago Jesus had sent Satan away and was ministered to by the angels. Mary went to ask him for help.

It was an odd situation, however. Her son, considered strange in many ways, had chosen to dwell in the wilderness for forty days only to return to mingle with fishermen—commonly regarded as members of one of the lowliest castes. His actions seemed especially unsuited to someone who had mastered the teachings of the East. So a question about what he was really doing may have been implied in Mary's statement, "They have no wine." (John 2:3)

Jesus knew that the moment for the full expression of his teachings had not yet arrived and told his mother his time had not yet come but nonetheless acquiesced to her entreaty and gave the commands whereby a miracle occurred. The Cayce readings speak of him changing the water into wine with a description meant for posterity: " . . . when water saw its master, blushed and became wine, even by activity! . . . " (3361-1) One of the key principles involved in the miraculous process that day was the idea of action. " . . . Only as it was poured out would it become wine," (3361-1) suggests Cayce—a concept that will become a running theme in the Master's ministry going forward. The presence of God is available to elevate and transform the world, but only when this divine energy is actively applied in loving service to others.

The Message

. . . Christ is not a man! Jesus was the man; Christ the messenger . . .
991-1

Like any good teacher, the Master tried to make his lessons come alive for his students using handy symbols and colorful stories. The parables attributed to Jesus are timeless allegories embellished with multiple layers of meaning. As a lecturer he had to walk an instructional tightrope and offer meat to his inner circle and those disciples already primed to hear the truth, while providing milk for the babes—souls still deeply entrenched in physicality and only beginning to wake up to the idea that human beings embodied more than mere flesh and blood.

His objective was to awaken the soul by teaching people that they had the capacity to construct a kingdom of harmony and peace for themselves and others. Jesus also told his followers there was nothing to fear because like the lilies of the field bedecked in natural splendor or tiny sparrows worth only a farthing in the marketplace, their Father was going to care for them each day. "Consider the ravens: for they neither sow nor reap; which neither have storehouse nor barn; and God feedeth them," he said. "How much more are ye better than the fowls?" (Luke 12:24) Every hair on their heads was numbered, and their needs would always be met by the same loving presence and Creative Force responsible for the spark of life, which animated the universe and was alive in them now. In a thousand different ways the Master attempted to draw a picture of the inner spiritual reality he had realized and what men and women could do to magnify its expression in the earth.

Prodigal Son

In one instance Jesus used a story found in various forms throughout the Middle East to explain the human predicament. The parable of the prodigal son tells the tale of a very rich man with two sons. The younger, beloved child leaves his father's house, a place (consciousness) of harmony, ease, and plenty to search for something better in the outside world—something he believes he does not have and sorely needs. But life away from his father's house does not unfold exactly as planned.

Luke's account in the New Testament says the young man pocketed his inheritance and journeyed into a far country where he wasted his substance with riotous living. After squandering his birthright, the young foreigner is set adrift just as a great famine arises in the land. All alone, destitute, and fallen from the heights of glory of his original condition as heir to a mighty fortune, the lost son hires himself out to feed the swine owned by a local citizen. The gospel describes him as being so hungry he would have "filled his belly with the husks the swine did eat: and no man gave unto him." (Luke 15:16)

The biblical narrative uses a powerful phrase to relate what happens next. The prodigal son "came to himself." He awakens to his true identity and acknowledges that if he had never separated himself and were still living with his father, he would lack for nothing. So the wandering child decides to return home to see if he can rejoin the household he had left behind. Yet even before he arrives at his destination, "when he was yet a great way off," his father runs to greet him and welcome him back, giving his child the finest robe and the ring of sonship to signify the young man's position in the family. As far as the father is concerned, there is nothing to forgive. His joy is manifold because a son who was lost has chosen to return to him. And the love and appreciation of the child who went astray intensifies after this reunion—because now he is able to more fully appreciate his heritage. (Luke 15: 17-24)

The boy's brother, the "good son" who never left his father's estate, is not happy about this turn of events, however, and feels slighted. He had not transgressed the rules or squandered his inheritance by carousing with harlots and yet his father never honored him with a special celebration. Jesus concludes his parable with a profound spiritual principle voiced by the father to his elder child: "Son thou art ever with me, and all that I have is thine." (Luke 15:25-31) The children of God never had to leave home (the divine state of consciousness) to find what they needed. As the progeny of a divine source, they are deeply loved and eternally sustained. And when a soul hopelessly lost in the material world is finally able make its way back to the realization of its true identity and rightful status, the universe rejoices.

Good Shepherd
⤳

The Master continually reiterated his conviction that human beings are children of a loving deity whose concern for its offspring is inescapable and endless. His depiction of this tender-hearted, devoted parent—the Spirit residing within the holy temple of man's inner being—provoked a fundamental shift in religious thinking and marked the beginning of a new era in human history. Discarding the old entrenched views of a distant God sitting on a throne somewhere high in the sky acting like a temperamental potentate prone to harsh discipline, fits of anger, and petty rule making, Jesus called the divine Spirit abiding within him—and in every living creature—the good shepherd.

Ever since the time of Adam and Eve whose son Abel was a keeper of sheep, the shepherd has played a prominent role in the chronicle of humanity's spiritual journey on earth. Moses watched his father-in-law's sheep and later became a shepherd to the Hebrew people leading them out of their captivity in Egypt. The psalmist David who slayed Goliath was a shepherd as were Lot, Laban, and Jacob among other star players in the divine drama. So, too, was a small band of shepherds—the first group to recognize the Christ newly born into the earth at the stable in Bethlehem. The shepherd is the ever alert guardian who gently guides his flock to green pastures where sustenance and shelter from storms and predators are found. He does not rely on force to lead his sheep to food and water and bring them safely home again, but calmly moves them along while steadfastly keeping a close eye out lest one of them strays too far afield. Jesus described the good shepherd as the devoted watchman who will leave the ninety-nine in the fold to go find a single lost sheep and bring it back—the protector who will lay down his life for the creatures under his care.

The Master's entire ministry was centered on making this shepherd, the gentle presence of the inner Christ, real for the human race. He taught the multitudes about a Spirit they could not see with eyes of flesh and blood but had experienced firsthand in the extraordinary events that seemed to follow this rabbi wherever he went. The supernatural deeds attributed to Jesus uncovered the operation of a power no one was able to comprehend but thousands identified as real because they saw it manifest in plain sight. In total, the Master spent three short years shepherding his earthly flock, yet during the course of that brief but remarkable career, the miracles he performed not only solidified his disciples' budding belief in the truth of Immanuel but also brought countless souls from every province and walk of life into the fold. The Spirit he radiated transformed everyone who had the good fortune to encounter him wandering the hills of Galilee.

And He Healed Them
⌒⌒

For, what is the source of all healing for human ills? . . . Each soul
has within its power that to use which may make it at one with
Creative Forces or God . . .   3492-1

Jesus' ability to heal and perform the other mystifying feats ascribed
to his ministry was a demonstration in the material realm of the invisible Spirit he had come to disclose to humanity. Because he consciously
had realized the presence of the divine, the omnipotent Creative Force
dwelling inside him, the Master could proclaim—and prove—"I and my
Father are one." (John 10:30) Such tidings were the gospel (good news)
his listeners both heard and experienced as he moved among them.

The atmosphere surrounding such an enlightened teacher must
have been magnetic. The gospels recount numerous occasions when
this simple preacher had captivated large audiences hailing from great
distances, irresistibly drawn to the aura of peace and reassurance that
exuded from his every footstep. Out of the blue lost souls, hungry
for spiritual nourishment, found themselves tagging along behind
the unorthodox rabbi. Moreover, the biblical narrative reports amazing healing powers flowing forth from Jesus into every corner of his
world—a clear sign of the validity of the principles he both embodied
and spoke.

Edgar Cayce describes the healing phenomenon as a process governed by universal law, which affects the consciousness of the person
requesting help to allow physical restoration to occur. He asks us to
remember that all healing—physical, mental, and spiritual—comes from
within and when these three aspects of ourselves are fully coordinated,
we are whole and thereby capable of fulfilling the purpose for which
we entered a material experience. (2528-2) " . . . For there is the ability
within the physical body to recreate or reproduce itself . . . ," the readings assert. (1663-1) Cayce further insists that within the human body
" . . . living, not dead—*living* human forces—we find every element, every gas, every mineral, every influence that is outside of the organism
itself. For indeed it is one with the whole . . . " (470-22) For this reason
the readings call attention to the importance of maintaining a creative,

constructive attitude because healing of every nature arises from within us. (1663–1) Cayce explains: " . . . For all healing . . . is attuning of each atom of the body, each reflex of the brain forces, to the awareness of the divine that lies within each atom, each cell of the body . . . " (3384–2) The power is in Him, the Creator. "The *power* as needed by all is the realization of abiding in His presence . . . " (262–33)

The readings note that there were many instances in the New Testament where individual healings were of an instantaneous nature such as the time Jesus said to the man sick of the palsy, "Son, be of good cheer, thy sins be forgiven thee." (Mark 2:5) And afterwards when questions about the incident arose as the Master knew they would, he provided a ready answer. " . . . 'Which is it easier to say, Thy sins be forgiven thee, or Arise, take up thy bed and go unto thine house?' *Immediately* the man arose, took up his bed and *went* unto his house! . . . " reports Cayce, adding that " . . . it was not by the command, but by His own personage that the healing occurred. For, the question was not as to whether He healed but as to whether He had the power to forgive sin! The recognition was that sin had caused the physical disturbance." (5749–16)

Not surprisingly the readings point out that the same healing power the Great Physician tapped into more than twenty-one centuries ago is still accessible today. Cayce contends that since the totality of life is the expression of the Creative Forces or divine influences within a material plane, the same power that creates is the only power capable of generating healing. He remarks that just as the garments worn by Jesus as a small boy would heal other children because his perfect body radiated " . . . health, life itself . . . " so, too, individuals today " . . . may radiate, by their spiritual selves, health, life, that vibration which is destruction to dis-ease in any form in bodies . . . " (1010–17) Healing is also said to exist in every herb and element in the universe that is " . . . creative within itself . . . " and " . . . gives that inclination for *healing* to a physical body . . . " It does not matter whether the application is by " . . . mechanotherapy, mechanical appliance, suggestion or even by the knife or the red hot irons . . . ," the underlying principle remains the same. (1458–1)

And while it is true that the divine animating life force exists as an element of every single atom found inside the fleshly body, physical restoration requires us to tune into that energy. The readings maintain that all strength and healing of every nature involves changing the vibrations from within or attuning to the divine, the Creative Energies, which are ever-present in the body's living tissue. " . . . This alone is healing . . . " Cayce asserts. " . . . Whether it is accomplished by the use of drugs, the knife or what not, it is the attuning of the atomic structure of the living cellular force to its spiritual heritage." (1967-1) The readings go so far as to point out that prayer is just as scientific as the knife and as effective as mechanical treatments in their individual fields which are of the same source as prayer, " . . . if applied in the same way or manner, or *with* the same sincerity." (1546-1) The operations, procedures, and medicinal remedies we regularly use to revitalize the physical body help to awaken the healing energies already lying dormant inside us. "Know that all healing forces must be within, *not* without!" state the readings, "The applications from without are to create within a coordinating mental and spiritual force . . . " (1196-7)

Furthermore, when asked whether supposedly incurable diseases could be cured, Cayce's response was affirmative. " . . . That which *is* was produced from some force . . . " he said, and " . . . there are in truth no incurable conditions, though the condition may be changed, or the mode of the plane's existence changed . . . " Everything that exists is and was produced from a first cause and may be met, counteracted, or altered because the condition experienced represents the breaking of a law and the healing forces necessarily comply with other laws able to meet the needs of a specific condition. Healing also depends in part on the attitude we hold toward the situation and our ability to discern these divine energies moving through us. (3744-2)

Elevating the sick to a higher state of attunement is what allowed Jesus to heal. In Cayce's comments about the Master's healings he notes that the consciousness of the individual was taken into consideration. It made no difference whether the affliction was a withered hand, an issue of blood, leprosy, blindness, fever, or some other discord caused by material law, mental disturbances, or sin. The Master's realization of the presence of God at that particular moment in time lifted the ill or injured into a new state of consciousness. Jesus met people where they were in their understanding and, serving as a mirror, reflected back to them their godlike natures. To experience the Christ essence of the Master must have been like sensing the oscillations of a humming tuning fork. And once the sufferer began resonating with that higher frequency harmony appeared.

Blind Bartimaeus
❧

Occasionally the process of conforming the physical and mental to the spiritual began with the Master asking the person soliciting his help what he or she wanted him to do. It occurred in the case of a blind beggar named Bartimaeus who happened to be sitting on the side of the highway one day as Jesus and his party left the city of Jericho. When Bartimaeus hears the commotion and discovers Jesus of Nazareth is passing nearby, he begins to cry out, clamoring for the Son of David to have mercy on him. Passersby try to shut him up, but every effort to silence the beggar compels him to shout even louder until the Master asks someone to bring the blind man to him. Mark's gospel describes what happened next. "And he, casting away his garment, rose, and came to Jesus. And Jesus answered and said unto him, What wilt thou that I should do unto thee? The blind man said unto him, Lord, that I might receive my sight. And Jesus said unto him, Go thy way; thy faith hath made thee whole. And immediately he received his sight, and followed Jesus in the way." (Mark 10: 50–52)

The episode in which Bartimeaus' sight is restored is the quintessential example of the Master's prowess as a healer and teacher able to use an unanticipated event as the springboard to impart a vital spiritual teaching. Unkempt, considered next-to-worthless due to his handicap and with no material goods to speak of, the blind man sits at the bottom of the heap in terms of rank and reputation. It was easy for the disciples shadowing the Master and the throngs of spectators milling around the area to brush him off. Yet Bartimaeus is the only one among the crowd who truly sees. Physical eyes were not necessary for him to ascertain the proximity of the Christ and seize the opportunity to approach this divine Spirit once he becomes aware of it crossing his path. His persistence in trying to reach the Master—the single power capable of blessing him—eventually pays off. After Bartimaeus succeeds in making contact with the Christ and is invited to come and kneel before its visible manifestation, the man who was a beggar casts away his old garment and "rises." And in an expression of loving concern, the sacred presence allows the lowly mendicant to ask for—and receive—the desires of his heart. "What wilt thou that I should do unto thee?" his Lord inquires. (Mark 10:51) A soul that was blind is ready to see.

Even before he spoke to Bartimaeus, Jesus knew exactly what the physical problem was yet he still sought confirmation that the sightless man was prepared not just to be cured of a bodily ill but to be elevated into a higher state of awareness. Every time the Master asked what an individual desired of him, he was looking for evidence the petitioner was open to the influx of Spirit and prepared to "re-form" the patterns and attitudes holding the soul in physical and mental bondage. Invariably Jesus' response was to raise the infirm and downtrodden to a heightened state of attunement and in the process solve the problem. Sometimes the rabbi also would admonish those forgiven or cured to "go and sin no more," (John 8:11) warning them that returning to their former ways of thinking and acting by feigning ignorance of the presence and power of God could result only in more pain and distress. Human ills are the byproduct of states of consciousness, and Jesus' healings proved there was a way out for people seeking to escape the shackles of a physical or mental ailment. They could wake up to who they truly are.

It is worth noting a few ancillary details that the Edgar Cayce readings mention in augmenting the story of Bartimaeus' miraculous healing. Called strong in body yet lacking in sight, the man is said to have received " . . . in the flesh—the benefits as were had by the acts of the Master . . . "(2124-3) Apparently the effects of the healing Jesus had induced on that roadside near the outskirts of ancient Jericho proved to have had a lasting impact on this soul, for the blind man's brief encounter with the Master continued to influence him lifetime after lifetime. The reading 2124-3 reports the episode that restored his sight built " . . . in the warp and woof of the entity's being . . . "and the desire " . . . to lift up, to aid, to succor, those in distress . . . " We also learn that following his cure the former beggar worked in metals and there, too, acted as " . . . a power to strengthen those that were weak . . . " Coming full circle to the twentieth century, Cayce advised the individual identified as having been Bartimaeus to use his current incarnation to bring peace, understanding, and aid to those who may be in the same situation he was thousands of years ago—seeking to awaken the inner man to the abilities that come from making contact by "calling *on* His name."

Do Thou Likewise
⁓

Q. Have I any healing power; if so, how may I develop it?
A. By raising those vibrations within self to the consciousness of the Christ-force, and giving it out through the hands and through the thoughts. 1222-1

Since the days of Jesus' ministry, most churchgoers and mainstream religious traditions have regarded the Master's ability to heal as something wholly disconnected from the rest of humanity. Seen as mystifying, "one-off" events which occurred thousands of years ago to a lucky group of long-dead people, healings the way the Master performed them are believed to belong exclusively to the sole representative of God on earth. But a closer examination of his cures unveils an eternal message of hope and deliverance for anyone capable of understanding it. Jesus' words and work revealed him to be a transparency for the divine. And the physical and moral regeneration which witnesses observed in his miracles were unmistakable proof that a consciousness wholly in tune with its Source will expose the radiance of Spirit to this world, enabling the "sun" of God to penetrate human experience. Thus did Jesus become the light of the world. Just as moths drawn to a flame, those who were afflicted, in pain, and searching for relief reached out to the luminous divinity shining through his person, and in the process were lifted up for one magical moment to the same beatific state of harmony the Galilean had attained.

Incredibly the Master told his disciples that they, too, must become windows to the divine by proclaiming that every child of God had both the capacity and the responsibility to do what he did. "Believe me that I am in the Father, and the Father in me: or else believe me for the very works' sake," Jesus had declared in the Gospel of John before acknowledging the astonishing works that were bound to succeed him generation after generation. "Verily, verily, I say unto you, He that believeth on me, the works that I do shall he do also; and greater works than these shall he do; because I go unto my Father." (John 14:11-12) Edgar Cayce adds a grace note to this statement of the Master's in advising us that " . . . we, as His brothers and sisters, as His emissaries, as true children of Light, may do likewise day by day . . . " (272-7) To succeed, we need only let go of all the worldly treasures and pleasures now standing in our way blocking the inner light of "Son."

Feed My Lambs
ᷝ

Traveling the countryside accompanied by the group of disciples he had chosen to help further the Father's work, Jesus saw his ministry expand as the crowds coming to hear him swelled and the number of people hoping to claim his services grew. The Master directed his gifts to meet the needs of everyone who asked: believers and non-believers, the doubters or merely curious waiting to be convinced, and those who were still struggling to accept this unusual man and his dangerous ideas but held back, hiding in the shadows out of shyness, fear, or shame. His words had incredible vitality and the power to profoundly touch individual souls as well as to inspire the masses gathered at his feet. The multitudes marveled at the evidence of something supernatural manifesting right before their eyes.

In at least two instances the New Testament recounts the Master feeding thousands of hungry people who had traveled great distances from their homes to hear him preach. As Mark describes one of the incidents, a throng of approximately five thousand had been sitting on the hillsides for most of the day with nothing to eat. When the disciples brought the problem to Jesus' attention and suggested he send everyone away because that deserted place offered nothing edible and there was not nearly enough money in the purse to buy bread for such a huge group, the rabbi asked them what food was available. The answer was five loaves and two small fishes. The Cayce readings say the request was made " . . . that there might be supplied from that in hand sufficient of the material needs to feed that multitude, with the loaves and the few fishes." (2549-1)

Jesus then proceeds to address their predicament. After directing his disciples to ask the people to sit down on the grass in an orderly fashion, he takes the loaves and fishes and after looking up to heaven with a blessing acknowledging the sufficiency of an omnipresent God, begins to break the bread and divide up the fish. The gospel reports that this action resulted in multiplication such that the amount of food distributed was plentiful enough for the entire group of men, women, and children to eat until they were full. The leftover fragments alone filled twelve baskets after the massive crowd had finished its meal. The Cayce readings comment on the meaning of what happened that miraculous day. Then came that experience " . . . when there were those gatherings about the mount in the wilderness and the call of the five thousand that they be sent not away in their weakness, but the supplying of the physical needs to the material man." (2549-1) (Biblical version is found in Mark 6:35-44.)

The miracle of the loaves and fishes encapsulates several universal truths about the Christ spirit and its activity in the earth. Before this wondrous event could occur, Jesus had asked his disciples to confirm what they had to work with: five loaves and two fishes. He then requests those present to assemble in an orderly fashion on the hillside—a nod to the reality of divine law in operation. This law is exact, systematic, and purposeful. And while appearances may have claimed the presence of lack in such an arid wasteland, the Master saw nothing of the kind. His essence or Christ identity had recognized a single, more potent reality at work within that seemingly barren site. With his confident attitude and profound understanding of and connection to his Source, Jesus had perceived the power of God right where he stood. He knew the divine kingdom was available to him as it is to anyone on this plane fully conscious of its existence. Limitless spirit is always nigh, and fulfillment was possible because nothing is ever missing from the divine kingdom, which is accessible now. The children of God need never want or fear. Spirit will unfailingly use whatever is at hand to bring forth the life-giving manna and accomplish its sacred purpose in the world.

Itinerant Preacher
∽⧽

. . . He wined, He dined with the rich, He consorted with the poor, He entered the temple on state occasions; yea He slept in

the field with the shepherds, yea He walked by the seashore with
the throngs, He preached to those in the mount—*all things*; and
yet ever ready to present the tenets, the truths, even in those forms
of tales, yea parables, yea activities that took hold upon the *lives of
men and women* in *every* walk of human experience!   1472-3

As he moved from village to village along the rural roads, the Master spoke to the multitudes about things they knew well, describing
his new kingdom and what they could do to attain it. Most often he
would use analogies and symbols drawn from agriculture and the
natural world to make his point about the value of looking beyond the
baubles of a material existence to recognize what has been true since
the beginning of time. Thus could men and women regain a connection to their Source and do what they saw him do. Thus could human
beings create a heaven on earth. But this evolution in consciousness
would not happen without effort even for those fortunate enough to
have heard the Master's doctrine directly from his lips. Many simply
would not understand. Others capable of comprehending his message
would choose not to embrace the new way he taught and start living
out from the internal light of their own Christ beings.

He told one group of listeners the story of a farmer sowing seeds.
Some of the farmer's seeds fell by the wayside where the birds ate them.
Other seed fell on stony ground and sprang up quickly from shallow
roots caught among the rocks. But because the roots did not reach
far enough into the soil, the sun scorched the young plants and they
withered away. Still other seed fell among the thorns, which choked
the vegetation's growth and kept it from yielding any fruit. But luckily
some of the seeds the farmer sowed dropped on fertile ground. This
seed bore much fruit and over time the harvest it produced increased
one hundredfold.

Jesus was trying to convey in language an agrarian audience could
understand how the truths he imparted would come to fruition in the
world. He knew many of his words would fall by the wayside for few
would be able to catch the essential meaning of his teachings on the
first hearing. Before his doctrine could take root within them, a portion
of the message would be carried away and lost. He was also cautioning
his students not to become religious dilettantes whose spiritual roots

are too shallow to produce anything of value. The dabblers heard a bit of truth and instantly resonated with it but lacked persistence and never allowed the principles to germinate within them. Failing to recognize who they really were beyond name and form, they quickly burned out, withering under the white-hot glare of egotism and personal desire. Other truth seekers were choked off from the Word because they could not unbind themselves from the entangling cares of a material world, and in the end they, too, yielded no fruit for the garden of the new Eden. But some of Jesus' words undoubtedly fell on fertile ground. And that made all the difference. These were the elect who ingested the seeds of truth and allowed them to flourish by watering them inside the garden of their own souls. The result was a flowering of the Christ in consciousness and spiritual fruitage spilling forth into the world.

Jesus was describing an evolutionary process of change for the planet initiated by those ready and willing to construct the new order he preached. The way of the Master was not heavy-handed or demanding. He did not plant seeds only to quickly dig them up to try to measure their progress or force results on the world. The punishing tactics of mental coercion and physical might were not the Christ way. No, his words would take root and blossom in an entirely different manner than past reformers had proposed. They would begin to grow in the heart like a mustard seed, the tiniest seed of all, which in due season matures into a mighty tree.

Chapter 6
As I Have Loved You

Seek and Ye Shall Find

... He *was* the light that came into the
world to show the way of approach to
the kingdom—as lies within . . . 428-5

With brief parables and easy-to-understand examples Jesus attempted to unravel for his listeners the inscrutable mystery of the spiritual kingdom he preached. He explained what it was like using graphic illustrations to show them how this kingdom would manifest in the earth as they and future generations chose to express the God light found within—in the without.

First, he said it was incumbent upon the children of God to search for their divine Source and actively take steps to reconnect with it. "Seek ye first the kingdom of God and His righteousness," Jesus instructed, "and all things will be added unto you." Do not be passive but "Ask, and it shall be given you; seek, and ye shall find; knock, and it shall be opened to you." (Matt. 7:7–8) The Master's injunction was to keep searching to recover what was lost, and when you find it, the universe will rejoice. " . . . What woman having ten pieces of silver, if she lose one piece, doth not light a candle, and sweep the house, and seek diligently till she find it?" he asked. "And when she hath found it, she calleth her friends and her neighbours together, saying, Rejoice with me; for I have found the piece which I had lost. Likewise, I say unto you, there is joy in the presence of the angels of God over one sinner that repenteth." (Luke 15: 8–10) The new kingdom of the Christ, the priceless inheritance of the wandering sons and daughters, is awaiting us now. Gaining it requires only the prodigal's decision to turn around and start heading towards home.

The Master compared this inner kingdom to a treasure hidden in a field, and when a man uncovers the secret fortune, he is filled with great happiness and will go sell everything he has to buy the field. Finding the divine in the midst of us is like discovering a pearl of great price—a jewel so valuable people will divest themselves of every other possession in order to purchase that single stone. Jesus constantly exhorted his students not to put their faith in princes and temporal domains or in the accumulation of material wealth, which moth and rust can corrupt and thieves might steal. Instead they must focus on reaching and knowing the sacred presence within. He compared obtaining the internal riches to receiving something unimaginable, heaped up and pressed down to overflowing. More importantly, he was able to prove what he said by tangibly demonstrating what it would mean when his new kingdom was magnified in the earth "as it is in heaven" and the reign of spirit finally and firmly took hold.

Power from On High
᷎

All power is given unto me in heaven and in earth. Matt. 28:18

Neither disease nor physical distance could dim the radiance and potency of the God force immanent in the man named Jesus as he would prove time and again throughout the gospel narrative. The presence of the Christ spirit on a ship was capable of quelling a storm at sea. Contact with it healed lepers, gave sight to blind beggars, and stopped an issue of blood in a woman who had been suffering for more than thirty years. Neither was the efficacy of his Christ light restricted to a particular time and place. When implored, Jesus answered the call of a faith-filled centurion seeking help for a servant who was not in the immediate vicinity but lying ill at home. Likewise, during the incident at the pool near Bethesda when he cured a lame man unable to reach the water on his own and who, like the other invalids, believed immersing himself in the pool was the only way to be healed, Jesus demonstrated that the activity of the Christ is not bound by man-made rules and human limitations. This spirit is universally present and available whether to restore the lost years of the locust or rejuvenate a crippled child of God.

The presence of the Master's elevated state of consciousness generated healing by awakening souls still asleep to the truth of their divine nature. His complete identification with this sacred reality lifted the individuals seeking his help to a higher state of awareness, and upon their perception of the truth about themselves, afflictions simply disappeared. Immanuel (God with us) had unstopped the ears of the deaf, restored harmony to the weak and afflicted, as well as comforted and fed the hungry and poor. It was able to exorcise malevolent unseen spirits by casting out discarnate entities selfishly invading human minds too weak to erect barriers against them. And in a very practical manner this same Christ spirit uncovered a coin in a fish's mouth to pay the Roman tax and render unto Caesar what Caesar was due.

Incredibly, the Bible also recounts the Christ in Jesus calling back the souls of several people who already had left their bodies and departed the earthly plane—raising them from the dead. The gospels report him restoring Jairus' daughter to life and summoning Lazarus from the tomb where the dead man had lain for four days. In each case due to the Master's conscious union with God, the soul which had inhabited that particular physical vehicle or body was able to reclaim the material form it had abandoned and walk among the human race again. The energetic force Jesus had tapped into—his realized oneness with the Source of the universe—set aside the laws of matter. He literally had become the law.

What the Master was asking of his disciples was their recognition of this same divinity within themselves. It was incumbent upon them as well to make contact with their Source and let it permeate heart and mind, because they were the ones chosen to serve as the conduits for his message. Again and again Jesus tried to make his students understand they could be like him and become transparencies through which the spirit of God—the spirit of love and healing—might flow into human circumstances. At the same time, he recognized that sincere believers enmeshed in familiar religious doctrines and under the spell of respected teachers and authorized institutions, people who knew only the distant ruler–God of the Torah, were not really free to make such a choice. It was time to release divinity from the confines of dogma, ritual, and spiritual superstition.

A Temple Not Made with Hands

For God looks upon the purposes, the ideals of the heart, and not upon that which men call convention.   1472-1

Across the great sweep of human history prior to the appearance of the Master on earth, Jewish patriarchs and prophets in touch with their own inner lights had imparted great mystical truths to the world. But sadly the wisdom they conveyed was now enshrined in orthodoxy, safely contained behind rigid walls of impenetrable dogmas, complex sets of rules for daily living, and blood sacrifices. All of it was held securely in place by a formidable religious establishment. Mysterious rites and doctrinal minutiae had successfully mesmerized religious devotees, imprisoning them behind the iron bars of doubt, guilt, and fear. It was evident to Jesus that if nothing changed, the limitless life of Spirit might never fully penetrate human consciousness. Conformity to custom and creed was an enormous barrier obstructing the inner sun of man's divinity and preventing it from shining forth. And without this light, the seeds of truth he was sowing could not flower in the earth.

He told his students not to look for divinity where it did not dwell. They would not find God by traveling to a holy mountaintop, solemnly observing liturgies, prostrating themselves before ornamental shrines and sanctuaries, performing litanies of prescribed duties such as ritual bathing, wearing sacramental robes, covering their heads, or growing facial hair. In short, holiness was not defined by the rigid fulfillment of every jot and tittle of an ancient law. Nor should they venerate the invisible "I am" by barbarically killing animals. God has no pleasure in your sacrifices he told them. The only acceptable offering was the gift of the human will placed on the altar of the divine.

Over the course of his lifetime, the Nazarene rabbi never formed a sect, instituted a ceremonial ritual, or established any doctrines. Neither did Jesus expect nor want his followers to construct temples and towers in his honor. Structures made of stone and glass erected to mark the sacred sites people appointed for devotion would arrive much later. "Consider, for the moment, that the Master was the creator, the maker of all that was," Edgar Cayce once remarked, "and yet in establishing the church did He ask any? Rather He gave His blood, His body, as the memorial . . ." Curiously, Cayce adds that as the idea of creating visible forms for worship began to crystallize in the minds and desires of those people who had the material means to build such edifices and " . . . from same arose spires, cathedrals, church buildings and schools." (1561-18) The Master had made it very clear he was going to build his church of trusted adherents on the rock of Peter's faith, the faith of those able to perceive the presence of God among men: Immanuel.

> When Jesus came into the coasts of Caesarea Philippi, he asked his disciples, saying, Whom do men say that I the Son of man am? And they said, Some say that thou art John the Baptist: some, Elias; and others, Jeremias, or one of the prophets. He saith unto them, But whom say ye that I am? And Simon Peter answered and said, Thou art the Christ, the Son of the living God. And Jesus answered and said unto him, Blessed art thou, Simon Barjona: for flesh and blood hath not revealed it unto thee, but my Father which is in heaven. And I say also unto thee, That thou art Peter, and upon this rock I will build my church; and the gates of hell shall not prevail against it. Matt. 16:13-18

In describing the man Jesus in whom Peter had perceived the presence of the Christ, the Cayce readings point out that the man born of Mary was " . . . tempted in all points like each soul and yet without offense to any." (3395-2) Even the gates of hell cannot prevail against those whose spiritual vision, like the apostle Peter's, rises above what can be discerned solely with eyes of flesh and blood. For such believers perceive through the eyes of the soul and are able to recognize the divinity animating every human being. Those who reach such a heightened state of awareness form the cornerstone of the universal church—built not on a foundation of shifting sand but on the bedrock of Christ truth.

Whitened Sepulchers
ೞ

It is not *what* one says that counts, but what one *is!*   524-2

Jesus knew sacred rites and liturgies were dead ends, but at the same time was astute enough to realize that telling people their precious beliefs and ingrained traditions were dispensable and that rabbinical interpretations of the holy scriptures were not the sole authority on who or what was of God would arouse anger among those with a vested interest in upholding the status quo. The religious establishment surely would fight back. Various accounts of the Master's ministry intimate that he reserved his scorn for the pillars of the orthodox religious community—the clergymen who profited from holding their brothers and sisters in bondage to a lie. All too often sanctimonious scribes and Pharisees caught up in displaying their fine robes and piously conducting temple ceremonies had used their positions to oppress the downtrodden and acquire money, homage, and power. Outwardly these so-called spiritual leaders looked like models of holiness. Inwardly they lacked the integrity to touch the divine.

Jesus referred to them as hypocrites and whitened sepulchers—ostensibly pure on the outside but rancid within. "Woe unto you, scribes and Pharisees, hypocrites!" he reprimanded, "for ye pay tithe of mint and anise and cummin, and have omitted the weightier matters of the law, judgment, mercy, and faith: these ought ye to have done, and not to leave the other undone." (Matt. 23:23) And when the same religious authorities tried to censure the Master because his disciples ate bread with unwashed hands or plucked ears of corn to eat on the Sabbath and when they criticized Jesus for healing a man with a withered hand on a Jewish holy day, he provided a ready answer about the rightful place of man-made offices and rituals in the eternal life of the children of God.

Eating without cleansing the hands does not defile a man he told them. Swallowing food is never what corrupts the soul because whatever enters the mouth simply proceeds into the belly and ends up cast out in the draught. Rather, those things that issue forth from the heart through the mouth and body—lies, evil thoughts, murders, adulteries, thefts—are what defile us. (Matt. 15:17-18) Upending traditional approaches to worship, the Master stressed that all the elaborate ceremonies and fancy trappings surrounding the temple practices were irrelevant. "The Sabbath was made for man, and not man for the Sabbath," he explained. (Mark 2:27) Rules and regulations existed merely on the surface of life and could be cast aside whenever it was convenient by the same people who had given them power in the first place. "John came neither eating nor drinking, and they say, He hath a devil," he observed. "The Son of man came eating and drinking, and they say, Behold a man gluttonous, and a winebibber, a friend of publicans and sinners." (Matt. 11:18-19) Man-made theories about the conduct of life simply have no effect on the presence of God.

The Master went on to denounce other customs as well. The one incident related in the gospels when we see Jesus become genuinely angry is the time he expelled a group of moneychangers hawking their wares inside the temple courtyard. Fed up with those who took advantage of the less fortunate under the guise of helping simple people venerate their God, he moved swiftly and decisively to indicate his displeasure at the egregious profit-making. The method of censure the rabbi employed that day was striking both for its severity and for the powerful message it sent, which was meant to last far longer than that single outburst displacing a few vendors sitting outside the temple doors. The Master was sending a signal about the idolatrous attitudes men and women must overturn and cast out of themselves in order to properly glorify their God, namely worshipping the golden calf of religious orthodoxy and external form.

The Least among You

Later in his ministry, after all the time he had spent with his disciples and everything he had taught them, when a group of his closest followers tried to establish petty criteria for assessing who was worthy enough to help advance the new kingdom, Jesus chastised them too. "Do not stop him from doing the work, he told his students when they truculently complained that someone, not of their own group, was healing in their teacher's name."[17] "Master, we saw one casting out devils in thy name," the apostle John informed him, "and he followeth not us: and we forbad him, because he followeth not us." To their surprise Jesus responds, "Forbid him not: for there is no man which shall do a miracle in my name, that can lightly speak evil of me." Then he pressed the point by declaring that he who is not against us is with us and whoever offers someone a cup of cold water in the name of the Christ is blessed. (Mark 9:38-41)

Their teacher refused to enact any hard and fast rules governing holiness or admission into the spiritual kingdom. Nor, as he told the mother of James and John when she inquired about the future status of her sons, did he pay any attention to rank or class. (Matt. 20:20-22) Whoever did the work of the Father was helping the kingdom unfold: believers, non-believers, atheists, theists, deists, agnostics. Every soul has a part to play. The divisive egotism and partisanship inherent in group affiliations, hierarchy, and clan must never stand in its way. The Edgar Cayce readings reinforce the Master's message by explaining what it means to be among the chosen people. " . . . Israel indeed is *all* who seek; meaning not those of the children of Abraham alone, but of every nation, every tribe, and every tongue—Israel of the Lord! For this is the full meaning of Israel." (2772-1) Like stalks of golden wheat waving in the sunlight, truth grows organically and will flourish with the help of every soul called into its service—until the moment arrives when the Christ reaps a great spiritual harvest in the earth.

---

[17] Janet Highland, "New Testament" (unpublished manuscript, 1979).

A New Commandment

> There has also come a teacher who was bold enough to declare
> himself as the son of the living God. He set no rules of appetite.
> He set no rules of ethics, other than "As ye would that men should
> do to you, do ye even so to them . . . "   357-13

Over and over Jesus emphasized that the new order he was instituting did not depend on outer appearances, man-made customs, or lavish
rites. Visible displays of holiness using loud prayers, fasting with long
faces, bragging about one's proximity to God, or arrogantly claiming
to be an important member of an exclusive "club" of believers had
nothing to do with regaining a conscious awareness of the Source. God
looks upon the attitudes and ambitions, the Master reiterated to his
disciples. Nearness to the divine will be judged solely by the innermost
intentions of the heart.

He understood all too well that formal ceremonies and audible
prayers to an unknown God dwelling somewhere in the external universe actually thwarted the evolution of the new kingdom. In ages past
Moses had discerned the reality of divinity alive inside him when he
awakened to the realization "I am that I am." Now it was time for the
rest of humanity to finally grasp this truth. Contrary to sacred beliefs
dating back to the earliest human beings who knew no better than
to bow down to a stone stele stuck in a rock, the Master repeatedly
hammered home the idea that God resided in a temple not made with
hands. And this divine Spirit would become evident in the world as
soon as people chose to express it. He was the living proof that what
he said was true.

Jesus' ministry set aside the time-honored system of Mosaic law
introduced in the Old Testament and replaced it with two simple yet
profound rules for living. Love God with all your heart, soul, and mind
he instructed his pupils. Then he followed up the first commandment
with its corollary: "Thou shalt love thy neighbor as thyself." (Matt. 22:39)
Rule number one requires us to discern where our treasure lies, then
give ourselves over to obtaining it by focusing attention on what is
real and eternal—Spirit—rather than venerating the external world of
appearances. The second commandment is its twin and parallels the

first. This was Jesus' unequivocal statement about the unity of all creation and the brotherhood we share with every other living creature
on this planet by virtue of our common ancestry as beloved aspects of
the divine.

The Ten Commandments presented to Moses on Mount Sinai had
induced the Jewish people, and eventually the world, to move beyond
the primitive approach to human affairs, which had held sway for
millennia, and embrace a more spiritually evolved code of conduct. In
addition to affecting social interactions, the Decalogue had unified the
community around a collective ethic. Complementing the ten were all
the other rules spelled out in the earliest books of the Bible (and later
deciphered in intricate detail in the Talmud), which interpreted God's
word to man on how he was supposed to live. The law and its manifold
expressions became central to Judaism, molding it into a system able
to survive intact for generations. But the Master was trying to elevate
his listeners then—and now—to a more expansive and highly evolved
state of consciousness—a place outside the boundaries of lifeless statutes catalogued in ancient texts or long lists of dos and don'ts covering
every trifle of mortal behavior. Jesus was saying we could no longer
afford to just be good human beings content with never violating the
tiniest letter of the law. While strict adherence to the Ten Commandments and other ecclesiastical codes might be noble, it dealt only with
the surface of life.

Hypervigilance in regulating one's personal conduct and rigid compliance with prohibitions and rules, without a corresponding change
in consciousness, was not good enough for the children of God. In
fact, the Master once made a shocking statement to his disciples, which
shed some light on his novel view of morality. During the course of
delivering an address about the law, Jesus discussed a violation of the
seventh commandment with this unusual take on the subject. "Ye have
heard that it was said by them of old time, Thou shalt not commit
adultery: But I say unto you, That whosoever looketh on a woman to
lust after her hath committed adultery with her already in his heart."
(Matt. 5:27–28)

The implications of his remark were stunning. From a spiritual
standpoint that which takes place in us internally is as important as the
external act. For whatever we do outwardly is merely the end product

of an interior process that originates in the mind and heart prior to manifesting in our external conduct and conditions. So in terms of its impact on the soul, the deed is already done. The only way to stop accumulating "sin" and achieve freedom is to rise in consciousness to a state above all the canons catalogued in the holy books by moving to a place where such transgressions virtually become impossible. Because every thought, word, and deed are perfectly aligned with the highest ideal: an unequivocal love of God and neighbor.

Prayer and Fasting
⤸

> And he said unto them, This kind can come forth by nothing, but by prayer and fasting. Mark 9:29

Jesus was the rabbi who discarded long-standing traditions and promoted radical ideas, upending codes of conduct endorsed by generations of devout Jews. Rejecting sanctioned Hebraic teachings, his philosophy fundamentally diverged from the ossified standards, which had governed religious behavior since the days of Moses. The Master understood that rules, ceremonies, and outer forms were merely the veneer and never could accurately reflect the ineffable spiritual reality he had touched. Leading a holy life was not based in an exterior process but an interior one. The Cayce readings describe the concept this way: " . . . that the soul is a body and the physical is the mere temple, the mere shell, the mere material manifestation of that which may not be touched by hands! . . . " (262-60) While proof of the existence of the divine might not always be evident to the five physical senses, the invisible Spirit nevertheless is real, silently working behind the scenes. And true reverence for the unseen God of Abraham, Isaac, and Jacob occurs inside the inner sanctum of man's own being.

Get in touch with your inner self—fast and pray—Jesus told his students, but do not have long faces or voice your prayers to be seen of men. That would be acquiescing to an outer form and its reward is human approval. Rather quietly fast from the things of this world. " . . . Get the truth of fasting! . . . " (295-6) echo the Edgar Cayce readings, explaining that it is " . . . not as man counts fasting—doing without *food*;

but one that would abase himself that the creative force *might* be made manifest . . . " (254-46) Jesus was telling his students to abstain for a time from indulging in rites and rituals, mind games, gossip, power plays, and the manifold attractions of the physical and mental appetites in order to make contact with a higher dimension—the domain of Spirit. " . . . For, fasting—as is ordinarily termed—is as the Master gave: Laying aside thine own concept of *how* or *what* should be done at this period, and let the Spirit guide . . . " (295-6)

"Go in secret into your closet to pray," he told his students, and your Father will reward you openly with spiritual fruitage: peace, patience, long-suffering, kindness, and love. These comprise the blueprint for creating the new Eden—a kingdom of wholeness and harmony—in the earth. And manifesting such attributes through mind and body is the singular expression of the sacred in this dimension and only acceptable sacrifice to place on the altar before our God.

Not by Appearances

> Behold, thou desirest truth in the inward parts: and in the hidden part thou shalt make me to know wisdom. Psalm 51:6

Jesus' constant counsel was to avoid judging a situation by its façade. Sumptuous rituals and perfunctory religious observances were lifeless forms, and now the Master also was admonishing his students to quit childishly clinging to old, worn-out theological formulas. Checking off items on a list or carrying out strenuous exercises in an attempt to win God's favor would neither transform them nor the world. Truth is dynamic; dogma, inert. And following the Christ way demands a total reorientation of thought. Human beings were to begin to take responsibility for the world they were creating together by taking responsibility for themselves.

The Cayce readings encapsulate the Master's philosophical system by defining it as a type of three-legged stool or three equally spaced points along the circumference of a perfect circle. God is love; love is law; law is God. This formula is the touchstone for living in the third dimension and presupposes a mode of existence built around the complete and active expression of charity along with a responsibility for self and others. Jesus offered a vivid example of living this way in one soul-stirring parable, which outlined in real-world terms exactly what it means to live a "holy" life, i.e., in loving service to the whole. The tale grew out of a question from a lawyer who was curious to know how he might inherit eternal life. Trying to put the Master to the test, he asked the rabbi who his neighbor was. Jesus responded with the story of the Good Samaritan.

The Good Samaritan
ᏯᎯ

One day a man walking from Jerusalem to Jericho was assaulted by robbers who beat and stripped him of all he had and then left him half-dead on the side of the highway. A priest who happened to wander by observed the injured man but quickly crossed to the other side of the road and continued on his way. Next a Levite who was walking the same route noticed the victim and did the same thing. But a Samaritan making the journey observed the afflicted traveler and was moved to pity. He bandaged his wounds, lifted the man onto his beast, and carried him to an inn, handing the innkeeper money to look after the suffering stranger. (Luke 10:25-35)

The Master's story was probably not the answer the lawyer had expected to hear. Steeped in the intricacies of the law, the man had replied correctly to the rabbi's original question about what God requires of man. But Jesus took that stock answer to another level and made it clear that love had to do with actions, not feelings. "It entailed giving time, compassion, and material possessions in the service of others, whenever and wherever the need might arise during the occasions of life. And, most importantly, this service was to be given whether or not the person assisted was of one's own clan, race, or belief. In using a Samaritan as the hero of his tale, Jesus made it plain that love must extend to those who ordinarily were looked upon as the opposition, the enemy."[18] After all, the commandment was to love your neighbor, not just your friends.

---

[18]Janet Highland, "New Testament" (unpublished manuscript, 1979).

At that time the people of Samaria were considered pariah by most full-blooded Jews who saw themselves as the only saved, enlightened people of their day and the Samaritans as outcasts—a kind of bastardized group not of the chosen people. "Yet the Samaritan traveler, victim of this kind of prejudice, had tended to the needs of the fallen Jewish man. It was the Samaritan who served God by serving his neighbor; it was the Samaritan who demonstrated love, the love that was a response to the needs of others, no matter who those others might be."[19]

In stark contrast, the priest and Levite, accustomed to obeying only the letter of the law, were incapable of comprehending such an attitude. Although they lived under the onerous weight of hundreds of rules and always strived to be letter-perfect in dispatching every religious duty said to please their God, this attitude conveniently freed them from a much greater obligation. Faultless, by-the-book "holiness" had alleviated them of the far heavier burden of being alertly responsible for the state of the world around them and their duty to care for their brothers and sisters who were children of the same divine parent.[20] Jesus wanted no part of such an attitude. His parable was a potent reminder that love unleashed is the one-and-only sign of godliness.

---

[19] Janet Highland, "New Testament" (unpublished manuscript, 1979).
[20] *Ibid.*

Chapter 7
About My Father's Business

> . . . to express love in thine activities to
> thy neighbor is the greater service that a
> soul may give in this mundane sphere.
>
> 499-2

Scattered throughout the four gospels is a series of incidents Jesus used to highlight the characteristics of those who had elevated their consciousness and had begun living a life rooted and grounded in spirit. The Master's own biography, especially the three years he spent teaching, testified to the legitimacy of his claims. And in an almost unbelievable assertion, he had told his students they would be able to do everything he could do—and more—if they were simply willing to pay the price of laying aside timeworn attitudes and beliefs. "He that believeth on me, the works that I do shall he do also," he promised. (John 14:12) But before this rebirth into the fullness of spirit could occur, the man of earth had to put on the white robe (pure consciousness) of a son of God.

Love and mercy sit center stage in the revolutionary order Jesus was describing. The new covenant he instituted to replace the ancient compact between Abraham and El Shaddai, the God of the Hebrews, was symbolized by atonement—at-*One*-ment. And to glorify that One, people faced the choice of either serving the good of the whole or their individual interests. Now instead of burnt animals given back as offerings to honor the Almighty, the children of God would immolate greed and pride on the altar of their inner temples by overcoming the desire to live exclusively for themselves. Eliminating any sense of separateness from their Creator through the surrender of personal will and desire, they themselves would become the purified sacrifices, cleansed not with water but by the renunciation of every thought and act born of divisiveness and egoism.

The Cayce material adds a unique dimension to the Master's general instructions about overcoming self with its novel approach to the concept of sin. The readings employ a clear-cut yardstick by which to measure the state of "sinfulness," neatly summing up the entire issue in one brief but brilliantly illuminating declaration. "*Know*, self is the only excuse. Self is the only sin; that is, selfishness—and all the others are just a modification of that expression of the ego . . . " (1362-1) The only sin is self and the choice to live according to the new, openhearted way the Master had outlined was just that: a choice, the consequences of which would have a distinct and very powerful impact on both the individual and the world at large. If and when his students chose to rise to the heights of spiritual awareness he hoped they might achieve, Jesus predicted that they, too, could begin performing the miraculous feats he had demonstrated and literally begin creating a heaven on earth. But the process of getting there required effort.

Love Your Enemies

But love ye your enemies, and do good, and lend, hoping for nothing again; and your reward shall be great, and ye shall be the children of the Highest: for he is kind unto the unthankful and *to* the evil. Luke 6:35

It is easy to pretend the Master was made of entirely different stuff than the rest of humanity. The tendency is to overlook his prior incarnations as well as all the years of study, exertion, and mental discipline demanded of him in preparing to fully manifest divinity through a corporeal body and complete his soul mission. The job required setting aside every particle of personal desire, every physical and emotional need in order to serve the universe of unawakened souls trapped in materiality. Before he was ordained to preach the good news of "God with us," Jesus had attained complete mastery over himself by resisting the three greatest temptations of human existence. The second Adam had crossed paths with the serpent again, this time disguised as the devil of the egotism, which had arrived to entice his soul to use its wisdom and spiritual faculties to satisfy mortal appetites and fulfill the secret longings of the heart. And he had sent it away. The Master had subdued the urge to use his gifts merely to better his own affairs by refusing to become ensnared in the seductive conceits of aggrandizing or deifying himself.

The Jewish rabbi had risen to a level of consciousness outside the range of the five physical senses to reveal a heretofore undefined state of being where the primacy of love is the complete and perfect fulfillment of the law. Love nullified the falsehood of duality—the lie that had lured Adam and Eve to their downfall and cast them out of Eden at the beginning of time. Jesus described the love of God and man as a boundless force. As such, it extended beyond the borders human beings had erected around it with their flawed notions of family, group, and nation, stretching to the furthest reaches of the imagination, even as far as caring for people they vilified and despised.

No longer were we supposed to pay back our foes with an "eye for an eye and a tooth for a tooth" (Matt. 5:38) or express the tiniest modicum of unjust anger toward a neighbor. Much to the surprise of an oppressed community caught in the grip of brutal Roman overlords, Jesus told his students their responsibility was to pay tribute to the principle of oneness by continuing to love without regard to circumstance or condition. They were to pray for their enemies. "Ye have heard that it hath been said, Thou shalt love thy neighbor, and hate thine enemy. But I say unto you, Love your enemies, bless them that curse you, do good to them that hate you, and pray for them which despitefully use you, and persecute you; that ye may be children of your Father which is in heaven: for he maketh his sun to rise on the evil and the good, and sendeth rain on the just and on the unjust . . . " (Matthew 5:43–45) In the kingdom of the Christ we pray for our enemies because the principle of Oneness by its very nature means there can be no enemies.

Similar passages in the New Testament reinforce Jesus' warning not to rip apart the fabric of the whole by rupturing the bonds between us with bursts of anger or the refusal to admit fault. He told his followers it was useless to try to contact the divine while still harboring an attitude of divisiveness. "Therefore if you bring thy gift to the altar, and there rememberest that thy brother has ought against thee; Leave there thy gift before the altar, and go thy way; first to be reconciled to thy brother and then come and offer thy gift," (Matthew 5:23–24) the Master had directed his followers. He wanted us to understand that since it is impossible for anyone to even begin to fathom the full depth and breadth of the cosmic plan, we must refrain from condemning what others may do—or fail to do—to us or for us. The Edgar Cayce readings elaborate: " . . . This is the first lesson ye should learn: There is so much good in the worst of us, and so much bad in the best of us, it doesn't behoove any of us to speak evil of the rest of us. This is a universal law, and until one begins to make application of same, one may not go very far in spiritual or soul development." (3063-1)

For She Is a Sinner
෴

. . . Those that find fault with others will find fault in themselves; for they are writing their own record—they must meet, every one, that which they have said about another; for so is the image, the soul of the Creator in each body, and when ye speak evil of or unkindly to thy brother, thou hast done it unto thy God. 487-17

Many of the people who most admired Jesus and were honored to be in such close proximity to a holy teacher never understood why their Master mixed with publicans and sinners, sometimes even accepting invitations to eat meals in their homes. But the example set by the Nazarene bespoke a vital spiritual truth. He was prompting his students to take control of the unchecked mind and refrain from indulging in human judgments and opinions. His unconditional acceptance of every genre of outcast proved that no matter what transgressions these so-called "sinners" may have committed, no one is ever so completely estranged from the Christ spirit that it will not answer the invitation to come and sup with them.

And when the Pharisees and several of his own disciples started to condemn the Hebrew prophet for allowing a reputed prostitute to wash his feet with her tears and anoint his head with precious ointments from an alabaster box, he spurned their criticism. Jesus simply refused to align himself with the world's opinion about the value of the woman prostrated before him. Then he underscored the gist of the lesson he wanted his students to grasp using a brief parable about a wealthy creditor who had two debtors. One of the debtors owed the lender five-hundred pence and the other only fifty, but neither had the means to pay. So the man who had loaned them the money forgave them both. Which one, Jesus asked, would love the creditor more? Simon correctly answers by saying the debtor forgiven the most would love the lender the most. (Luke 7:36-50)

The Master was teaching his students that they must never attempt to gauge how far away someone is from God by blindly accepting the false pictures presented to the carnal eye. They were to view life from a higher perspective, knowing that whatever man calls sin counts as nothing in the omnipresent realm of divinity and is already forgiven. Though the world may criticize and condemn us for our transgressions, nothing we are doing now or have ever done in the past—only our own consciousness—can ever separate us from our Creator. In this case, the "fallen" woman represented every soul, because every soul has the opportunity at any moment to rise in awareness to humbly approach and honor the divine in man. Just as she was blessed, so, too, are we blessed whenever we turn our lives around to present our gifts at the altar of love again.

It is reported in the Cayce readings that the woman who washed the Master's feet was completely transformed by her experience. "With the cleansing of the body-mind, through the association and experience, the entity then joined again with those of the family from whom she had been separated in Bethany, and became then again of the household of those that dwelt there." (295-8) The story of Mary washing the Master's feet provides additional evidence of how eminently practical the Son of Man was. By taking advantage of an unforeseen situation and choosing the right parable, he had grounded his message in a concrete example so its inner meaning would hit home. Jesus' constant mantra to his disciples was to keep a sharp eye on the occupations of the disapproving mind and weigh every thought and action on the scale of love first before proceeding, because human judgment means naught in the divine computation. Love is the critical factor and the sole benchmark by which to measure progress in fulfilling our heritage as sons and daughters of God.

Forgive Us Our Debts

Who gains by being forgiven and by forgiving? The one that forgives is lord even of him that he forgives.   585-2

The mere presence of Jesus moving among the swarms of people who followed in his wake is the foremost example of how a human being ought to navigate the world. Blameless and free of desiring anything from anyone—even a "good" reputation within the community—his Godly countenance illuminated the dark corners where the shadows of ignorance had held sway. As the Master roamed the hills and coasts of Judea, he came face to face with countless lost sheep from his Father's fold, and due to his prodigious intuitive faculties and acute understanding of the human dilemma was able to arouse their soul forces and affect change. The desperately lost suddenly woke up to recognize the snares that had caused them to lose their footing on the road back home. "Sins {were} of commission and omission . . . ," (281-2) forgiven or called to mind, observes Cayce.

Yet this humble preacher never condemned anyone who had missed the mark but told his followers neither he nor they should judge other people. His instruction was to look to ourselves first before criticizing our brothers and sisters—and never to condemn either one. "And why beholdest thou the mote that is thy brother's eye, but perceivest not the beam that is in thy own eye?" he rhetorically asked his disciples. (Luke

6:41 and Matthew 7:3) Their duty was to forgive not just once but in every case: seventy times seven. Edgar Cayce expounds on the Master's concept of mercy and mending broken relationships by urging us to become like the child who quickly forgets any slights or slurs, noting that the failings we perceive in another are mirror images of what we refuse to see in ourselves. " . . . The faults ye find in others are reflected in thine own mirror of life . . . ," (3395–2) he declares, which recasts the idea of forgiveness from a virtuous act conferred upon someone else to an opportunity for self-realization, which ultimately sets us free.

Debtor Servant

In speaking of forgiveness, Jesus compared the kingdom of heaven to a king who decided to clear up the outstanding accounts run up by his servants. After reckoning the totals the monarch realizes the first man brought before him owes him ten thousand talents, but does not have the means to pay. So the lord of the house issues a directive proclaiming that the debtor along with his wife, children, and the whole of his goods will be sold to cover the unpaid bill. Losing hope, the distraught servant falls down and worships his master saying, "Lord, have patience with me, and I will pay thee all." This heartfelt plea moves the king to compassion and causes him to change his mind and set the servant free, forgiving the man his entire debt.

Soon afterward, however, the liberated servant goes out and finds one of his fellow servants who happens to owe him a hundred pence. Taking his debtor by the throat the man snarls, "Pay me that thou owest." The second servant prostrates himself at his co-worker's feet, beseeching him to have patience and promising to pay everything he owes. But the servant whom the king had forgiven says no and has his colleague thrown into prison until the debt is settled. When the other servants in the household learn what has happened to their friend, they feel sorry for him and proceed to tell their master the entire story. Consequently, the king becomes very angry and has it out with the first servant. "O thou wicked servant, I forgave thee all that debt, because thou desiredst me: Shouldest not thou also have had compassion on thy fellow servant, even as I had pity on thee?" Then the lord of the

house delivers the ungrateful servant to some tormentors until the
man can pay his debt in full. Jesus ends his parable with these words
of warning. "So likewise shall my heavenly Father do also unto you, if
ye from your hearts forgive not every one his brother their trespasses."
(Matt. 18:23–35)

Jesus' core teaching about the indispensable nature of forgiveness
is crystalized further in the Gospel of John during a dramatic moment
when the great Teacher not only preaches about the idea of mercy but
also illustrates its meaning in very tangible terms. When the scribes
and Pharisees bring a woman taken in adultery before the Master to
test him and rightly claim the law of Moses condemns the adulteress
to death by stoning, Jesus remains unfazed. He has no interest in judging her life's path or acquiescing to the letter of a primitive law utterly
devoid of love and used as a bludgeon to harm a precious child of God.
The rabbi confronts the mob by silently reflecting back to them their
own failings and asking any member of the group who is without sin
to cast the first stone.

Interestingly, Edgar Cayce references two separate episodes involving
an adulterous woman. According to the readings in one instance Jesus
squatted down in the dirt and wrote, "' . . . Medi (?) Medici (?) [Cui?]'—the
expression of mercy and not sacrifice . . . ,'" which demonstrated to the
onlookers " . . . the individual awakening of the entity . . . " In the second
" . . . that written was that which made the accusers recognize their *own*
activities." (5749-9) Cayce remarks that Jesus wrote "That which condemned each individual, as each looked over His arm—or as He wrote,"
(295-8) which quickly caused the would-be rock throwers to disperse.
"And they which heard it, being convicted by their own conscience,
went out one by one, beginning at the eldest, even unto the last," (John
8:9) reports the Gospel of John.

"Neither do I condemn thee," the Master tells the stricken woman after her accusers have fled. Then he cautions her to keep her consciousness uplifted and to "go and sin no more" lest something worse befall
her down the road. (John 8:11) The readings proceed to describe how
his words had " . . . awakened, *will* awaken within the soul of the entity,
more of the love, the oneness of the force or power able to cleanse when
condemnation is not in self." (295-8) The lesson was clear. Censure is
no part of the Christ spirit embedded in the human heart. The Cayce

material then amplifies the story of Jesus' merciful interaction with the adulterous woman with a powerful and provocative statement about self-forgiveness, explaining that we must never condemn ourselves. " . . . For as the entity and each soul learns, condemning self is condemning the abilities of the Master . . . " (295-8)

Poor in Spirit

. . . And prove me now herewith, saith the Lord of hosts, if I will not open you the windows of heaven, and pour you out a blessing, that there shall not be room enough *to receive it.* Mal. 3:10

The great Galilean teacher used every method at his disposal to decipher for his pupils the characteristics of the reborn state of consciousness he heralded while dispensing nuggets of truth about exactly what it means to live that way. Among the many topics covered, Jesus spoke about the proper relationship to material possessions. When the Master reminded his students to take no thought for "your life," he was trying to paint a picture of a mindset in which possessions, normally prized for the self-worth and bodily comforts they offer, would become the portals for serving others.

The reason for owning any object reflected a greater purpose than just meeting the physical needs of a material life. The things that surround us are part of the toolbox we can access to help fill the needs of the whole, the One. Nor did Jesus subscribe to the idea that the materially destitute were innately better or holier than those who had accumulated some riches. In fact, the Cayce information describes the Master's own family as members of what today might be called the upper middle class. The critical element to consider in pursuing wealth in any form, be it status, reputation, or physical objects, is the attitude held toward that possession and most importantly, whether or not it stands between us and the conscious realization of our God.

Sitting near the temple treasury one day noticing how much money the richest members of the community were casting into the till, Jesus watched a poor widow humbly approach and drop two mites into the cache. Her meager contribution amounted to a mere farthing, worth next to nothing at the time. Perceiving her sacrifice, the Master called together his disciples to draw attention to the offering and noted that the impoverished woman had contributed more than all those who had left behind large sums of money. For they had given of their abundance while she had cast in everything she had—even all her living. The woman owned nothing from a material standpoint but had contributed anyway. (Mark 12:41–44)

The rabbi's lesson was targeted at exposing the role of money as no more than a physical representation of an inner supply and state of mind. He was showing his pupils that the amount tendered is never as important as what lies behind the scenes— the internal attitude or ideal which prompts the giving. And no matter how depleted our external circumstances may appear to be, true acts of charity flow out from that which we have in hand and are willing to bestow upon one another. "Tell me what thou hast in the house?" the Old Testament prophet Elisha had asked another poor widow who had nothing left at home but the scantest amount of oil—before every vessel she owned and pots borrowed from the neighbors were filled to the brim with a supply of oil that never diminished. (2 Kings 4:1–3) That which is present and available to us now is the access point for pouring forth a stream of help and healing balm into the world. Giving that arises from the depths of the soul is what counts.

Rich Young Man
ᝏ

> . . . For, know, the earth and all therein is the Lord's. All thine own
> is lent thee, not thine but lent thee. Keep same inviolate . . .
>
> 2622-1

A related lesson occurs later in the Master's ministry at the time Jesus and his disciples, aware of the dangers looming in Jerusalem, had withdrawn to the city of Ephraim near the wilderness before moving to a spot across the Jordan. Paralleling the biblical account, the Cayce material says a rich young ruler by the name of Nicholas approached the rabbi while he was in the area to ask him a question. "Good Master, what shall I do to inherit eternal life?" he inquires. The Master's initial response is to correct the young man about the source of all good, saying that no one is good—not even Jesus—only God. Then he follows up by advising the young man to obey the commandments, which Nicholas informs the Master he already does. But Jesus indicates strict adherence to the law is not sufficient either, and points out the one thing the seeker still lacks. "Sell all thou hast," he says, "and distribute it unto the poor" in order to gain the treasures of heaven. Then come and follow me. In other words, divest your consciousness of all its material aspirations and obsession with visible possessions, which tie you to the ways of the world, and come live by Spirit, the way of the Christ. (Luke 18:18–23) The rich young man, apparently fearful of continuing without the security of his vast fortune, leaves in sadness.

The Edgar Cayce readings speak at length about this young ruler, starting with a tongue-in-cheek explanation that refers to him as " . . . that one about whom much speculation has been in the minds of many, over what was written there in the records, concerning which many a verbose orator has proclaimed much about which he knew so little . . . " (2677-1) For, though Nicholas went away sorrowing at that moment, Cayce says it is important to remember another line: "Then Jesus beholding him loved him." (Mark 10:21) He interjects that indeed anyone the Son of Man has favored in mind or purpose may count his soul as fortunate, noting that " . . . blessed indeed is the entity to whom or about whom it was said, 'As the Master looked on him, He loved him.'" (1416-1) Jesus had instructed the wealthy young man to "Sell that thou hast and come and follow me." And subsequently the readings report, Nicholas "did just that. He came later and followed." Further on they disclose an interesting bit of information about the future activities of this remarkable pupil of the Master's during the period of persecution of the disciples. "Much might be said as to that period of sojourn, and as to the helpful forces that came into the lives and experiences of many owing to the activities of that entity . . . ," (1416-1) remarks Cayce.

An oft quoted line from the story of the rich young man is Jesus' pithy aphorism, "It is easier for a camel to go through the eye of a needle, than for a rich man to enter into the kingdom of God." (Mark 10:25) These words, frequently misinterpreted, represent the Master's summation of another universal truth, once again spoken in reference not to the outer conditions but to the state of consciousness held within. Material items—money, homes, clothes, jewelry, automobiles—are never the problem; the issue turns on where one has placed the attention of the heart. It is impossible to lower the head and enter the narrow gate of the inner kingdom while endeavoring to haul in the heavy baggage of the world behind us weighed down by fear of losing what we have. "No man can serve two masters," Jesus explained, "for either he will hate the one, and love the other; or else he will hold to the one, and despise the other. Ye cannot serve God and mammon." (Matt. 6:24) Excessive love of objects or "mammon" is a huge obstacle blocking the prodigal's progress on the road back to the Father's house. Sadly, it is an obstacle of our own making.

Render unto Caesar
⌒ℛ⌒

The earth is the Lord's, and the fulness thereof; the world, and they that dwell therein. Psalm 24:1

In the course of their exchanges in the world, the Master expected his devotees to attend to earthly concerns but to keep them in their proper place. There is a story in the gospels about the time several Pharisees hoping to entangle Jesus in his speech dispatched a few of their most loyal acolytes to try to trip him up. The wily group approached the rabbi saying, "We know that thou art true, and teachest the way of God in truth, neither carest thou for any man: for thou regardest not the person of men. Tell us therefore, What thinkest thou? Is it lawful to give tribute unto Caesar, or not?" Recognizing their deceit, Jesus replies, "Why tempt ye me, ye hypocrites?" before asking to see a piece of the tribute money. He looks at the penny coin for a moment then inquires, "Whose is this image and superscription?" When the men correctly answer it is Caesar's, Jesus replies, "Render therefore unto Caesar the things which are Caesar's; and unto God the things that are God's." Taken aback by the Master's words, his questioners quickly walk away. (Matt. 22:15-22)

Seen from its instructive angle, Jesus' retort is a warning to his disciples about spending too much time trying to parse the manifold complexities of man-made systems and rules. God is not a jealous potentate who requires his subjects to neglect their legitimate responsibilities or dismiss family, home, and business in order to come and honor him. "Suffer it to be so now," Jesus had declared at the time of his baptism in the Jordan in assenting to the demands of that moment. (Matt. 3:15) So, too, must his disciples fulfill their duties as honest citizens of the human community: pay taxes, settle accounts with the landlord and vendor, feed and educate their children, and spend time and money caring for the elderly and infirm. "If therefore ye have not been faithful in the unrighteous mammon, who will commit to your trust the true riches?" he asked them in the Gospel of Luke. (Luke 16:11) Joyfully fulfill whatever you are given to do each day, but do not let those obligations distract you from your true purpose. Rather infuse each activity, however exalted or mundane, with the light of the sacred flame of your inner countenance, remembering that every thought or deed undertaken in a spirit of love is your finest tribute to the one God.

Treasure in Heaven
☙

> What then cometh of thy barns, of thy store of riches, of thy power, of thy money, of thy position, of thy exalted place; yea, even of thy good name, lest it be that having been in the true Knowledge thou hast been indeed a channel that hath opened the eyes of those that had been dimmed by the vicissitudes of life that brought fear and distrust . . .   262-97

Jesus was speaking to the same principle when he began another discourse on the subject of supply using the parable of a rich man who brought forth plentifully. Evidently the wealthy landowner's provision was so huge that he did not know where to store all his bounty. "What shall I do, because I have no room where to bestow my fruits?" the man asks himself. So he decides to pull down his old barns and build new, larger storehouses to contain everything he owns, thinking that by having laid up enough material goods to last a lifetime he would spend the rest of his days eating, drinking, and being merry. But God has other plans and says, "Thou fool, this night thy soul shall be required of thee: then whose shall those things be, which thou hast provided?"

Jesus' sermon underscores the point that all of his disciples' sweat and struggle to "make things right" on the material plane means little in the grand design of the universe. Constant worry about fulfilling one's bodily needs and the compulsion to make every detail in life fall neatly into place—instead of harking to the still small voice within—is a delusion. "Which of you with taking thought can add to his stature one cubit?" the Master inquired of his students. Never be fooled into thinking the best and most grandiose personal plans the human mind concocts ultimately results in anything more than a dead body turning to dust in a grave. (Luke 12:16–25)

And as his disciples applied their God-inspired talents and began to make headway in the world, the world might sit up and take no-tice, tempting them to sell out to the ego rewards of self-aggrandize-ment and profit-making. But they were to resist that temptation too. Whatever success his followers achieved in material terms was given to them to serve the whole, not their egos. The call of the Christ was to subdue the kind of self-centeredness that seeks to turn every gain, every advance, toward selfish ends. The job was difficult, but their teacher enjoined them to do it.[21] "Be of good cheer," he proclaimed, "I have overcome the world." (John 16:33)

Children of the Most High
ॐ

> For the experience becomes rather as a very delicate instrument
> of music upon which the chords of life (which is God) are played.
> 1436-2

The philosophy the Master espoused concerned itself with how his disciples might live on the earth as the children of God. No matter what happened in their external circumstances, the sons and daughters of the Most High would assiduously turn inward to reaffirm their unity with the omnipresent, incorruptible "I am." Jesus had fed the multitudes from this limitless source and now he wanted them to offer the sacred bread of truth to spiritually famished souls by drawing from the same cache he had proven to be forever at hand. Pounding away at the idea

---

[21]Janet Highland, "New Testament" (unpublished manuscript, 1979).

that an infinitely loving, divine being—the God he had come to know intimately—never withholds from its offspring, he repeatedly reminded his students that those living out from the wellspring of their inner Christhood need never fear privation because it is virtually impossible to lose what is real. And contrary to how any situation may appear on the outside his disciples, rich or poor, embodied the capacity for measureless giving.

" . . . As ye would that men should do to you, do ye also to them likewise," Jesus commanded. (Luke 6:31) If you express love to someone who already loves you, what value does it add to the whole he asked, for even sinners love the people who love them. The same principle holds true whenever we scratch the back of someone certain to return the favor. "And if ye lend to them of whom ye hope to receive, what thank have ye? for sinners also lend to sinners, to receive as much again." (Luke 6:34)

The new covenant the Master preached was the agreement to love both the stranger and the enemy, to do good and lend one's all without any hope of a return, and to show as much mercy as their Father/ Mother God in heaven is merciful by demonstrating kindness alone to the ungrateful and evil. "For the words that He has given are simple, 'inasmuch as ye do it unto the least, ye do it unto me,'" (938-1) Edgar Cayce reminds us. The reward our Teacher promised for meeting this lofty standard was incalculable. He said we would be "children of the Highest." We would become as he is, a Christ. (Luke 6:35)

Chapter 8
Prepare Ye

Then said Jesus to them again, Peace *be* unto you: as *my* Father hath sent me, even so send I you. John 20:21

The Master had reached the stage where he had taught his students as much as they could absorb and the day had finally arrived for them to begin using the truths they had learned. A moment of delay was a moment lost to building the new kingdom. He had indicated as much one day when a disciple asked permission to stay behind for a funeral saying, "Lord, suffer me first to go and bury my father." Jesus' response was unusually brusque. "Follow me; and let the dead bury their dead," he told the man. (Matt. 8:21-22) His followers had to steel themselves against the temptation to get caught up in the myriad complexities and ever-changing circumstances of the exterior world. Their highest priority was to expend time and treasure revealing the inner Christ.

Jesus had amassed a group of workers aware of the tripartite nature of body, mind, and spirit and willing to accept the job of reopening the gates to the lost Eden. He began by sending out a relatively small group of adherents culled from those capable of perceiving the deeper meaning of his message. Because the truth implanted in their consciousness had found fertile ground, these initiates were ready to leave their teacher's side and begin sharing the good news with a wider circle. And as little by little they began to apply the principles gleaned from all the hours they had spent with the Master, exposing his words to as yet unknown audiences open to hearing the truth, the ideas he preached would begin to blossom like tightly bound buds unfurling under the rays of a warm sun. Edgar Cayce described the method by which Christ-truth manifests in the earth in commenting on the expansion of his own work. " . . . Let the work be presented in a manner to a great number of peoples in the proper way; that is, through the channels first of individuals, then of groups, classes and masses . . . " (254-15) Thus does seedtime grow into an immense spiritual harvest.

Luckily for the disciples listening to Jesus then and for us today, their teacher had provided instructions on every possible contingency they might encounter traveling the road back to the Father's house. In preparing his apprentices to step out on faith and roam the byways of the world, the Master had forewarned them about prospective hazards along the way. And scattered among all the bits of practical advice was his charge to continuously maintain the connection to their Source—the fount of all wisdom and power.

Go Forth
✑

The time draweth near, the time is at hand, when there is more
and more seeking for the light and understanding.   262-51

As Jesus spoke to his students to equip them for the passage by pairing them two by two, bestowing power over unclean spirits, and directing his pupils to impart his teachings to others, his primary focus was on outfitting a state of consciousness. The Gospel of Mark reports the Master "commanded them that they should take nothing for their journey, save a staff only; no scrip, no bread, no money in their purse: But be shod with sandals; and not put on two coats." (Mark 6:8-9) The followers of the Christ way were not supposed to worry about filling their coffers or their bellies before embarking on the assignment he had delegated to them. Concerns about money and clothing only served to confound and distract. And after everything his disciples had seen him do, if they still did not recognize omnipresent divinity as the bottomless wellspring of their supply, they had not understood his message very well. Take no thought for the ways of man the Master was telling his trainees but rather place your trust in the unseen forces, which cause the manna to fall from heaven day by day. "And when ye trust in Him, ye are sure," reaffirms Edgar Cayce, "and need never be afraid of the material things. For, does He not feed the birds of the air? Does He not give the color to the lily, the incense to the violet? . . . " (3333-1) Those attuned to the inner Christ always will have enough to carry them forward, " . . . for the workman is worthy of his meat." (Matt. 10:10)

Much more important for these spiritual ambassadors than worrying about the physical accoutrements of life was staying alert to the situations around them, cognizant of potential pitfalls in the path. "Behold, I send you forth as sheep in the midst of wolves: be ye therefore wise as serpents, and harmless as doves," (Matt. 10:16) Jesus cautioned. Wise as serpents, his followers did not have the luxury of being otherworldly types, naïve of the practical workings of a material world. His advocates must be shrewd enough to avoid the traps laid down by cunning adversaries intent on tripping them up. The Master had warned the disciples they might be delivered up to councils, beaten in the synagogues, or brought before rulers and kings because of the Christ spirit they disclosed. But they were not to worry. Even in the midst of those challenging circumstances they could count on the God he had revealed to them. "Take no thought beforehand what ye shall speak," he advised his students. "Neither do ye premeditate: but whatsoever shall be given you in that hour, that speak ye: for it is not ye that speak, but the Holy Ghost." (Mark 13:11)

When confronted by the beastly nature of the insensitive and unaware eager to attack, they were to remain "harmless as doves," using only evolutionary, nonviolent tactics to achieve their ends. The dove, symbol of the divine principle descended to earth and of the energetic

force and wisdom of infinite Mind, was to be united with the serpent— symbol of the movement, knowledge, and power of the physical
dimension.[22] Time and again Jesus had shown his protégés how he was
able to stand his ground and endure yet remain gentle and blameless
in both word and deed. This was how he wanted them to act.

Beware the Leaven
∼≈∽

The Master's counsel on the perils of the duplicity and deceit his
followers might encounter included a warning about placing too
much confidence in the priests or other purported spiritual leaders of
the community. This particular lesson came about one day when the
rabbi and his band of followers had taken a ship over to the coast of
Magdala and the disciples realized they had forgotten to bring along
any bread. So Jesus decided to make use of the situation to impart a
little wisdom by telling them to "Take heed and beware of the leaven
of the Pharisees and of the Sadducees." Clueless, his students miss the
point, reasoning amongst themselves that their teacher must be referring to the missing loaves of baker's bread. Aware of their confusion,
Jesus comments on their lack of faith and the fact they assumed he was
worried about procuring groceries. The frustrated rabbi then proceeds
to ask, "Do ye not yet understand, neither remember the five loaves of
the five thousand, and how many baskets ye took up? Neither the seven
loaves of the four thousand, and how many baskets ye took up? How
is it that ye do not understand that I spake it not to you concerning
bread, that ye should beware of the leaven of the Pharisees and of the
Sadducees?" Only then does it dawn on the group their teacher was
not talking about actual yeast and wheat, but warning them to be wary
of the doctrines promoted by members of the high-ranking religious
classes. (Matt. 16:6–12)

Matthew's gospel lays out several more components of the Master's
game plan in noting his command to the disciples to speak first to their
own people—the Jews—the nation of the one God. Do not go among
Gentiles or the Samaritans "rather to the lost sheep of the house of

---

[22]Janet Highland, "New Testament" (unpublished manuscript, 1979).

Israel," Jesus directed as he set the stage for their departure to distant shores to preach the good news of the kingdom. (Matt. 10:5-6) He also had forewarned his emissaries that not every home they entered would necessarily be ready to accept the message they carried. Yet no matter what type of reception his disciples received, they were to remain untroubled and centered within. "And when ye come into an house, salute it. And if the house be worthy, let your peace come upon it: but if it be not worthy, let your peace return to you," (Matt. 10:12-13) Jesus decreed. His followers were not supposed to waste time giving "that which is holy unto the dogs" or cast their pearls of wisdom before the swine, "lest they trample them under their feet, and turn again and rend you." (Matt. 7:6) If certain households or even an entire city showed no interest in hearing what his envoys had to say, they must not get caught up in drama and recriminations but simply shake the dust of that place off their feet and move on.

Their teacher himself had faced enormous amounts of skepticism, criticism, and outright disbelief especially among the people who knew him best and thought it blasphemous that a man with his background, someone who shared the same ancestral bloodline, could claim to do the things he did. The gospels describe how this mistrust came to a head one Sabbath day when Jesus began teaching in the local synagogue. Astonished at his words, his listeners started murmuring, "From whence hath this man these things? and what wisdom is this which is given unto him, that even such mighty works are wrought by his hands?" What the assembled congregation saw before them was the local carpenter's boy whom they knew as the son of Mary and Joseph and a brother to people still living in their village. Disregarding the magnitude and eloquence of the statements they were hearing with their own ears, many in the audience took offence. Jesus' response to their cynicism was instructive. "A prophet is not without honour, but in his own country, and among his own kin, and in his own house," he told them. The Bible reports that because of the locals' unbelief he was unable to do mighty works in that place, except to lay his hands on a few of the sick and heal them. Marveling at their doubt, the Master continued on his way about the neighboring villages, teaching. (Mark 6:1-6)

Set Thine House in Order

. . . Set thine *own* house in order, and through the results of that
obtained by *setting* thine house in order, let thy *works* constrain
thine *brother* to do likewise!   257-20

Jesus had warned his disciples it would not be easy for advocates
of the Christ way to hold their own in a frenzied world spellbound by
physical and mental power. Sometimes it would feel as if they did not
belong anywhere and figuratively (or even literally) were homeless. It
had happened to him, their teacher. Once when the Master was surrounded by the multitudes and a scribe approached him announcing
he would follow the rabbi wherever he went, Jesus replied, "The foxes
have holes, and the birds of the air have nests; but the Son of man
hath not where to lay his head." (Matt. 8:20) The Christ spirit present
among us has no permanent foothold in a material world. Its residence
is with the angels.

Yet despite the challenges that arose, his disciples were to retain a
positive attitude and no matter what happened, keep pressing forward.
According to the Edgar Cayce readings we fail only when we stop trying. (3292-1) Their contention is that stepping out on faith to make a
contribution—the attempt or effort put forth—is just as valuable as
reaching the goal. " . . . To not know, but to do the best as is known,
felt, experienced in self, to him it is counted as righteousness," (1728-2)
Cayce insists. The Master encouraged the workers he was sending out
to labor in the fields of the Lord not to entertain doubt or sink into fear
but to keep the faith and tenaciously persist. It was the same advice
he had given his apostles when they started to panic as the waves of a
raging sea began crashing around them.

Doubt and Fear
⤪

. . . Then don't worry about what's going to happen! . . . When you
get to the place where you would worry . . . stop and pray! For why
worry when you can pray? . . .   2823-3

One of the most dramatic accounts recorded in the New Testament is the story of Jesus and the twelve sailing across the water when their boat runs into a terrifying tempest. Mark describes the scene in his gospel: "And there arose a great storm of wind, and the waves beat into the ship, so that it was now full." Apparently the Master was asleep on a pillow at the back of the boat as the storm whipped up and unaware of the deteriorating situation. Growing more and more distraught by the minute the disciples finally decide to wake him up crying, "Master, carest thou not that we perish?" So Jesus rises, rebukes the storm and says to the sea, "Peace, be still." And upon his command the wind ceases and a great calm settles over wave and sky. Afterwards he follows up with the unnerved men by asking his friends, "Why are ye so fearful? how is it that ye have no faith?" His questions cause the group to become even more frightened and start mumbling among themselves, "What manner of man is this, that even the wind and the sea obey him?" (Mark 4:35–41)

The Cayce readings offer an interesting addendum to the message communicated in the story of the storm at sea. They suggest that when something which would make us afraid enters our hearts tempting us to falter, we, too, must awaken the Christ spirit slumbering inside. Only this spirit can quell the waves of fear that threaten to engulf us and bring peace to our turbulent world. " . . . Fear is of the earth," asserts Cayce. "The spirit of truth and righteousness casteth out fear." (397-1) He adds that anyone who is apprehensive has " . . . lost consciousness of self's own heritage with the Son . . . ," referring to fear as the "first consciousness" of sin entering the door. The important point to remember is that through the Christ we are heirs to a heritage far greater than anything in the material realm that might cause angst or alarm. (243-10) By the same token, the readings counsel that when fear of the future, the past, or what other people may say arises, we should immediately set our dread aside using a specific prayer recited not merely by rote with the lips or in thought, but in body, mind, and soul—

> "Here I am, Lord—Thine! Keep me in the way Thou would have me go, rather than in that I might choose."   2540-1

And when asked how to prevent doubt and fear in the first place,

Edgar Cayce's response cut right to the heart of the matter. "By the application of that thou knowest to do today, putting the trust in Him, *making* the *personal* application of that thou knowest to do in *His* name." (524-2)

If the World Hate You
ལ

His representatives were to continue doing the work of the Christ spirit in spite of any resistance they might encounter. "If the world hate you, ye know that it hated me before it hated you," he reminded his students before explaining that if they had not been spiritually transformed but still thought and acted like everyone else under the thrall of egoism and materialistic concerns, their friends and neighbors no doubt would approve. But because they approached life from a higher standpoint, the unenlightened souls fearful of ideas they could not comprehend and anxious about losing their prized possessions might rebuff and revile them. Remember, the Master added, "The servant is not greater than his lord. If they have persecuted me, they will also persecute you; if they have kept my saying, they will keep yours also." (John 15:18-20)

Jesus had foreseen the level of doubt and disbelief his teachings would arouse. Introducing the way of Spirit could incite fierce opposition and in some cases might even provoke bodily harm. No doubt a portion of any group would resonate with what his followers had to say while others would merely be indifferent to their speech. But for a certain number the content of their remarks would touch a chord deep inside and cause alarm, stirring up controversy and generating irrational amounts of anger. Hostile audiences vehemently resistant to change might strike out and verbally assault his emissaries with sneers, rebuking them as tools of the devil just as they had done to him, or attack the messenger using physical force. Jesus had predicted these volcanic responses when he uttered the phrase, "Think not that I am come to send peace on earth: I came not to send peace, but a sword." (Matt. 10:34) The line of demarcation between an existence based exclusively in materiality and one rooted in the inner Christ was as sharp as a razor's edge. And the sword of truth his disciples wielded firmly and forever severed the connection between one's former way of life and the pattern demonstrated by the Master. The weapon could even sunder the relationship between mother and child.

Who Is My Brother?
✍

What separates ye from seeing the Glory even of Him that walks with thee oft in the touch of a loving hand, in the voice of those that would comfort and cheer? For He, thy Christ, is oft with thee.

5749-6

Apprentices under the Master's tutelage had to stay vigilant, ever alert to the possibility their relatives and friends might misinterpret or reject the changes in them. Suddenly and quite unexpectedly his disciples might find themselves estranged from the people they loved. The way of the Christ did not serve parochial interests or honor a personal investment in culture, race, or national origin. It demanded a higher and more expansive view of human relationships—one not easily understood by those deeply immersed in material modes and means. The two approaches mixed like oil and water. The Master's pronouncement that he had come with a sword foreshadowed the discord he envisioned his teachings might spark in hearth and home. He was putting his students on notice. "For I am come to set a man at variance against his father, and the daughter against her mother, and the daughter in law against her mother in law. And a man's foes shall be they of his own household." (Matt. 10:35-36)

As the followers of the Christ way became more active in the world, they had to be prepared to deal with dissension cropping up in both their physical and psychic abodes. Parents, siblings, aunts, uncles, cousins, and close companions unable or unwilling to accept the invitation to start living life from the inside out might disown them, unraveling longstanding bonds. The Master himself had had to steel himself against this same kind of emotional fallout when he left his family behind to travel the countryside and fulfill a mission his relatives did not always agree with or understand. His personal situation was proof that his followers might be called upon to distance themselves from prior affiliations too. But if and when that happened, they should remember what their teacher had said about who family really was.

A story chronicled in the Gospel of Mark describes the time Jesus was preaching inside someone's home and such a large crowd had gathered around him that there was not enough room to even eat. When several of his friends heard about the situation, they set out to take charge of the Master, fearing he might be out of his head. Meanwhile, some scribes, newly arrived from Jerusalem, claimed the rabbi was possessed by the devil Beelzebub. After Jesus assures the group of Jewish teachers that this was not the case, he used a parable to question the men about their unfounded accusations. "How can Satan cast out Satan? And if a kingdom be divided against itself, that kingdom cannot stand. And if a house be divided against itself, that house cannot stand. And if Satan rise up against himself, and be divided, he cannot stand, but hath an end." (Mark 3:23–26)

A little later we learn Jesus' brethren and mother Mary, who must have been worried about her son, were standing outside calling for him. But when the people perched closest to the Master informed him his relatives were present and would like to speak with him, Jesus' unabashed response reflected the central choice he had made about whom and what he served. "Who is my mother, or my brethren?" he asks. Then he looked at the multitudes sitting around him, proclaiming "Behold my mother and my brethren! For whosoever shall do the will of God, the same is my brother, and my sister, and mother." (Mark 3:33–35)

A Kingdom Divided

It is worth noting the circumstances surrounding the Master's use of the metaphor of a divided kingdom. The gospel story indicates family and friends were concerned about his sanity so the lesson Jesus' imparted was twofold. It was a reproof to a disingenuous group of scribes hoping to undermine his legitimacy and a platform for instructing his followers on how to maintain their sanity in an unbalanced world. Those who choose to carry the Christ light into the darkness must keep a laser-like focus on the task at hand because it is impossible to preserve one's inner integrity and remain whole (sane) while attempting to serve more than one master. Trying to hold onto two diametrically opposed positions—living as the man of earth and a child of heaven—is like trying to move in two different directions at the same time. It cannot be done. And the dissension and division the internal conflict engenders is bound to rip us apart. Once we have allowed the enemy, the resistance known as Satan, to set up camp inside our castle walls, a battle ensues, weakening its structural defenses until our spiritual household crumbles and falls into ruin.

Interestingly, immediately after Jesus responds to the group of scribes by asserting his undeviating fidelity to God, the gospel account highlights an incident, which compels him to reconfirm his commitment to releasing every tether tying him to the past. A chapter out of his personal history reappears in the form of several relatives who show up at the gathering and start calling out to him trying to attract his attention. But Jesus ignores their pleas. As appealing as a mini-reunion with members of his family might be, he does not abandon his post nor allow the pull of an emotional bond to overshadow his mission by bestowing undue attention on blood relations. The Son of Man has made a choice and by extension was teaching his disciples that they must also sever any leftover ties to partisanship—be they familial, religious, social, cultural, or political.

The followers of the Christ way unquestionably were charged with a responsibility to love and nurture the souls entrusted to their immediate keeping, but they were not supposed to sell out to exclusivity. Unquestioned devotion to a special group or caste subverted the mandate to love everyone and dulled one's sensitivity to the plight of those outside the clan. So, too, did upholding the allegiances to culture, race, and class extract a high spiritual price in return for the physical and psychic comfort these associations offered. The cost was a delay in the heavenly kingdom reflected in the earth.[23]

The Master understood the inclination to limit sympathy and support to a favored group, but the children of the one heavenly Father/Mother God were not to succumb to that temptation. "The security and peace such arrangements promised were spurious at best. It was

---

[23]Janet Highland, "New Testament" (unpublished manuscript, 1979).

the quiet of decay, the calm of stagnant backwaters—a condition that by its very nature excluded the vital force of the living waters of Spirit. And as such it was a peace their teacher rejected."[24] The way of life the Master preached did not permit anyone to ignore the responsibility to assist those outside the boundaries of kith and kin. His students were to advance the work he had pioneered "with the vision cleared of tribal taboos and their energies freed from narrow, egoistic interests."[25] The Christ way skewed toward unity, and Jesus' command to his students was to serve the entire family of God—not just those who belonged to the small, insular communities which counted them as members. From then on anyone doing the work of the Spirit—the will of the One—was their brother, sister, mother, or father.

Come and See

Do not attempt to force, impel or to even try to impress thy knowledge upon another. Remember what the serpent did to Eve.

5753-2

In the process of tutoring his best students on how to carry the good tidings of "God with us" out into the world, Jesus had handed over the keys to the kingdom of heaven. At the same time, he issued a warning to his students about using the spiritual knowledge they had attained to try to impress or dominate their sisters and brothers. Those ordained to minister to the multitudes were to approach their divine siblings with humble hearts and minds filled with compassion. They would lead his fold as gently as the guardian shepherd who carefully guided the flock to fertile pastures before steering them safely home again.

After unveiling the secrets of the universe to his most ardent pupils, Jesus no longer regarded them as novices, but fully trained emissaries of the divine. And whether they moved among the teeming rabble or mingled with the highborn and powerful, his envoys knew how to conduct themselves because they had apprenticed with a master. Their teacher was relying on this group to stay grounded in its commitment

---

[24]Janet Highland, "New Testament" (unpublished manuscript, 1979).
[25]*Ibid.*

to the Christ way and meet every demand and condition as a present opportunity to demonstrate the truth of God and man as one.

Jesus' protégés had had the chance to watch their teacher up close interacting with the sick and destitute as well as the religious authorities and well-heeled among society. And amid all of them, the modest Nazarene had stood firm, resolute in his own knowingness while at the same time exhibiting an infinite amount of tender concern toward the weak and the lost. His was the quiet calm of a deep lake. Never didactic or overbearing, the Master's teaching method was to defer to the silent promptings of the soul. "Thy gentleness hath made me great," (Psalm 18:35) the psalmist David, his royal ancestor, once sang. So, too, must the enthusiasm and energy with which his disciples carried out their assignments be tempered by loving-kindness.

To earn the respect and trust of the as-yet unschooled and uninitiated was a delicate dance, which necessitated listening to the hushed whisper of the divine before speaking or making a move. People whose egos took control and started behaving in a patronizing or autocratic manner or those who tried to manipulate his message in order to build temporal empires for themselves were perverting his words. The life of service he proposed did not employ a battering ram to storm the barricades and conquer defenseless souls or try to invade others' spiritual homes uninvited to purloin their goods. The Christ knocks on the door, then patiently waits to be beckoned into the inner sanctum. This was the approach Jesus was directing his followers to take.

The Cayce readings closely parallel the Master's guidance. One soul-stirring reading unambiguously states that " . . . individuals *must be free* to *choose* for themselves the manner of life they would live; or the Lord, the God they would worship." (2540-1) Since man was created as a free agent endowed with choice, no one had the right to eradicate the autonomy of another in dealing with his fellow man or woman. When asked how to present his own work to people of the orthodox faith, Edgar Cayce's answer was exceedingly simple: "*Come* and *See*! . . . " The correct method is not to impose our ideas on others by pressuring them to acquiesce and see things our way, but to invite everyone to come and see. And the ones searching for answers to the questions nagging from within will heed the call. Conversely, " . . . If they are satisfied in their own mire, or their own vomit," states Cayce, "then *do not* disturb. For only the *father* may quicken. But so live in thine *own* life, in thine own associations; not finding fault . . . " He closes that portion of the reading with a thought–provoking question. " . . . If thy Father, God, had found fault with every idle word or every unkind act in thine experiences, what opportunity would *ye* have had in this experience?" (254–87)

My Sheep Hear My Voice

> How beautiful upon the mountains are the feet of him that brin-geth good tidings, . . . that publisheth salvation; that saith unto Zion, Thy God reigneth! Is. 52:7

It would be difficult to invoke a more inspiring incident among the four gospels than the story of the centurion who approaches Jesus while he is teaching in Capernaum to beseech his help for a servant grievous-ly sick of the palsy. True to form, the Master tells the centurion he will go and heal the suffering man. But upon hearing the rabbi's response, the soldier respectfully demurs and in so doing utters an extraordinary statement of faith. "Lord, I am not worthy that thou shouldest come un-der my roof: but speak the word only, and my servant shall be healed. For I am a man under authority, having soldiers under me: and I say to this man, Go, and he goeth; and to another, Come, and he cometh; and to my servant, Do this, and he doeth it." (Matt. 8:8–9)

The Bible describes Jesus as marveling at the centurion's words and remarking to his followers, "Verily I say unto you, I have not found so great faith, no, not in Israel." Then the Master follows up with this enigmatic footnote: "And I say unto you, That many shall come from the east and west, and shall sit down with Abraham, and Isaac, and Jacob, in the kingdom of heaven. But the children of the kingdom shall be cast out into outer darkness: there shall be weeping and gnashing of teeth." Jesus ends his brief lecture by assuring the centurion he can go on his way because according to his belief, it will be done unto him. "And his servant was healed in the selfsame hour." (Matt. 8:10–13)

Besides exposing one man's unwavering faith in the transcendent, transformative power of Immanuel, the episode in Capernaum provides yet another clue as to how Jesus' disciples were supposed to conduct themselves when interacting with the seekers who crossed their paths. The centurion was both a Roman and a soldier—neither a member of their community nor someone who would normally be interested in what a Jewish rabbi had to say. Yet even Jesus was astounded by the words that came out of the soldier's mouth and his profound understanding of the principle of divine authority. The man's keen insight and conviction of the truth—his recognition of the omnipresence of the Christ spirit—was an extraordinary testament to the level of his spiritual development. In turn, this chance meeting crystalized for the Master's pupils hearing the exchange the danger of jumping to conclusions about the readiness of any soul to embrace the truth.

A majority of the Hebrews, including the apostles, likely regarded the Roman army officer as the enemy—an interloper with no real perception of the God the Jewish people worshipped. But it was this religiously illiterate Roman who exhibited a greater understanding of the unseen power of Spirit than all the good Jews steeped in the knowledge of Yahweh and the law. Jesus predicted that many would come from the East and West ready to take a seat at the table with the prophets of old. And when they did, the "children of the kingdom" had to overcome the inclination to judge who rightfully belonged there. Preconceived notions about what any other soul was capable of grasping merely promoted a false sense of superiority. The Master expected his disciples not only to accept every man, woman, and child as is, but to also faithfully serve these divine surrogates in order to learn from them.

Counting the Cost

"For which of you, intending to build a tower, sitteth not down first, and counteth the cost, whether he have sufficient to finish it?" the Master asked his disciples in the Gospel of Luke. "Or what king, going to make war against another king, sitteth not down first, and consulteth whether he be able with ten thousand to meet him that cometh against him with twenty thousand? . . . So likewise, whosoever he be of you that forsaketh not all that he hath, he cannot be my disciple." (Luke 14: 28, 31, 33) All too soon Jesus was going to complete the work appointed him to do in the flesh and depart from his students' sight. They would not have access to him physically anymore.

Just as a mother bird encourages her fledglings to abandon the safety of the nest in order to become airborne and begin circumnavigating the globe, so, too, his disciples were ready to spread their wings and fly. Seen in this light, the Master's brief remarks about the cost of building a tower or preparing for war were words to the wise about carefully assessing the price of such a journey before embarking upon it. While his companions had tremendous love for the teacher who had helped them soar to breathtaking spiritual heights, the emotional bond they felt toward the man Jesus would carry them only so far. The kingdom he preached was not of this world and achieving it required casting aside everything on the material plane they had clung to in the past for support, including his presence in a bodily form. Would they keep going anyway?

From now on the lives of his disciples were no longer their own, but belonged to the whole, the One. And the job of maintaining a continuous state of God awareness 24/7 was intense; it brooked no holidays. Edgar Cayce provides an interesting perspective on the depth and breadth of the commitment Jesus was demanding of his followers in a telling remark about the Master's healing work. "Some might easily ask the question: If He were the healer, why was it necessary that Joseph pass away? Did the Master come to be about *his* work or His Father's work? As individuals, as representatives of the Master, as brothers, as heirs with Him, do we go about our Father's work or our work? There is the variation." (5749-16)

The readings remind us not to put off today that which will bring hope and help to the mind of another, noting that God never says " . . . in a more convenient season I will hear thee." The thing delayed becomes a joy unfulfilled. (877-9) " . . . Live each and every day as if the evening was to be spent with *thy* Creator . . . " declares one forthright reading. (4185-3) The underlying principle is that for as long as we walk this planet, our every thought and action is either adding to the emergence of His Kingdom or preventing it from manifesting here and now. " . . . For we are each His agents, His soldiers in the strife through that we call Life," (911-6) maintains Cayce. And a good soldier never deserts his post no matter how painful or costly the battle becomes, but is well armed beforehand both physically and mentally to withstand the protracted struggle ahead.

Make Haste Slowly
❧

In your patience possess ye your souls. Luke 21:19

Jesus was counting on his agents to work hard but at the same time to be patient and understand that the results of their labors might not be immediately apparent. The efficacy and transformative power of the Christ spirit is not always evident to the human eye nor was the work he wanted them to do designed to be the avenue for amassing money, fame, and position. The Master compared the kingdom of God to a man casting a seed into the ground. He could sit and watch the spot where the seed lay buried all day long and rise throughout the night to keep an eye on his field, but what he had planted would spring up and grow "he knoweth not how. For the earth bringeth forth fruit of herself; first the blade, then the ear, after that the full corn in the ear. But when the fruit is brought forth, immediately he putteth in the sickle, because the harvest is come." (Mark 4:23–29)

While their teacher had given his disciples the job of planting seeds, they were not to spend precious time and energy worrying about how those seeds were exactly going to flower. For long periods the earth would seem to close over their efforts and show no signs of the development taking place beneath the soil. But they were to remain undaunted and remember that in due season the seeds they had planted would extend roots and sprout. It takes time for a grain of wheat to fall to the ground and die so that the life force dormant within it can burst forth from its casing and allow new growth to appear. The Edgar Cayce readings counsel the same approach: " . . . Be not over hasty in word or deed, for it *is* line upon line, here a little, there a little; for it is the *little* leaven that leaveneth the whole lump, and such compared He to the *kingdom* of God . . . " (262-12)

Worldly minded people no doubt would seize upon the seeming failure, the delayed fruition, to rationalize their refusal to follow the Christ way, letting the "strident sounds of ego demands drown out the still small voice of wisdom,"[26] which valued constancy and forbearance.

---

[26] Janet Highland, "New Testament" (unpublished manuscript, 1979).

The skeptics would no more understand the tactics of sowing and reap-
ing than primitive peoples "had understood the efforts of those among
them who first sought to institute agricultural practices."[27] Many were
the failures of the quixotic few hoping to implement progress through
their plantings. Time and again the seeds they placed in the ground
showed no signs of growth, "and the derision of the more 'practical'
and 'realistic' members of the tribe likely added to the weight of their
confusion and failure, making defeat difficult to endure. Yet, still, they
persisted. They refined their techniques, learned from their failures,
sought new methods to implement their dream, and eventually, the
patient people prevailed. And with their success human beings finally
were freed from the tyranny of the hunt—a tyranny that had kept the
race at the lowest level of development by exhausting all of its energies and capacities in an endless search for food and survival."[28] Patient
perseverance transformed everything.

Wheat and Tares

ᑲᑭ

... But find not fault in thine friend nor in thine enemy; for, hath
not He, the Father, allowed the tares and the wheat to grow up
together? ...   440-4

Expounding on the lesson of patience, the Master likened the kingdom of heaven to a landowner who had sowed good seed in his field.
But while the man and his household slept, his enemy secretly slipped
into the field and sowed tares in the ground. So when the first blades
sprang up bringing forth their fruit, tares began blooming right next
to the stalks of wheat. Surprised by this turn of events, the landowner's
servants said to him, "Sir, didst not thou sow good seed in thy field?
from whence then hath it tares?" Their master responds by saying it
must have been his enemy that had done it. His servants proceed to
ask him if they should go and gather up the tares. "Nay," the house-

---

[27] Janet Highland, "New Testament" (unpublished manuscript, 1979).
[28] *Ibid.*

holder replies, "lest while ye gather up the tares, ye root up also the wheat with them. Let both grow together until the harvest: and in the time of harvest I will say to the reapers, Gather ye together first the tares, and bind them in bundles to burn them: but gather the wheat into my barn." (Matt. 13:24–30) Jesus then compared the kingdom of heaven to a net some fishermen had cast into the sea, which gathered up fish of every kind. And "when it was full, they drew to shore, and sat down, and gathered the good into vessels, but cast the bad away." (Matt. 13:47–48)

The patience Jesus promoted was a reference to the restraint his disciples needed to maintain living in a world composed of light and shadow. Growing up in tandem with the tenets they represented—and alongside souls already caught up in the net of Christ truth—would be doctrines, religious leaders, and philosophies representing the antithesis of their teacher's words and work. Fearless and unfazed, his students had to accept the fact that such seemingly incompatible ideas would continue to exist side by side. Their duty was not to search out and eliminate all the so-called sinners and false prophets or try to uproot the untold numbers of flawed precepts implanted by the enemies of truth and now flourishing in the earth.

Like the drops of rain descending from heaven, the benefits of the new far reaches of thought their Master had preached would fall on the just and the unjust alike.

Counterfeit ideas were going to blossom right next to genuine off-shoots of the Christ. Yet when the time came to gather in the yield, those principles which bore no spiritual fruit or were inedible would be separated out and discarded. Consumed in the fires of truth, the lies would vanish into the atmosphere like wisps of smoke. Jesus charged his followers to keep doing the constructive work he had entrusted to their keeping, realizing that slowly, reluctantly consciousness was going to change and the harvest would increase. Remarkably, the Master's lessons of perseverance, of trying, of keeping faith in the eventual efficacy of the work they were called to do extended much farther than even his closest disciples possibly could have imagined. He wanted them to understand that death itself did not mark the finish of his—or their—most effective work. "Except a corn of wheat fall into the ground and die, it abideth alone: but if it die, it bringeth forth much fruit." (John

12:24) Jesus had told them.

His students could not know it then, but more than twenty-one centuries after their leader had departed from the earth, the ways of the Spirit he taught would become more and more a fact of life. So much so, that even some of the most ethically retrogressive among the human race would pay lip service to the idea of loving one's neighbor and grudgingly acknowledge the positive impact the social gospel had on the world. Even those "who misunderstood who and what Jesus was, who despised him as a symbol for all the ills they hoped to eradicate from the planet, would, nevertheless, be building on the foundation"[29] of the three brief years he had spent teaching in an obscure corner of the Middle East. People everywhere are still using the blueprint of love and responsibility for self and others this great Master preached—a sure sign his work is bearing fruit to this day.

---

[29]Janet Highland, "New Testament" (unpublished manuscript, 1979).

Chapter 9
Consciousness Reborn

The Way of the Cross

The way of the cross is not easy, yet it is
the tuneful, the rhythmic, the beautiful,
the lovely way.   1089-6

Those closest to Jesus and privy to the hidden mysteries were relatively few in number, yet the Master expected great things from the
coterie of true believers he had assembled around him. They were the
ones who would ensure the continuation of the work he had started by
sharing the good news liberally with others. The esoteric concepts their
teacher had disclosed to his most trusted confidants were concealed
from the masses and the learned priests and scholars who traded in
the currency of inconsequential facts while boasting about the depth
of their erudition. Such men lacked the capacity to understand what
God reveals to babes. "No man knoweth who the Son is, but the Father;

and who the Father is, but the Son, and he to whom the Son will reveal him," the Master had confided to his inner circle before stating, "Blessed are the eyes which see the things that ye see. For I tell you, that many prophets and kings have desired to see those things which ye see, and have not seen them; and to hear those things which ye hear, and have not heard them." (Luke 10:22–24)

Their teacher had provided a solid footing in truth for his students and now he expected them to begin to build on that foundation by making his words real in the earth. Jesus compared what he was asking his disciples to do to a man who had constructed his home on a layer of bedrock. "Whosoever cometh to me, and heareth my sayings, and doeth them," he explained, " . . . is like a man which built an house, and digged deep, and laid the foundation on a rock: and when the flood arose, the stream beat vehemently upon that house, and could not shake it: for it was founded upon a rock." In contrast, those who had heard what the Master had to say but failed to "dig deep" within themselves to erect their lives on the solid substratum of the inner Christ were "like a man that without a foundation built an house upon the earth; against which the stream did beat vehemently, and immediately it fell; and the ruin of that house was great." (Luke 6:47–49)

Born Again
❧

> . . . Be not other than that thou wouldst have thy fellow man be
> unto thee . . .   262-72

During his tenure as a traveling preacher, the Master had employed any number of analogies to clarify the gist of his lessons about the new direction he wanted people to take. In one case he used a phrase that evoked some consternation when he told a Pharisee named Nicodemus, a fully grown adult, he must be "born again." Taken aback, the learned man asked if the rabbi expected him to return to his mother's womb. (John 3:1–5) But Jesus was explaining how extraordinary the change would be for those making the transition from living as a man of earth wholly steeped in materiality to living from the inside out. The key to the new kingdom was to die inwardly to an existence based on external appearances and dense physical forms and be reborn into an awareness of the nonmaterial aspects of life, the Spirit, or essence of God.

Whoever loses his life—the earthbound existence fed by the mind—the Master noted, by laying down his worldly all, gains something far greater than what a majority of the population values in terms of the normal human state of affairs. Moths and rust cannot corrupt this spiritual kingdom nor can it ever be consumed in a fire. Like the seed that falls to the earth and appears to die, we, too, must be willing to divest ourselves of the shell of our former ways and make the transition to begin life anew. " . . . Ye must be born in flesh, in spirit again, that ye may make manifest that ye have experienced in thine own soul!" echo the Cayce readings. (262-60) After incarnating into the material dimension the man of flesh whose "breath is in his nostrils" (Is. 2:22) must reform—*re-form*—into a being fully cognizant of its supernatural heritage and prepared to express the soul faculties alive within. Be " . . . born of the spirit where ye may make manifest the fruits of the spirit. Where? In the earth!" the same reading commands.

Jesus had also warned his students that they would not be successful by merely pretending to have made this fundamental change. Thinking lofty thoughts or affecting a different posture while continuing to hang onto outworn attitudes and beliefs would not work. The vessel must be emptied. "No man also seweth a piece of new cloth on an old garment: else the new piece that filled it up taketh away from the old, and the rent is made worse," he explained before adding, "And no man putteth new wine into old bottles: else the new wine doth burst the bottles, and the wine is spilled, and the bottles will be marred: but new wine must be put into new bottles." (Mark 2:21-22) The Master was emphasizing how important it was to begin life anew and live by Spirit. It is impossible to hang onto old habits and prior ways of thinking and acting, acquiescing to the methods and means of a material world, while still hoping to inherit the blessings and peace of the new kingdom. The path is straight and narrow that leads to this new life and deviating from it by attempting to place heart and mind under the authority of two different rulers is destined to fail. A kingdom divided against itself cannot stand for long.

Choose Thou

... There is today, every day, set before thee good and evil, life and death—choose thou. For only self can separate you from the love of the Father ...
3581-1

Jesus did not mince words in spelling out for his disciples the interior conversion necessary to claim rights to the title of a follower of the Christ way. First, all human sense of pride had to disappear. "If any man desire to be first, the same shall be last of all, and servant of all," (Mark 9:35) the Master decreed. In addition, his followers must purge themselves of every speck of insensitivity and cruelty no matter how minor or well hidden, eschewing harsh words and the propensity toward violence. And under no circumstances would they ever defile the innocent, especially a child. "And whosoever shall offend one of these little ones that believe in me, it is better for him that a millstone were hanged about his neck, and he were cast into the sea," (Mark 9:42) the rabbi had pronounced in the Gospel of Mark. Their duty was to reject every thought, word, and deed that reeked of selfishness by scouring clean the squalid recesses of hate and corruption still living inside them—especially those vices they tried to conceal from the world.

Adherents of the Christ way do not yield to anger or spew mental pollution into the atmosphere by venting prejudicial ideas. Neither would they humiliate another or take advantage of the uneducated and less fortunate. (254-87) Their teacher had given his disciples explicit orders to never let any element of the external world lead them astray. "And if thy hand offend thee, cut it off: it is better for thee to enter into life maimed, than having two hands to go into hell... And if thy foot offend thee, cut it off: it is better for thee to enter halt into life, than having two feet to be cast into hell ... And if thine eye offend thee, pluck it out ... " (Mark 9:43, 45, 47) Those individuals who know the mysteries of the kingdom of heaven—souls reborn into the new state of consciousness—bear an enormous responsibility. To whom much is given, much is expected and the demand is to proactively cast aside every bit of debris now sullying the holy sanctuary from which the light of divinity is meant to shine.

The Father lives within us, notes Edgar Cayce, and will rightly guide

us in our seeking and the steps to take day by day once we have removed all the garbage littering our temple's interior and eclipsing the
glow of its sacred flame. " . . . If thou keepest the temple cluttered up
with those things that bespeak rather of the flesh, only the flesh can
answer—but if thou keepest the temple clean and decorated in the
spirit of love, and in the light of truth, then it will shed its light abroad
. . . " he explains. (440-4) The question we are to ask ourselves is this:
" . . . Are the courts of my temple a dwelling place of the living God?
Or have I rather set up those idols of the earth that are earthy? . . . "
(331-1) The readings maintain that we will find the way made clear by
keeping our "courts and temple" cleansed. They warn us not to make
the Father's house a den, parroting the Master's protest in the Gospel
of Luke when he proclaimed, "My house is the house of prayer: but ye
have made it a den of thieves." (Luke 19:46)

Be strong and upright the readings instruct, " . . . that *He* may come
in the heat of the day or the cool of the evening and converse with
thee in the courts of thine own temple . . . " Thus does our God speak
to us and thus do we come to know that which casts out fear. (333-1)
Referencing the scene in the chapter 17 of Exodus when God directed
Moses to smite the rock at Horeb and open up a tap for the water to
flow, Cayce states that " . . . as the rock that casts shadows for those
that are athirst, and brings forth its waters . . . ," supplying souls seeking refreshment in its shadow, " . . . so in *this* temple of thine know He
will guide, guard and direct in the way that *thou* may become a rock
for thine brother . . . " His counsel concludes by urging us to " . . . *keep*
the way clear." (333-1)

Meeting Self
&

Selfishness is the mindset despoiling the house of the Lord by filling
it with dross that crowds out the authentic and pure. Thus removing
"self" becomes the first order of business before attempting to assist
anyone else. " . . . What action should be taken? *Correct* thine own *ways!*"
(1828-1) one abbreviated reading practically shouts. Cayce goes on
to inform us that the experiences we are having in the earth present
countless opportunities to meet self. Remember, he notes " . . . that all

are tried as in the fires of self ... ," (3292-1) emphasizing the tremendous value in learning to stand aside as often as possible to watch self pass by, even when it may be a torment to examine our actions so closely.

The readings direct us to let our lives become a pattern others may use as a light along the path. Equally significant, their across-the-board guidance is to sustain a level of consistency—not being too hard or too easy on ourselves but understanding that no matter how far afield we may have drifted in the past, the opportunity for reconstruction is readily available. " ... Do not condemn self ... ," (3292-1) Cayce declares because indulging in self-condemnation is considered sin from the standpoint of the readings. " ... While selflessness is the law, to belittle self is a form of selfishness and not selfless," (2803-2) he declares, pointing out that condemning oneself is as much of an error as condemning others. (3292-1) In seeking to apply the principles revealed by the great Teacher of teachers, Edgar Cayce catapults us into action with one additional sage piece of advice: " ... Never think too highly of yourself and never belittle yourself too much ... Then use the abilities that you have, and you have many ... " (3689-1)

The representatives the Master has delegated to complete his work must be clear-eyed about who they are, honest about purging the inner sanctum of its filth, and ready to model the unassuming Galilean in both word and deed. The promise is that those attuned to the Christ way are certain to succeed in their missions because they have access to a fountainhead of unlimited compassion, wisdom, and strength at their disposal. "Are ye not all children of God? Are ye not co-creators with Him? ... " the readings inquire. " ... Have ye not been with Him from the beginning? Is there any knowledge, wisdom or understanding withheld if ye have attuned thyself to that Creative Force which made the worlds and all the forces manifested in same? ... " The spirit of God is ever-present and accessible to all. It never abandons its offspring nor does it reflect the slightest trace of a desire to punish those who may have missed the mark. " ... Thinkest thou that the arm of God is ever short with thee because thou hast erred? Though ye be afar, though ye be in the uttermost parts, if ye call I will *hear!* and answer speedily.' Thinkest thou that speakest of another, or to thee?" (294-202)

Fit to Enter
⌒ֆ⌒

For as He chose to enter, so *ye* have entered. As He chose to live,
so may ye live . . .   262-103

The approach to daily living the Master outlined was not a job for
the faint of heart. "Bless them that curse you, and pray for them which
despitefully use you," the Son of Man had instructed. "And unto him
that smiteth thee on the one cheek offer also the other; and him that
taketh away thy cloak forbid not to take thy coat also. Give to every
man that asketh of thee; and of him that taketh away thy goods ask
them not again." (Luke 6:28–30) For the umpteenth time Jesus was describing the highly evolved state of consciousness that would prevail
in his new kingdom. Because his disciples understood the principle
of Oneness, they would not take offense no matter what treatment
befell them but would turn the other cheek, dismissing the slight and
showing no resistance or reaction. Due to their perception of the truth
his representatives on earth would be able to recognize the divine
countenance hidden behind the ego–mask of the offending party and
respectfully walk away.

Never withhold anything in consciousness from others was the
overriding message of the Christ. Understand what your brothers and
sisters think they need in order to find their way back to the Father's
house—and provide it. Present your coat to the thief who has stolen
your cloak because it is not given to anyone to judge someone else's
spiritual path, no matter how convoluted it may appear to be on the
surface. Fretting over the exchange of personal possessions or hoping
to get even reflects an egoistic attitude of "I, me, mine" and negates
the reality of man's true being. Conversely, turning the other cheek or
divesting oneself of the very object considered indispensable to our
own happiness is an act of far greater spiritual power than fighting
back. The Master was not telling his students never to lock their doors
or to impoverish themselves at the hands of manipulative con artists.
Rather they should stay alert and keep consciousness open to every
opportunity to meet the needs of those unawakened souls who lacked
the benefit of the esoteric knowledge they had received.

In unraveling the mysteries he had imparted to his pupils, the Master had left behind explicit criteria to gauge those fit to inherit the kingdom prepared from the foundation of the world. "For I was an hungred, and ye gave me meat: I was thirsty, and ye gave me drink: I was a stranger, and ye took me in: Naked, and ye clothed me: I was sick, and ye visited me: I was in prison, and ye came unto me." (Matt. 25:35–36) And after his disciples asked him point blank when they had ever seen him—Jesus—hungry, thirsty, sick, or in prison or when he had been a stranger they took in and clothed, their teacher offered this candid response. " . . . Verily I say unto you, Inasmuch as ye have done it unto one of the least of these my brethren, ye have done it unto me." (Matt. 25:40) His followers were not to confuse having the physical presence of the man Jesus in front of them to fulfill the charge to live as active expressions of the Christ spirit in the earth. They had to look beyond appearances and recognize this same divinity in everyone, knowing that whatever they were doing to aid others, they did in the name of the One.

As children of God we are not simply creatures; we are creators who have been given the opportunity to express every modicum of divinity we possess. This is what our elder brother accomplished with his lifetime and He expects no less of us. " . . . The good shepherd feedeth the sheep; he tendeth the lambs," (262-51) acknowledged Edgar Cayce during one of his readings, charging us to attend to the needs of the flock the Master had entrusted to his followers. " . . . To express love in thine activities to thy neighbor is the greater service that a soul may give in this mundane sphere," he asserts. (499-2) Today and every day good and evil, life and death are set before us and the readings exhort us to choose well, for in the final analysis a soul's progress will be measured against the ideal the Master set.

To that end, the readings warn us to keep in mind whom we are actually dealing with when offering aid and solace to our neighbor. "Know that in the manner ye mete, or do to thy fellow man, so ye do unto thy Maker," (2599-1) they declare, for the brethren Jesus was referring to are, in truth, material manifestations of " . . . that Creative Force {*God*} in a material world . . . " (524-2) The upshot of this single, inescapable reality is that genuine charity is never about exalting oneself, but about honoring the Creator. The Master had predicted many would announce they had prophesied and cast out devils in his name yet he would reply he never knew them, (Matt. 7:22–23) indicating that those who used his teachings merely to elevate themselves or to advance a personal agenda already have their reward. But " . . . they that have ministered that the God–force, the soul that is the image of the Maker *might* be glorified have done so unto the Lord . . . , " (524–2) observes Edgar Cayce.

According to philosophy promulgated in the readings, the purpose of each situation experienced on earth is to glorify that which is good and of the one source, God, for that alone is eternal. And whenever we decide to assist someone else, magnifying the good and minimizing what is false, we grow in grace, knowledge, and understanding. (2599–1) Cayce insists that as we give of ourselves through different fields of activity—in the home, street, marketplace, and our associations with people from various walks of life—we will begin to better understand the Master's teachings. Such circumstances present " . . . the channels or the places or the experiences or the opportunities . . . " whereby we can apply " . . . that which has been given as the whole law and the prophets: Ye shall love the Lord thy God with all thine heart, thine soul, thine body, and thy neighbor as thyself." (524–2)

Come Out and Be Separate
༄

> . . . Wherever Truth is made manifest it gives place to that which is heaven for *those that seek* and love truth! . . .   262-87

One day focusing the attention of those gathered around him on a young child, Jesus remarked that it was the innocent ones, the guileless few, who never would consider misusing the power of mind and body to exploit others for personal gain and who are considered the greatest in the spiritual kingdom. Cayce echoes this sentiment in commenting that Jesus' words " . . . 'Suffer little children to come unto me' is indeed the greater promise to the earth . . . " The Master was making the point that unless and until we became as gentle and innocent as children, willing to learn as they do, we cannot enter in. " . . . No faults, no hates remain in their experience," the readings explain, "until they are taught to manifest such . . . " (1992–1) Contrary to the elaborate rites and rigid sets of rules religious sects imposed upon their followers, the great Galilean teacher made it clear that our singular obligation is to emanate the unblemished purity of the soul in everything we think, say, and do—to become like little children.

The children of the Law of One were expected to maintain a fundamentally different attitude and approach to life than the progeny of Adam and Eve, the offspring of duality, who lived purely from the standpoint of matter and mind. The Master remarked that followers of the Christ way would be as merciful "as your Father also is merciful" (Luke 6:36)—a generative, bottomless well of infinite love and compassion. They do not swagger or boastfully announce to others what they are doing in the name of the kingdom by showing their alms before men nor do they regard themselves as better than anyone else. The last shall be first, Jesus counseled. Humility was their byword while patience with themselves and others was a sign of how well they had digested his teachings. Become a little more patient, a little more tolerant, a little more humble the readings counsel. " . . . But . . . not a tolerance that becomes timid—this would make a rebellion in self. Not a patience that is not positive. Not an humbleness that becomes morbid or lacking in beauty. For as orderliness is a part of thy being, so let consistency—as persistency—be a part of thy being." (1402-1)

Those walking the path the Master trod will remain still, trust in God, and unfailingly exude peace. They are the ones who put up their swords and "resist not evil" (Matt. 5:39) by laying down the weapons of the world and bearing only the armor of Spirit. Displaying the forbearance of a Job, his disciples will confront every difficulty sustained only by the "weapons" of kindness, serenity, long-suffering, and goodwill toward all. And when harmed by their brothers and sisters, these spiritual warriors will turn the other cheek because they understand the outcome of any situation pales in significance to sustaining the connection to their Source, which never changes. As the transparencies by which the spirit of God enters the world, their sole duty is to retain an attitude of helpful hopefulness, letting nothing stand between the inner light of their consciousness and its manifestation in the earth.

In one insightful commentary, Edgar Cayce describes in more detail the attitude a true member of the community of the Christ way is expected to display. Repeated throughout the readings is the observation that it is not enough for us to merely listen to the gospel and pontificate on its words, we have a work to do—

> ... not only to proclaim or announce a belief in the divine, and to
> promise to dedicate self to same, but the entity must *consistently*
> live such. And the test, the proof of same, is longsuffering. This
> does not mean suffering of self and not grumbling about it. Rather,
> though you be persecuted, unkindly spoken of, taken advantage of
> by others, you do not attempt to fight back or to do spiteful things;
> that you be patient—first with self, then with others; again that
> you not only be passive in your relationships with others but ac-
> tive, being kindly, affectionate one to the other ...   3121-1

Break Forth into Joy

Smile always—and *live* the smile!   1819-1

Although at first glance the price of pursuing the sort of existence
espoused by the Master seems inordinately high, yet in reality submission to the Christ way yields untold rewards. But gaining the passkey
to the treasure trove our teacher promised depends to a large degree
on the attitude we adopt during our passage through the earth. Most
of us do not realize the impact our disposition has on the direction and
success of our interpersonal relationships and daily activities. A single
unguarded word or morose facial expression, an agitated demeanor,
testy exchange, or hate-filled screed can stir up waves of feeling, which
ripple outward in ever-widening circles pulling family, friends, and
strangers into the emotional wake. Luckily, joy and peace are just as
infectious and help to calm the rough waters on the seas of life. From
the perspective of the Cayce material, the fallout from the attitudes and
emotions we project during the ups and downs of daily life not only
multiplies geometrically, landing unbidden on everyone around us,
but also renders an eternal imprint on the ethers. The temperamental
drama aired today is creating the conditions we must face tomorrow.

Helpful and hopeful are the catch phrases the readings employ to
describe the proper approach to living, suggesting that the soul's sojourn in this plane should be the creative song of a joyous worker. " ...
Ye can make thyself just as happy or just as miserable as ye like," asserts

Cayce. "How miserable do ye want to be?" (2995-3) He goes on to define happiness as the love of something outside of self, remarking that it may never be obtained by loving only the things that reside within our own domain. (281-30) Furthermore, happiness is not something set apart from us, but the condition by which we approach that in hand to be done. (5563-1) His prescription is to cultivate the ability to see the ridiculous and laugh often, insisting that only in those whom God has favored is there the ability to laugh when the clouds of doubt or disturbance start to gather. " . . . For, remember, the Master smiled—and laughed, oft—even on the way to Gethsemane," (2984-1) he notes. The readings emphasize the importance of brightening the small corner of the world we inhabit and never letting a day pass by " . . . without speaking to someone with the smile of the face and eye reminding them that somebody cares, and it is Jesus!" (3357-1) An attitude of gratitude is the cornerstone of constructing such a joy-filled life, for the fact remains that He (the Christ spirit) is an ever-present reality—healing, helping, restoring hope—even during those moments we may find ourselves walking "in the valley of the shadow of death." (Psalm 23:4)

An incident in Luke's gospel recounting an extraordinary healing of the Master's underscores his perspective on the importance of sustaining a continuous state of gratitude. It happened one day when Jesus was on his way to Jerusalem passing through Samaria and Galilee. Upon entering a certain village the rabbi was met by ten lepers standing afar off and calling out to him for mercy. Acknowledging their distress, the Master bids the ten to "Go shew yourselves unto the priests." So the lepers proceed on their way as directed until, much to their surprise, the group realized that their leprosy had disappeared. Immediately upon seeing evidence of his cure, one of them went back "and with a loud voice glorified God, And fell down on his face at his [Jesus'] feet, giving him thanks . . . " Interestingly the gospel reports that the leper who returned to honor the source of his healing was a Samaritan. Jesus responds to the grateful man by asking, "Were there not ten cleansed? but where are the nine? There are not found that returned to give glory to God, save this stranger." The story ends with this final truism from the Master: "Arise, go thy way: thy faith hath made thee whole." (Luke 17:12-19)

Two aspects of the tale about the ten lepers combine to create a compelling spiritual lesson. Outwardly Jesus does nothing but ask the group to go show themselves to the priests, indicating that the inner workings of the divine are revealed to those steeped in the sacred mysteries—the "priests." Second, the story emphasizes the significance of maintaining an appreciative attitude by remaining ever mindful of the causative force behind every action in the created universe. With the expression of gratitude for his cleansing, the leper who came back was recognizing the power from which his recovery had derived. The spirit of God in man had initiated this transformation, which had released him from bondage to a form of bodily illness. Jesus' dismay at the other nine who never returned to express their appreciation was not because he craved human approval. His reproach reflected a much more profound teaching. To celebrate the release from captivity into a place of divine harmony is humanity's delight, but all must honor the source of their deliverance. "Arise," the Master commanded the soul prostrated before him. The risen consciousness of the Samaritan restored to health—his faith—had made him whole.

Stepping Stones
⤳

. . . And there *shall* it be *told* thee from within the steps thou shouldst take day by day, step by step. Not that some great exploit, some great manner of change should come within thine body, thine mind, but line upon line, precept upon precept, here a little, there a little . . .   922-1

Jesus knew his students were bound to face countless difficulties traversing the peaks and valleys of myriad incarnations on this planet. And the attitude they held while meeting those challenges was crucial to their spiritual progress. Paralleling the teachings of Buddhist masters who train their students to stay focused on the now, the readings also recognize the tremendous value in remaining unruffled by calmly accepting each experience as an opportunity to grow. Cayce explains how important it is to be cool-headed, never letting the vexations of life deter or drag us down, but rather meeting every situation with as much joyousness as if it brought pleasure. A positive attitude alters both heart and mind, which in turn can pave a path to resolution.

The readings regard this effect as conforming to a universal law. " . . . For that which is is a result of the thinking of individuals as related one to another . . . " (610-1) they declare. Similarly Cayce urges us not to allow our everyday problems to become humdrum or perceive them merely as issues to be fought through by questioning their purpose and utility in our lives. For " . . . then the life becomes rather as a drone, as of one drudging, coming through toil . . . " (1968-5) he observes. Seen from the vantage point of the Cayce philosophy, when hindrances or troubles arise in life, the summons is to turn those stumbling blocks into stepping stones. Otherwise a " . . . soul falls backward rather than progresses." (2331-1)

"Take my yoke upon you, and learn of me; for I am meek and lowly in heart: and ye shall find rest unto your souls," Jesus had declared, implying that those in touch with the inner Christ never have to carry their load alone: "For my yoke is easy, and my burden is light." (Matt. 11:29-30) Likewise, the readings' steady drumbeat is to work hard but hold fast to optimism and joy while regularly tuning into the higher realms for inspiration and support. Taking that tack, we will not bedevil but contribute to uplifting the whole—and enjoy the journey in the process. "Let the light of His countenance rest upon thee and bring thee peace . . . " is their rallying cry. " . . . Let His ways be thy ways. Let joy and happiness be ever in thy word, in thy song. Let *hopefulness*, helpfulness, ever be thy guide. The Lord is thy shepherd; let Him keep thy ways." (938-1)

Atmosphere of the Christ

> Jesus " . . . wept with those who wept, and *rejoiced* with those that did rejoice. He joined with those who made merry, partaking of those things that made merry for the material *body*, yet when sorrow and those things that made afraid came into the experience of others, so He *also* joined with them—but giving life *to every* condition . . . "   451-2

For thirty-three years the Master had lived his life drawing support from the deep well of compassion and peace he had found inside himself while filling the environment around him with harmony, vitality, and joy. Religious institutions are inclined to paint a portrait of Jesus as a benevolent yet slightly unapproachable teacher prone to regarding himself alone as the one and only son of God. They overlook his happy nature and infectious sense of humor. The Cayce readings describe Jesus as jolly even as he approached his death and remind us to emulate this attitude of the Master's.

People reborn into the dynamic life of Spirit are not psychologically closed down, prickly, or dour. They do not regard the rest of the world as not good enough or push away other people as if their human failings were contagious. No, they wholeheartedly embrace life. " . . . For how did He give? . . . " the readings ask, " . . . Not as of old, as they who shut themselves away; but in their laughter, in their sorrows, in their joys, in their pleasures did He join...." Edgar Cayce depicts a Jesus who ate, drank, and lived among people in such a way that " . . . whether they were of the street or in palaces . . . " all were blessed by His presence. (1632-2) He was " . . . mindful of friends, He was sociable, He was loving, He was kind, He was gentle. He grew faint, He grew weak—and yet gained that strength that He has promised, in becoming the Christ, by fulfilling and overcoming the world! . . . " (2533-7) The energy and demeanor of a true follower of the Christ radiates this same aura of lightness and warmth. They draw souls to them like moths to a flame. And they laugh—heartily and often.

The Master no doubt would need to retain his upbeat attitude and faith-filled frame of mind as the waves of destiny sweeping across Judea began to crest during the final weeks before his Crucifixion. Jesus and his disciples were on the far side of the Jordan as the time of the Passover drew near, and he said to them, "Behold we go up to Jerusalem." (Matt. 20:18) Although the members of his inner circle were apprehensive about the potential dangers his presence in that city might arouse, the group nonetheless began its journey toward the final chapter of their Master's story—a saga which would soon culminate in the unveiling of the resurrected Christ. Edgar Cayce summed up the sense of the uncertainty and the arguments that arose among his worried followers during those anxious days preceding their entry into Jerusalem. " . . . We find those periods of much disturbance among the disciples who were of Galilee and those who were of the Judean ministry. These were in disputation as to what was to take place when he, Jesus, was to go to Jerusalem. Yet He chose to go, entering through the period of rest at Bethany with Mary, Martha, Lazarus; and *there* the triumphal entry and the message that was given to those throngs gathered there." (5749-10)

For the disciples who had been with Jesus since his first miracle at Cana, the active ministry of their teacher was coming to a close. Now it was time for him to prove to them and to everyone else that Spirit, which had entered into matter in the beginning, was never bound by the limitations of mortality. It could rise to the heights of glory and return in full consciousness to dwell with the Father again.

Chapter 10
Bread of Life

There should be the reminding that—
though He bowed under the burden of
the Cross, though His blood was shed,
though He entered into the tomb—
through that power, that ability, that
love as manifested in Himself among
His fellow men He broke the bonds of
death; proclaiming in that act that *there
is no death* when the individual, the soul,
has and does put its trust in Him.

5749-13

As the feast of Passover drew near, Jesus and the disciples started moving from the other side of the Jordan towards Jerusalem where he would impart some of his most profound teachings in the fleeting time he had left on earth. The Master no doubt realized the enormity of the events he was walking toward but had set the wheels in motion any-way. The momentum behind the conspiracy to eradicate the charismatic rabbi and his teachings had started gathering steam long before those final fateful days, which Christians now revere as Holy Week. According to Edgar Cayce, over the course of the three years of his ministry Jesus had drawn a constant barrage of " . . . those trials, those temptations, those activities and those desires for the ability of those in authority to trap him." (1436-2) Questions kept arising about this harmless-looking yet powerful preacher who had captivated the hearts of the masses with a message that potentially could topple the status quo.

As the rumors about his miracles spread around the region, Herod Antipas, the Tetrarch of Galilee, had caught wind of them and the ruler's interest turned into dread. One of the rumors said that John the Baptist, whom Herod had beheaded, had risen from the dead. Other people believed Jesus was one of the ancient prophets, perhaps Elias, who had returned to perform new wonders. Likely due to an enormous amount of guilt and fear on his part, Herod apparently held more to the belief that the rabbi's arrival in their midst was indeed the reappearance of John. Not surprisingly, Jesus also came under constant scrutiny by the temple authorities. For the miracles he had wrought, the great following he had assembled as well as his association with his cousin John who headed up the Essenes, a persecuted sect, the Master had long aroused the interest, concern, and anger of the Pharisees. Cayce alludes to their antagonism in one reading by saying " . . . there was so much concern from the teachings of the Master, or Him who walked in Galilee, Him who made for the strifes among the sects of the Pharisees, the Sad-ducees, the Essenes." (830-1) Due to the risks the different political and religious elements in Jerusalem posed—and the fact that the time had not yet arrived for him to take leave of his body—the gospel writer John reports that for the most part Jesus "walked in Galilee, for he would not walk in Jewry, because the Jews sought to kill him." (John 7:1)

The Bible, however, does reveal the Master secretly traveling to the holy city for the Feast of Tabernacles and portrays him teaching in the temple during that festival. (John 7:2-10) John's gospel also indicates that after the feast he continued to teach in Jerusalem for the next few months. It was during this previous visit prior to his triumphal entry on what is now labeled Palm Sunday that Jesus had healed the man born blind by mixing spittle with clay (a demonstration of the insignificance of matter in the presence of Spirit) and had told a group of faithful Jews that the Christ spirit he represented was greater than their beloved patriarch Abraham. He remarked that the prophet Abraham would have rejoiced to see his day when the God-in-man was made manifest in the earth.

Because of his insolence in having pushed the father of the Jewish nation off his pedestal and generally affronting their religious sensibilities, several angry spectators claimed Jesus had a devil and tried to stone him. The gospel reports that Jesus "hid himself, and went out of the temple, going through the midst of them, and so passed by." (John 8:59) And when the Master subsequently proclaimed his Oneness with the Father and asked those gathered before him to believe the words from their own scriptures—"I said, Ye are gods" (John 10:34)—many accused the Hebrew rabbi of blasphemy and tried to seize him a second time. Immediately following this second incident, Jesus left Judea for Perea and the land beyond Jordan where his cousin John had baptized. The Master remained in that area and did not return to the city again until Lazarus passed away.

Lazarus, Come Forth
༄

... When He spoke, death itself gave up that it had claimed ...
5749-16

The death and resurrection of Lazarus is a pivotal moment in the Master's story for two reasons. First, it unequivocally proved the presence and power of the Christ spirit at work in the material realm, and second, it solidified the belief of many who were still wavering, unsure what to think about this extraordinary teacher named Jesus. Questions have arisen as to why the Master delayed his arrival when he was first notified that Lazarus was ill. If he were capable of healing his sick friend, why didn't he save Lazarus and spare the grieving family all those days of sorrow? The likeliest reason for his hesitation was to allow the requisite circumstances to unfold. Jesus' delay was part of essentially the same process he had described to his disciples when they asked him why a certain man had been born blind. "That the works of God should be made manifest," (John 9:3) he had told them. A seemingly tragic human situation was going to allow the presence of God to be glorified in the minds and hearts of untold numbers.

The Cayce readings indicate that Lazarus " . . . was ill of a fever—that today would be called the slow fever, or typhoid . . . " (993-5) and augment the reason for the Master's absence with some additional commentary on the larger purpose of Lazarus' death and resurrection. "While much has been said as to his {*Jesus'*} visits, his friendship with Mary, Martha, Lazarus, we find that much remains to be said as to how that friendship with those brought so much into the hearts of men at that experience, many who never followed, save as afar; and as to how closely this may illustrate how His being may be to the children of men even in this experience." (1986-1) It is worth noting that Cayce provided a similar interpretation when speaking about the death of Jesus' father, Joseph. He had this to say on the subject: "Some might easily ask if he were the healer, why was it necessary that Joseph pass away?" And the answer is implied: Did the Master come to be about his work or the Father's work? "As individuals, as representatives of the Master, as heirs with him, do we go about our Father's work or our work? There is the variation." (5749-16)

It is difficult to reconstruct twenty-one centuries after the fact what it must have felt like for the spectators crowded around Lazarus' tomb to see Jesus, the simple Nazarene who walked among them, demonstrate dominion over death. As Cayce expresses it, " . . . as experienced by those who stood about the grave of him, the brother of those whom the Lord loved—when he spoke, death itself gave up that it had claimed, even though the sister had warned that there had not been the embalming . . . Instantly the activity brought life. For He *is* life; He *is* health, He *is* beauty. He *is*—not was, not will be, but *is*." (5749-16) On a more prosaic note, the readings also add rare details to the picture with a couple of comments about unwrapping the grave clothes from the revivified man: "To Lazarus we find He called, 'Come forth!' yet he was not able to unbind himself." (1158-14), and "Yet with the breaking of the bonds of death, the breaking of the material bonds—the binding about the head—must needs be done by others." (5749-16) Needless to say, the raising of Lazarus, a precursor to Jesus' own resurrection, had an overwhelming impact on those who observed it firsthand as it does on almost anyone hearing the story today. According to Edgar Cayce, the experience " . . . brought about a change which made for a *new life*, a new understanding, a new conception of the manifestations of the Creative Force, or God, among the children of men." (1158-4)

Witnesses to Lazarus' release from the tomb were awestruck by the incident and word of Jesus' amazing feat no doubt began moving through the region like wildfire. The religious authorities became especially concerned about this turn of events for they knew all too well of the healing miracles Jesus had performed and the loyalty of his many followers. The fear was that the upstart rabbi might accumulate too much power and incite a rebellion, causing people to sever their allegiances to the temple. The Cayce material implies that the episode of calling forth Lazarus from the tomb, more than any other, was the catalyst or turning point, which sealed the Master's fate.[30]

The readings also provide a much more comprehensive portrait of the immediate aftermath of Lazarus' reappearance among the living and the astonishment it generated in the general populace than the accounts reported in the Bible. There were " . . . great turmoils about those of the city of Bethany when Lazarus was raised from the grave . . . ," states Cayce, " . . . when those of the followers, those of the sisters—Martha and Mary—made preparations for the supper after the resurrection or the bringing to life of the brother." A neighbor's child by the name of Susane is said to have noticed the sense of bewilderment and panic among Jesus' followers when some of the authorities appeared in their midst to interrogate the group, trying to verify what had happened. She " . . . saw the fears created by those in authority who questioned Susane and the parents and those about the feast." (1179-2) It is no surprise that this official line of questioning instilled concern among the Master's camp. As written in the gospels and confirmed by Edgar Cayce, both the life of Jesus and Lazarus were now in danger. The chief priests and the Pharisees were acutely afraid that if more people started following this miracle maker, the Romans would nullify their own authority and perhaps even destroy the Jewish nation. So they

---

[30] Anne Read, *Edgar Cayce on Jesus and His Church*, ed. Hugh Lynn Cayce (New York: Warner Books, Inc., 1970), 117.

consulted together and began to scheme about putting Jesus to death. Cayce adds that they also started plotting against Lazarus, since it was because of him many more Jews now believed in Jesus. Aware of the impending danger, the Master and his disciples decided to withdraw to Ephraim before continuing to an area across the Jordan.[31]

Death of the Son
ᑰ

> O Jerusalem, Jerusalem, thou that killest the prophets, and stonest them which are sent unto thee, how often would I have gathered thy children together, even as a hen gathereth her chickens under her wings, and ye would not! Matt. 23:37

Prophecies from the Old Testament and his own words had predicted the trajectory of events in this, the last chapter in the story of Jesus' incarnation in Galilee. In a parable related shortly before his Crucifixion, the Master spoke to his disciples about a householder who had planted a vineyard. After hedging it well, digging a winepress, and building a tower on the land, the owner lent out his vineyard for husbandmen to steward while he traveled to a far country. Months later, when the harvest was ripe, the landowner sent several servants to gather up the fruits of his holdings. But the husbandmen beat and stoned his servants, even murdering one of them. Undeterred, the owner sends a second group of servants to collect his harvest but the overseers do the same thing. Finally, he sends his son, someone who embodies the father's very essence and authority, saying "They will reverence my Son." But the husbandmen kill the young man, too, in an attempt to steal his inheritance. (Matt. 21:33–39)

Jesus is foreshadowing what is going happen to him, the first son, who most fully epitomizes humanity's heritage as children of God. Before the Master had arrived on the scene to live as Jesus, many of his Father's servants had appeared on earth to disclose the true relationship between the lost souls and their Creator. Throughout the ages

---

[31] Anne Read, *Edgar Cayce on Jesus and His Church*, ed. Hugh Lynn Cayce (New York: Warner Books, Inc., 1970), 117.

messenger after messenger had arrived to help human beings reap a bountiful harvest of spiritual awareness, but those divine emissaries were either ignored or slain. The ones the Father had entrusted with husbanding the vineyard of the earth had rejected his servants, craving only material riches and temporal power. And now Jesus was intimating that he, too, was going to be murdered by the same destructive forces at work in the world. The harvest time was nigh, but people still refused to acknowledge the primacy of Spirit and accord it its due. Yet despite the worst machinations of those who had chosen to remain unconscious and intent on wiping out the truth, three days after leaving his body, the first son would prove that nothing could ever "kill" the Christ, because the spirit of God in man was eternal. And just as our elder brother had foretold more than 2,100 years ago, this same Spirit, the stone the builders had rejected, would become the cornerstone of a new kingdom of love and healing in the earth. (Matt. 21:42)

Stones Will Cry Out

Later, as the feast of Passover drew near and Jesus decided to return to Jerusalem, he and his disciples began moving toward the city. This was when the Master directed two of them to go into a nearby village and untie the colt of an ass they would find tied there, telling anyone who might question their actions that the Lord had need of the animal. The Gospel of Matthew says this was done so the prophecy could be fulfilled: "Behold, thy King cometh unto thee, meek, and sitting upon an ass, and the colt the foal of an ass." (Matt. 21:5) The Cayce readings describe in some detail the portrait of Jesus riding down from Bethany where he was staying with friends to make his triumphal entrance into the Holy City. The roads were filled with travelers from around the region. " . . . There were those gatherings from all the lands nigh unto the Galilean, the Phoenician or Syro-Phoenician, Tyre and Sidon and all the peoples of the faith of the Jews had come as *one* for the days that were counted as holy." (1301-1) Local residents along with visitors making the pilgrimage to celebrate the religious holiday witnessed the spontaneous procession and heard the shouts of acclamation as the Master entered Jerusalem just days before his execution. Interestingly, Edgar Cayce also mentioned that the swarm of people that glorious day was composed primarily of women and children: " . . . For, though man would have most {people} believe that there were great throngs, they were mostly women and children . . . " (3615-1)

As Jesus approached the city gates on the back of the little colt, members of the crowd had spread their garments across his path and cut down fronds from the trees, waving the branches and strewing them on the ground in front of him. The multitude was overcome with excitement from having seen or heard the rumors about the rabbi's mighty works. Recognizing the hope and miraculous power the man represented, they cried, "Hosanna to the Son of David: Blessed is he that cometh in the name of the Lord!" (Matt. 21:9) This was the moment in his thirty-three years when Jesus, at the zenith of his notoriety, could have used his fame to stoke a cult following among the people and set himself up as king. Instead he chose not to arrogate power to himself. Meanwhile those gathered along the roadway instinctively were honoring a reality which no longer could be denied: the presence of God among them. Their souls could not help but hail the divinity manifested in the person of Jesus while he, their leader and teacher, sat quietly on a lowly ass, making no move to exploit the situation. "If these should hold their peace, the stones would immediately cry out," the Master subsequently tells a group of Pharisees when they command him to rebuke his followers for their cries and salutations. (Luke 19:39-40)

My Kingdom Is Not of This World
ᏽ

The thought of their Master finally receiving the recognition he deserved undoubtedly had revved up his disciples. This was a pregnant moment in the history of Jesus' ministry, the moment when all the hopes and dreams of the rebels and glory seekers who never gave up believing he was the Messiah who would overthrow Roman rule, crashed headlong into the reality of their teacher's message. The readings explain that it was during this condensed period of time linked to the final journey into Jerusalem when those who had misunderstood the Master's meaning and still hoped for political emancipation became disenchanted. Their disillusionment was due to the fact that they sought release "*not* from the bondage to sin but from the material bondage to the power of Rome," according to Edgar Cayce.[32] He describes the hopes of one young Syro–Phoenician woman among the milling crowd who had journeyed to the area with a group of visitors from that province. Having heard about the miraculous activities of Jesus, she believed " . . . there was to be either the establishing of the material kingdom by that man, or there were to be the understandings of what those teachings were to bring into the experience of others." (681-1)

Conversely, the Cayce information also discloses that many of the spectators celebrating that day gained a more profound understanding of what " . . . was being presented to a stiffnecked people" and their hearts, minds, and lives were deeply touched by the experience. (1151-1) The readings speak movingly of one discouraged onlooker who was confused about why Jesus did not seize power until he was able to look into the Master's eyes and finally understood the reason this extraordinary teacher had come to earth: To bring about man's " . . . *closer* associations with his Maker . . . " In one spellbinding moment the man realized that " . . . man as man may be far from God, but man as a god and acting godly may be close to the divine." (1301-1) Along those same lines, the readings divulge the true meaning and purpose of the Master's declaration that if the people did not honor the manifestation of the Christ among them, the very stones would cry out in jubilation at its presence in their midst. "For, even as he gave on that memorable day, if the people do not proclaim him—or if the people had not cried 'Hosanna'—the very rocks, the very trees, the very nature about, would cry out *against* those opportunities lost by the children of men, to proclaim the great day of the Lord." (1468-1)

Several of Jesus' most stalwart disciples, including Judas, understandably were disappointed at his refusal to claim kingship for himself and deliver the Jews from their onerous servitude and the burdensome taxation of Rome. Others who followed the Master mostly for the sake of being close to a genuine miracle worker who provided benefits such as free bread and fish also wanted to crown him king. But that was not to be. Fomenting civil revolution was not the Master's domain, and he had already discouraged the hangers–on who merely coveted

---

[32] Anne Read, *Edgar Cayce on Jesus and His Church*, ed. Hugh Lynn Cayce (New York: Warner Books, Inc., 1970), 122.

more perks by pointing out that they were not really seeking God. "Ye seek me, not because ye saw the miracles, but because ye did eat of the loaves, and were filled," (John 6:26) he explained, and filling their bellies was not the reason he had come to earth. His soul mission was much more exalted than winning factional political battles or satiating the superficial desires of today for people who would just crave more goods tomorrow. As Edgar Cayce summarizes the Master's purpose, " . . . He gave, not for self, not for material gain, but that *all* should know the truth that would make *all* men free under *every* circumstance in a material plane." (1179-8)

The readings also pick up the story of the innkeeper's daughter Sarapha by placing her at the scene that day on the road to Jerusalem. Sarapha had been present at the birth of Jesus in Bethlehem some three decades earlier and had personally experienced the phenomena sur- rounding that momentous occasion. The inn where she worked was located on the same road by which the Master passed when he returned to the Holy City. Cayce says she was " . . . among that mighty throng that cried, 'Hosanna in the Highest—the King cometh!' And there again she met those disappointments when that mighty force, that glorious creature, that mighty man among men was not proclaimed king . . . " Sarapha was discouraged that Jesus seemed to exert so little of " . . . that necessary material application of a glorious power and might . . . ," which she knew he had demonstrated over sickness, doubt, and fear. Many of the people healed by the Master were known to her and she was especially close to the blind man Bartimaeus whose sight the Master had restored. Bartimaeus, " . . . strong in body, yet lacking in sight, a worker in those things pertaining to the metals . . . " had often rested close to the wayside inn where Sarapha lived. (1152-3)

Another witness that day identified in the readings as Mariaerh had traveled to the big city along with her parents and Mary's cousin, Elizabeth, where she heard for the first time about the astonishing events that had resulted in the raising of Lazarus. The young woman was said to have been struck by " . . . not merely that triumphal entry but the humbleness—yet the graciousness, the glory, the dignity of the Man, who—with His disciples—waited among friends . . . " who were seeking " . . . from a material angle . . . " to protect Jesus from exposing " . . . the physical Man . . . " to danger. Yet even in that perilous situation the Master was acting exactly as he had counseled and preached in living out the purpose for which he had come into the world. He " . . . as a man must stand forth for what had been the purposes for His entrance," (1468-2) assert the readings. Mariaerh was able to discern the Master's underlying message by catching " . . . that concept of how each soul must in each experience live as the grain of wheat, as the grain of mustard, as the seeds of every nature, fulfilling that purpose for which it enters into an experience in a sojourn, irrespective of self's individual or personal desires . . . " It meant letting the personality of "self" become lost in the individuality of the Christ purpose—" . . . as he so magnificently gave in that way from Bethany to Jerusalem!" (1468-2)

Final Lessons
ごえ

In the days immediately following the triumphal entry, Jesus taught openly in the temple, answering questions and assisting those who sought his guidance. Although the religious authorities still conspired to put him to death, they did not dare seize the rabbi publicly for fear of the great crowds surrounding him. Not surprisingly, the Master taught some of his most profound lessons during the relatively brief span of time he spent in Jerusalem before the chief priests and elders took him into custody.

In the evenings he would withdraw to the Mount of Olives and the home of friends who lived in Bethany. And along the way he would instruct the disciples concerning the things that must come to pass—his death, resurrection, and signs of the coming of the end of the age. The readings say that one of his statements in particular brought confusion and questions to many of them. "Verily I say unto you, This generation shall not pass, till all these things be fulfilled," their teacher pronounced in the Gospel of Matthew. (Matt. 24:34) According to Edgar Cayce, the meaning of these words becomes apparent when considered from the standpoint of the bigger picture and how life in this dimension evolves across the ages. Jesus was alluding to the fact that "Those individuals that were in hearing and in keeping of those things presented by the Master . . . would be in the manifested form in the earth . . . " during that era in the future when his prophecies would be fulfilled. " . . . Not in what is termed as generation of four score and ten years . . . " but centuries later when the Son of Man's words were destined to come to completion. (262–60)

Last Supper

The time had come for the Passover celebration and the victory of the resurrection—when the icy grip of death would lose its hold on the children of God. Knowing the moment had arrived for the next and final step in his human journey, Jesus once again sends a couple of disciples into the city and tells them they will meet a man bearing a pitcher of water. The two are to follow the servant until he stops at a certain house then ask the goodman of that house if Jesus and his party might use its guest chamber for their Passover meal. The two disciples are shown to an upper room (Mark 14:13–15), which, as explained in the Cayce material, was located in the home of John's father, Zebedee.

Discrepancies exist among the four gospels about exactly when the Last Supper took place. John states that the apostles gathered prior to the Passover. And considerable evidence exists to support the theory that Jesus and his apostles did, indeed, eat their infamous meal on the day before the Passover feast, the day of preparation, based on the type of food they ate and what happens later that same evening. Supporting this hypothesis is the fact that both the disciples and the mob were reported to have carried weapons; the Jewish tribunal, the Sanhedrin, met to try to condemn the Master; the High Priest tore his robe to protest what he considered to be blasphemy; and Jesus was executed and his body prepared for burial. A passage in John reads, "Then led they Jesus from Caiaphas unto the hall of judgment: and it was early; and they themselves went not into the judgment hall, lest they should be defiled; but that they might eat the passover." (John 18:28) These details provide some fairly impressive proof that the critical events leading up to the Crucifixion may have taken place earlier than previously believed because such activities would have violated Judaic law and the sacred customs associated with that holy day.

The Meal
&

Edgar Cayce fleshes out several striking details about the setting in the upper chamber and the disciples seated around the table for what will be their last meal together with their teacher. The text also adds a fascinating sketch of Jesus along with its description of the venue. "The whole robe of the Master is not white but pearl gray—all combined in one—the gift of Nicodemus to the Lord. . . . The Master's hair is most red, inclined to be curly in portions, Yet he is not feminine nor weak—*strong*, with heavy piercing eyes that are blue or steel-gray. His weight would be at least a hundred and seventy pounds. Long tapering fingers, nails well kept. Long nail, though, on the left little finger. Merry—even in the hour of trial. Joke—even in the moment of betrayal." (5749-1)

The readings explain that Martha, the wife of Nicodemus, had fashioned the Master's robe. Martha happened to be the older sister of Peter's mother-in-law, and when word spread about Jesus having healed his wife's sister of a terrible fever, Nicodemus had experienced a fundamental change. This was when Martha began weaving the garment. Since the couple was associated " . . . with the temple and the service of the high priest . . . ," that connection had influenced the general pattern or style of the robe, which " . . . became a part of the equipment the Master had . . . " It did not expressly mimic the priestly robes in color rather was pearl-gray, " . . . woven in one piece with a hole in the top through which the head was to be placed, and then over the body, so that with cords it was bound about the waist." The selvage was " . . . woven around the neck, as well as that upon the edge, as over the shoulder and to the bottom portion of same; no bells no pomegranates {*as upon the robe of the high priest*}, but those which are woven in such a manner that into the selvage portion of the bottom were woven the Thummin and Urim. These were as the balance in which judgments were passed by the priest. But these were woven, not placed on top of same. Neither were there jewels set in same." (3175-3)

The readings then proceed to describe the meal. " . . . See what they have for supper . . . ," Cayce remarks, " . . . Boiled fish, rice with leeks, wine and loaf. One of the pitchers in which it was served was broken—the handle was broken, as was the lip to same." Again, this menu does not include food traditionally served for Passover, which involves eating the meat of a lamb slaughtered the preceding day as the main dish. (5749-1) The concept of the sacrificial lamb is a critical element in unraveling the esoteric meaning of the Last Supper, however. When they were slaves in Egypt, God had directed the Hebrews to slay a lamb and sprinkle its blood on the lintels and doorposts of their homes to shield them against the death of their first born. The blood of the lamb displayed at the threshold on what would turn out to be the final night of Jewish captivity ultimately proves to be the key to unlocking their passage to freedom.

Thus Jesus, whose life's blood is spilled on the day prior to the ritual commemorating death passing over, comports with ancient biblical symbolism. Similar to that fateful night in Egypt when death found no foothold in those houses marked with the sign of the innocent lamb, the timing of the sacrificial slaughter of the crucified Lamb of God carries enormous significance. It harks back to the moment in Jewish history " . . . when the angel of death covered that land {*Egypt*} . . . ," (2476-1) and that which had separated man from Life itself passed over all who partook of the sacrifice.

The Twelve
&

The readings also provide a snapshot of a few of the physical characteristics and personality traits associated with some of the apostles. In addition to noting the differences in their disposition toward cleanliness, Cayce adds several interesting details about their facial features and what they generally wore. "The better looking of the twelve, of course, was Judas, while the younger was John—oval face, dark hair, smooth face—only one with short hair. Peter, the rough and ready—always that of very short beard, rough, and not altogether clean; while Andrew's is just the opposite—very sparse, but inclined to be long more on the side and under the chin—long on the upper lip—his robe was always near gray or black, while his clouts or breeches were striped; while those of Philip and Bartholomew were red and brown. The sack is empty. Judas departs." (5749-1)

Each of these twelve men is fated to play a part in the upcoming

Crucifixion and Resurrection drama and its aftermath. They will also color the history of the church in conveying their unique perspectives on the meaning of the Christ once the resurrected Jesus has ascended and leaves the earthly scene. Twelve is the mystic number denoting completeness and perfection as well as the combination of forces bringing strength to the world to replenish it. (5751-1) Judas, still seeking a terrestrial ruler, is called upon to play perhaps the most difficult role as the plot develops representing all those who are tempted to sell out their Christhood in exchange for temporal power and the fading baubles of a material world. As deciphered by Cayce, Judas' betrayal was the result of his desire to force Jesus to assert himself as king and establish his kingdom then and there. (2067-7) In spite of everything their teacher had taught them, Judas like many of the Master's followers never fully understood the true nature of his mission. Fittingly, in a nod to the past life Jesus spent in an earlier incarnation as Jacob's son Joseph, the innocent, beloved son once again will be traded into captivity for a bagful of silver pieces.

After Judas leaves, the eleven continue eating their supper until the Master pauses to pass around bread and wine. After "the last is given of the wine and loaf," says Cayce "with which He gives the emblems that should be so dear to every follower of Him . . . ," Jesus tells his students to remember his words whenever they partake of these substances in the future. (5749-1) From then on, ingesting bread and wine will stand as the eternal symbol of assimilating the Christ spirit into every cell of the mind and body. The Master then uses the concluding moments of the meal with his friends as one last opportunity to reinforce the central message of his ministry. Jesus surprises the group by kneeling down and modeling the behavior he expects of them to illustrate his disciples' true purpose in the world: serving one another. His students are taken aback. Their revered leader, the renowned rabbi who just days before the masses had wanted to crown a king, humbles himself to minister to a band of lowly fishermen and tax collectors by washing their feet.

The Master " . . . lays aside his robe which is all of one piece—girds the towel about His waist, which is dressed with linen that is blue and white . . . " and picks up a basin of water. Cayce elaborates: "The basin is taken as without handle, and is made of wood. The water is from the gherkins [gourds], that are in the wide-mouth Shibboleths . . . that

stand in the house of John's father, Zebedee." (5749-1) Jesus rolls back
the folds of his garment and initially kneels at John's feet then moves
onto James before approaching Peter who at first refuses his teacher's
ministrations but quickly relents.

The Master's unusual act was a subdued but soul-stirring " . . . dis-
sertation as to 'He that would be the greatest would be servant of all,'"
(5749-1) states Cayce. For "though he were their leader, their prophet,
their Lord, their Master, he signified—through the humbleness of the
act—the attitude to which each would come if he would know that true
relationship with his God, with his fellow man." (5749-10) With their
teacher's final lesson fresh in his students' minds, Jesus is ready to take
leave of his companions for a while to let them digest everything he
had imparted. The gathering starts drawing to a close with the words
" . . . It is finished," according to Cayce. (5749-1)

They conclude the evening with a hymn. We discover through the
readings that the Master was a musician who played the harp and
accompanied the group as it sang the ninety-first Psalm. " . . . He that
dwelleth in the secret place of the Most High shall abide under the
shadow of the Almighty. I will say of the Lord, He is my refuge and my
fortress: my God; in Him will I trust," (5749-1) they sang. The Cayce information also indicates that while a few of the disciples may have had
an inkling of what Judas was planning to do after he disappeared, the
group did not appear to be frightened as they exited the room. There is
" . . . little seen in the faces of the eleven about him {*as they leave the upper
chamber*} of that fear that was created by the leaving of Judas; but rather
that as was experienced in the heart and mind of all when He gave, 'My
peace I leave with you—in my Father's house are many mansions—if it
were not so I would have told you—I go to prepare a place, that where
I am ye may be also.'" (1424-3) Jesus heads to Gethsemane.

Chapter 11
Cross and Crown

. . . Remember, brother, there are no shortcuts to God! Ye are there—but self must be eliminated.   5392-1

In the final hours of its incarnation as the man Jesus, the Adam soul finds itself in a garden again. This time the place is Gethsemane on the Mount of Olives where the Master will grapple with and overcome the psychic pull of his humanhood one last time by unconditionally submitting his will to the will of the One. Jesus asks three of his most faithful disciples—Peter, James, and John—to remain with him to lend moral support as he retreats to a nearby corner to pray. Unbeknownst to the three, their teacher is wrestling with himself, trying to find the necessary strength to face the ugly, painful process he knows awaits him.

Not surprisingly, given the late hour and heaviness of the meal they had just eaten, the apostles promptly fall asleep. The Master proceeds to wake them up before removing himself to a solitary spot to continue praying in seclusion only to have to rouse the men a second time after he finds them slumbering again. The oblivious disciples present a striking metaphor for the human condition. Those who are cognizant of the Christ are asked to stay alert and uphold its presence in the earth. But instead, saddled with the weight of bodily appetites and day-to-day concerns, all too soon they fall asleep, ignoring their responsibility by descending into a state of unconsciousness.

The biblical account goes on to describe the intense interior battle Jesus was fighting to fully accept the cup he had chosen to drink until, settling the issue within himself once and for all, he regains his peace and stands up to leave. And for the third time that evening finds his companions sleeping. But this time he decides to let them rest, knowing the night will be physically and emotionally draining for everyone. The image of the three apostles who for all intents and purposes had abandoned their friend in exchange for a few minutes of rest is not a very flattering picture yet it serves to communicate a crucial message: To support the spirit of the Christ in this world, we must stay awake.

The readings provide a glimpse into the incredible inner resistance Jesus had to confront staring down his doubts and fears while working to divest himself of every last shred of personal desire. Cayce claims that the most difficult trial for the Master was the struggle in the garden when he realized " . . . that He had met every test and yet must know the pain of death." (5277-1) From the perspective of the readings, it is far easier to achieve success in our external circumstances and careers than to bring the will under submission. Yet nothing is more important for us to do than to align heart, mind, and will with a higher calling. "Know that no influence surpasses the *will* of the entity. Make that will, then, one with that which is the entity's ideal," (1089-30) they advise.

The internal tug of war and agonizing choices Jesus had to make wondering whether his faith in God would abandon him or if he had the strength to complete the mission his soul had assumed for the world, reflect perhaps the most demoralizing phase of the entire episode of the Crucifixion. "Those periods in the garden—these become that in which the great trial is shown . . . " suggests Cayce in referring to the Master having to endure the emotional toll of the apparent indifference and loss of " . . . one in whom trust and hope had been given . . . " And at the same time knowing he needed to fulfill " . . . all that had been in the purpose and the desire in the entrance into the world." (5749-10)

When asked to clarify the difference between a desire of the heart and a desire of the will, the readings offer an interesting juxtaposition of the two in discussing those difficult moments in the Garden of Gethsemane, where the second Adam was forced to meet himself again. Cayce explains that the heart, ordinarily considered the seat of life in the physical body, is connected to the material sphere while the will is a motivating factor within the mental and spiritual realms. The two may be made one only when " . . . the will of self and the desire of the heart are selfless in the Christ Consciousness. Even as He gave in the shadow of the day when the Cross loomed before Him on Calvary, when the desire of the heart and the will of self were made one . . . " (262-64)

Prisoner
ॐ

As recorded in the gospel narrative, Jesus' visit to Gethsemane is what starts the sacred drama progressing in earnest toward its tragic denouement. Suddenly Judas along with "a great multitude with swords and staves, from the chief priests and the scribes and the elders" (Mark 14:43) enter the garden. Meanwhile the Master stands ready for whatever may come, calmly awaiting the advancing search party as it moves closer in pursuit of its quarry. Then Judas approaches the rabbi to kiss him on the cheek and with that kiss enters history as the consummate villain.

Since the first century AD religious believers of every stripe have unapologetically condemned Judas for his traitorous behavior. Yet that moment on the Mount of Olives is telling both for the stoicism Jesus displayed and the fact that the Master never once denounced his apostle. Reading the gospel text one can almost imagine the same words he had uttered to the adulterous woman reverberating off the page: "Neither do I condemn thee." (John 8:11) Nor is it likely Jesus would have disregarded the pivotal role Judas was playing in launching a chain of events that would alter the course of human history. Even at that instant in the garden when the disciple walks up to embrace his teacher as a signal to the armed men ready to take their prisoner into custody, Jesus addresses Judas as someone he knows well and loves. Exhibiting no animosity either in his demeanor or his language, the Master calls him friend. "Friend, wherefore art thou come?" (Matt. 26:50) he inquires, knowing full well what is about to transpire.

The Hebrew rabbi's composure is undisturbed. It is almost as if he were standing back from all the commotion more as a casual observer watching the scene of his apprehension play out. In fact, he immediately rebukes one overzealous follower, whom the gospel writer John identifies as Simon Peter, for pulling his sword and slicing off the ear of one of the high priest's servants. Jesus promptly heals the wounded man and reminds his disciples that their leader does not rely on material ways and means. "Then said Jesus unto Peter, Put up thy sword into the sheath: the cup which my Father hath given me, shall I not drink it?" (John 18:11) Rattling sabers and placing one's trust in earthly powers are not the way of the Christ. The Son of Man has no need for weapons of iron with the spirit of God and its twelve legions of angels at his beck and call.

On Trial
ᴄᴂ

> Then, when ye abide in His presence, though there may come the trials of every kind, though the tears may flow from the breaking up of the carnal forces within self, the spirit is made glad; even as He in the hour of trial, the hour of denial, *smiled* upon him . . . "
> 262-33

Following his arrest Jesus is bound and initially taken to the home of a high priest named Annas where the scribes and elders plotting against him had assembled for an impromptu hearing. Soon after they lead their prisoner to the palace of Annas' son-in-law, Caiaphas, who at that time was serving as the ruling High Priest. (The more formal trial in front of the Sanhedrin, which had jurisdiction over the province of Judea, will occur the following morning.) The Master's accusers run into problems, however, when the false witnesses they had lined up are unable to agree on the charges. Cayce mentions that the sole charge of which Jesus stood condemned was that he had said he was the son of God. Since this accusation was not a criminal offense under secular law, the group needed to dig up a more concrete allegation in order to rid themselves of the rabble–rousing rabbi.[33]

Yet despite the dearth of hard evidence in the end, the Jewish council, which lacked the power to put anyone to death, decides to turn Jesus over to the Roman authorities to be tried and executed. " . . . So did the High Priest condemn thine Lord!" states Cayce, "So did those of the Sanhedrin wreak their own purposes upon Him . . . " (262–61) This is when the Master is dragged before Pontius Pilate who serves as the regional Roman governor. In Luke's account of the hearing before Pilate it says that Jesus was accused of "perverting the nation and forbidding to give tribute to Caesar." (Luke 23:2) Edgar Cayce corroborates this version of events. There were claims made by " . . . ones in authority that there had been a neglect to pay tribute, or that there had been first that attempt upon the part of those that were as the followers of same to prevent the tax, the levies to be paid. *This* was the manner of presentation rather than much of that as ye have recorded even in Holy Writ." (1151–3)

The Bible also reports that Pilate's wife had warned her husband to have nothing to do with "that just man [Jesus]: for I have suffered many things this day in a dream because of him." (Matt. 27:19) The Cayce material sheds new light on her statement by divulging a prior connection between the Master and the Roman prefect's wife. Apparently she was well aware of the Hebrew rabbi and his activities and very likely first came to know about him through a woman named Agatha who was a close associate of their household and outspoken in her beliefs. Agatha had been a longtime follower of both John the Baptist and Jesus and had served as some sort of liaison between the Jewish and Roman cultures. "Hence the entity Agatha, as it grew to maturity in years, became not as a servant (as would be termed in the present) but rather as an instructress, a teacher, in the garrisons of the Roman *and* the Galilean peoples; to interpret for the wives, the companions of the Romans, the customs of the Samaritans and their relationships with the Jewish portion of their acceptance." (603–2) In addition to Agatha's

---

[33] Anne Read, *Edgar Cayce on Jesus and His Church*, ed. Hugh Lynn Cayce (New York: Warner Books, Inc., 1970), 130.

reports, Pilate's wife had had a much more direct experience with Jesus due to an illness in her family. According to the readings, a man called Romoluon, who was one of her companions or guards, had " . . . brought their afflicted or epileptic son to the Master for healing." (1217-1) There is little wonder then why the woman would be so disturbed that her husband, the father of this boy, might condemn to death the same man who had healed their child.

Another item taken from the readings reveals that several people in the household of Herod Antipas, the ruler " . . . that made for such destructive influences in the minds of many as respecting those relationships with the activities of the Master . . . ," (324-5) had witnessed the healing of Pilate's son. But in spite of Jesus' countless good works recognized even by a contingent of powerful Roman citizens, momentum kept building toward a death sentence. Whether motivated by the temple authorities moving among the spectators in order to stir them up or merely the brutal fallout from an agitated, bloodthirsty mob, the throng of people amassed outside the palace walls that day disregarded any naysayers and called for the release of the prisoner Barabbas instead of Jesus, shouting "Crucify him!" (Mark 15:13) at the top of their lungs. While the relative few who might have spoken out in the Master's defense fled away in fear.

What strikes a reader most from the gospel chronicles depicting what happened during Jesus' sham trials is his demeanor throughout the grueling hours of intimidation and torture. The Prince of Peace never wavers and never answers back. He neither turns on his accusers nor withers under the white-hot glare of their physical and verbal abuse, but maintains a sense of humble acceptance throughout the ordeal. His presence is meek, courageous, and calm.

It is also instructive to note the unique perspective the Cayce readings bring to the usual interpretations of Jesus' dealings with Pilate. They report that although the circumstances were difficult to bear, the proceedings before the Roman official were not the worst situation the Master had faced on the long road to Crucifixion. "In considering that which materially passed through the mind of the Master and those experiences leading to the way of the Cross: the decisive point in Peraea [?] [Berea?] was the more trying even than the trial . . . ," (5749-10) states Cayce. Equally painful was having to take leave of his closest disciples

" . . . after the establishing of the emblems of his body and blood . . . " (5749-10) at the Last Supper. Cayce also told one woman who had come to him for help that she was part of the throng at the trial before Pilate, and seeing the face of the Master " . . . saw that tenderness with which He felt and experienced His aloneness when deserted by those who had been close to Him . . . " (2620-2) The hearing before Pontius Pilate itself was not with " . . . the pangs of pain as so oft indicated . . . " according to the readings, rather the experience was the Master glorying in the opportunity of "taking upon self that which would *right* man's relationship to the Father . . . " Edgar Cayce maintains that through free will sin had entered the activities of the children of God and now the first begotten son " . . . was bringing redemption through the shedding of blood that they might be free." (5749-10)

Crucified
⤜

Crucify in self, then, that which might in any way hinder thee, or
that might influence others to doubt or to fear . . .   993-5

After he is condemned to death, several Roman soldiers lead the Master outside the walls of the city lugging a crossbeam on his back, which somewhere along the way they will hand over to a great soul, Simone of Cyrene, (Matt. 27:32) who is pressed into service to help bear its weight for their prisoner. As Jesus moved through the process, Cayce says, he laughed " . . . even at those who tormented him. This is what angered them the most." (3003-1) Unlike much of the literature written about the Master, the readings describe him as someone who " . . . smiled—and laughed, oft—even on the way to Gethsemane." (2984-1) They mention him joking " . . . to those about Him, about the beauties of the garden . . . " (1158-14)

The four gospels go on to report in some detail the agony the Son of Man experienced climbing the steep path to Golgotha, the place of the skull, surrounded by a screaming mob, wounded, losing blood, and bent under the burden of his cross. Symbolically the wooden beam Jesus carried harks back to the tree of the knowledge of good and evil, which represented his soul's undoing in the garden at the beginning.

Ironically, after the Crucifixion and Resurrection, the conjoining limbs of this "tree" will come to signify the way back to that paradisiacal state. The cross, comprised of two pieces, has a vertical plank denoting the divine spirit in man, the unbroken link between heaven and earth. The horizontal beam represents matter and the judgmental mind—that which impedes the upward movement of consciousness as it ascends toward complete reunification with the divine.

As the first son, Jesus had assumed the responsibility for rising high enough in awareness to break through the barrier of mental constructs and material forms and in so doing fashioned a way of escape for souls still entombed in matter. In crucifying self—his human will—on the "Tree of Life," this entity, the "Lamb slain from the foundation of the world" (Rev. 13:8) was revealing to the human race how it might reunite with its Source and reclaim Eden.

A Ransom for Many
᙭

... If thou dost exalt self, thou dost crucify thy Lord. If thou dost exalt thy Lord, thou dost bring peace and joy and happiness into thine life.   934-1

While most faith traditions view the saga of the Crucifixion as a heartrending tragedy, they also tend to interpret the event as the payment God extracted from the human race as restitution for its sinfulness and corruption. These believers attach great significance to the physical suffering the Master endured at the hands of his captors, commemorating its violence and gore as the brutal ransom that one individual—Jesus—had to pay in order to cleanse the world of "sin" and deliver salvation to the rest of us. In a strange way, this commonly held theological belief comes close to conflating the shedding the Master's blood on the cross with the bullocks and goats slain on the altar stones of old as offerings to appease a deity who demanded the sacrifice of actual flesh and bone. Needless to say, such traditional interpretations of the Crucifixion widely miss the mark.

A limited reading of the word "blood" merely as vital bodily fluid narrows the scope of what Jesus actually had accomplished. It all but negates the years he spent following the straight and narrow path of mindfulness saying yes to what each moment demanded of him. The metaphysical meaning of "shedding the blood" is indeed a letting go—dying to this world by divesting oneself of every claim to mental constructs and physical forms and conditions. As it was with Abraham who at the final moment did not have to physically murder his son Isaac in order to worship and honor his God, omnipresent spirit has no need for the bloody remains of a lifeless corpse. The only offering ever exacted is the sacrifice of the human will.

" . . . There is nothing in heaven or hell that may separate the entity from the knowledge or from the love of the Creative Force called God, but self . . . " (5023-2) maintains the readings. The Master had walked away from every attempt to crown him a ruler-king or set himself up as a false idol people should worship, but rather he lived his life in a continuous state of awareness of and submission to his God. This was the ultimate sacrifice—the death of the ego. And as such it becomes our reconciliation and atonement too. As Edgar Cayce explains, "At-one-ment may be given even as atonement. At-onement, then, is making self's will one with the Creative Forces that may become the impelling influence in thought, in mind, that is the builder to every act of a physical, mental or material body." (262-45)

From the beginning Jesus' fate was to one day pass from the mortal body because his mission was to demonstrate the omnipresence of life even at the center of what human beings call death. The important point was not the fact that he died, but that he had lived. For physically dying was by no means the Master's sole or greatest sacrifice. The surrender of self had begun more than thirty-three years earlier, prior to even his own birth in Bethlehem, when the new Adam, the first soul, had chosen to reenter this plane as the Son of Man. Accepting the cross was merely the culminating act of love and service by someone whose entire earthly incarnation was spent heeding the call of the still small voice of divinity and aligning his will with the will of the One. The Master chose to leave his body just as he had entered it—acting out the role assigned to him to help advance the spiritual evolution of the world. And his lifetime of work as the man called Jesus had succeeded. He had set the pattern for conquering the only sin there ever was: selfishness.

Suspended on the Tree of Life
ᶜᵃᵉᵒ

... It was *necessary* that Christ, *physically*, becomes a Loss, that the
Spiritual Man be made alive, see? ...   900-171

Once the journey up the hill to Golgotha was finished and the soldiers had nailed and hoisted him up on the cross, Jesus experiences
several agonizing hours with his body hanging in public view on the
man-made tree—exposed not only as an object of scorn but also as a
warning from the iron-fisted Romans to other potential miscreants. Still,
the innocent prisoner held his peace. The irony is that the Master could
have removed himself from the situation with a single word, but instead
chose to submit to the purpose and inevitability of the moment.

For three years, people all over Judea had heard his words and witnessed the miracles this Master had performed, which had proved the
presence of Immanuel. His days spent among them had demonstrated
that the divinity found inside themselves was their salvation from
every type of affliction and misery. Yet he would not come down from
the cross and relieve his own suffering during those awful hours on
Calvary because this, too, was a lesson—a testament to the presence of
love even at the center of the hell produced by human ignorance and
cruelty. Jesus not only allowed the experience to continue to fulfill its
larger purpose for the world, but he also forgave the perpetrators who
had caused him so much agony because they "know not what they do."
(Luke 23:34) The guards standing at the site on Golgotha simply did not
understand how close they were to the Christ—either hanging from that
cross or within their own souls.

Although the readings say this incident was likely the first cross or
literal crucifixion the entity called Jesus had experienced, Cayce tells us
that in the figurative sense that was not the case. For eons the Adam
soul had borne the "cross" of humanity's need to be released from its
imprisonment in matter. " ... In the beginning He was the Son—*made*
the Son—those of the Sons that went astray ... " note the readings. This
soul had journeyed through space and time overcoming the world by
living out a whole variety of experiences, bearing his cross in each and
every one of them until he reached " ... the *final* cross with *all* power,

all knowledge in having overcome the world—and of Himself *accepted* the Cross . . . " (262-36)

At the same time it would be a mistake to interpret Jesus acquiescing to such agony as confirmation of the misguided notion that torture and pain make a person holier or more pleasing to God. The Master allowed that particular scenario to continue—to "suffer it to be so now" (Matt. 3:15)—because conditions could not be otherwise given the choices he had made lifetime after lifetime. Calvary was what his soul had called forth unto itself. His Crucifixion would teach humanity how to willingly meet the effects of what they had created with their minds and even in that extremity find their God. Because human suffering, while never a spiritual requirement, might serve as the gateway to better understanding where selfishness has ruled us in the past. And when the Master's grueling ordeal was finally over, he would prove that the instrument of torture and worst situation imaginable could become the doorway to resurrection and ascension.

Why Hast Thou Forsaken Me?

... For what is the pattern? He gave up Heaven and entered physical being that ye might have access to the Father ...   5081-1

The readings fill us in on a few more details about the harrowing hours the Master spent hanging from the cross and the physical and emotional anguish he felt in separating from his body. " . . . Yet in that day when the voice was raised on the Cross, He said, 'Father, why—why the way of the Cross?' This is indeed the pattern that is interpreted in 'I perceive that the heart of man is to do evil—the spirit is willing, the flesh is weak.'" (3188-1) " . . . Not only was He dead in body . . . " state the readings, " . . . but the soul was separated from that body . . . " (5749-6) Cayce talked often about the manifestation of the physical, mental, and soul bodies in the earth so it was no surprise given the Master's elevated state of awareness that he was very likely fully conscious of the separation of the three. It must have felt as if he were being ripped apart. " . . . Is it any wonder that the man cried, 'My God, my God, why hast thou forsaken me?'" he inquires. (5749-6) Still Jesus neither blamed others for his troubles nor faltered in his determination to fulfill his purpose in choosing to enter this plane. And in the process this deliverer set an exceptionally high bar for all those who hope to follow in his footsteps.

The Gospel of John provides another ostensibly minor yet telling appendix to the story of Jesus' death when the entity known as Pontius Pilate refuses a request by the chief priests to change the sign at the top of the cross which read JESUS OF NAZARETH, THE KING OF THE JEWS. [John 19:19] Hoping to cast further doubt on the validity of the Master and his work, the temple leaders were trying to make sure his followers understood that the crucified Hebrew rabbi, a descendent of the royal House of David, had only alleged to be a king. Little did Pilate realize at the time what his decision would mean to posterity. In acknowledging Jesus as the king of the Jews, the Roman ruler unwittingly had recognized a new reign of spirit in the earth. He had confirmed the supremacy the Christ, the anointed one, whose kingdom constitutes the life of man and whose benedictions are bestowed on all who will acknowledge and honor the one God.

Holy Women
⌒⌒

The Cayce material subsequently calls attention to the disciples who had gathered at the foot of the cross in solidarity and support of their teacher and friend. One of them was a woman named Ulai who, after experiencing the raising of Lazarus, had been " . . . among those seeking to know something of the heart and the experience of the Mother {*Mary*} . . . " Ulai had missed the Master's triumphal entry into the Holy City because she was the one who " . . . made the journey to notify the mother of that taking place in Jerusalem . . . " In addition, the readings describe her as being " . . . among those that saw and heard and spoke to the Master on the way to Calvary." (993-5) Also present that afternoon was Josie who had tended to Jesus when he was a little boy. Following the Master being taken prisoner, it was Josie who went and persuaded " . . . the Mother, Mary, when there was the arrest, to come to Jerusalem." (1010-17) Many others from the circle of holy women among his followers were present, distraught, and weeping, including

Mary Magdalene and someone named Sophie. Sophie apparently had been part of the assembly in the Essene community compound decades earlier and had witnessed the vision on the stairs " . . . when the first choice of the maidens was made," (2425-1) indicating Mary would become the mother of the Messiah. Jesus' friend Martha also was part of the group of relatives and friends standing near the cross and is said to have been " . . . one of those upon the right hand of Mary, the Mother of Jesus . . . " (3175-3)

As he, the Master, the savior of the world, hung upon the cross says Cayce, " . . . He called to those that He loved and remembered not only their spiritual purposes but their material lives . . . For He committed unto those of His brethren not only the care of the spiritual life of the world but the material life of those that were of His own flesh, His own blood . . . " (5749-6) The Gospel of John describes the moment when Jesus places the care of his mother Mary into the hands of his beloved apostle John. "When Jesus therefore saw his mother, and the disciple standing by, whom he loved, he saith unto his mother, Woman, behold thy son! Then saith he to the disciple, Behold thy mother! And from that hour that disciple took her unto his own home." (John 19:26-27)

Passage from the Earth

> Thus in this hour of despair . . . let all take heart and know that this, too, as the hour upon Calvary, must pass away; and that as upon the wings of the morning there comes that new hope, that new desire, to the hearts and minds of all who seek to know His face.
> 5749-13

The purpose and meaning of the second Adam's mission as a bearer of the Christ light to the world comes sharply into focus during those final hours on Calvary when a series of astounding events occur, especially as his spirit leaves the physical form and our teacher dies. The Bible says darkness covered the earth beginning at noon that day and lasted for three hours until the Master's passing. (Luke 23:44) Darkness is the metaphor for the state of the world whenever the ego tries to snuff out the Christ spirit, the light—condemning humanity to live in darkness without the sun (Son) to illuminate the earth. As Jesus cried out for the last time and "yielded up the ghost," the gospels report that the temple curtain hiding the Holy of Holies was ripped apart. "And, behold, the veil of the temple was rent in twain from the top to the bottom; and the earth did quake, and the rocks rent; and the graves were opened; and many bodies of the saints which slept arose . . . " (Matt. 27:50–52) recounts Matthew. Not only are the dead released from their graves as Jesus' soul is released from his body, but the curtain that had shrouded the temple's inner sanctum in mystery and blocked entrance into the Holy of Holies is split in two. Jesus' life and work had healed the breach between heaven and earth, reopening the passageway to that sacred space where man will meet his God: in the inner sanctuary of the human heart.

Once Jesus has made the transition and the soldiers realize he is gone, one of them thrusts a spear into his side to make certain their prisoner is dead. "And forthwith came there out blood and water," (John 19:34) states the Bible, a reference to the commingling of the physical (blood) and the spiritual (water). Then they divide the Master's garments among them except for the beautiful seamless robe Martha had woven. The men decide to do a little gambling for Jesus' cloak, each wagering he would be lucky enough to win the most valuable piece. And with their game of chance the Roman guards unknowingly fulfill another scriptural prophecy. "They parted my raiment among them, and for my vesture they did cast lots." (John 19:24)

It Is Finished
ᴄ↢

For, as has been given, it is not all of life to live, nor yet all of death to die. For life and death are one, and only those who will consider the experience as one may come to understand or comprehend what peace indeed means.   1977-1

With the sorrowful day of the Crucifixion nearing its end and dusk just a few hours away, the Master's friends prepare his body for burial according to the local customs and lay it in an unused tomb belonging to a wealthy man named Joseph of Arimathea. During that period in the Middle East corpses were wrapped in linen cloths with spices, with a separate cloth or napkin used for the head. The readings speak of a woman named Veronicani who apparently had the opportunity to bathe the face of the Master, saying she gained an ability to heal and help " . . . those with or for whom the entity may pray or seek to aid in an hour of turmoil" from that blessed experience. Cayce then expressively adds, "What more could be asked for than to have bathed the face even of a dead Lord! . . . " (489-3)

According to the readings, the wrappings for the final anointing of Jesus' body were prepared by Andra, the daughter of Elois, who had been one of the companions of Mary when she was a young girl in the Essene temple. " . . . Rather the wrappings than the spices, for Josie and Mary Magdalene and Mary the mother of the Lord prepared these . . . " (649-1) explains Cayce before making a telling comment about Josie. " . . . Is it any wonder that when there were those preparations of the body for burial, Josie was chief among those who brought the spices, the ointments that were to consecrate the preparations of this body for which she had cared through those early periods of his experience in the earth?" (1010-17) The readings go on to describe a number of other specific details about the burial clothes. Among the wrappings Andra had prepared were the napkins placed around Jesus' head that had " . . . those seals that were later made as raised figures . . . " (649-1) These figures are described as "the seals of the Holy One, as the seals of the son of David: the pear with the bell, with the pomegranates on either side." (649-2)

The small band of female disciples who had gathered to help the family was also said to have " . . . acted . . . as mourners for Mary . . . " (587-6) One in particular, Sarapha, played an important role for the group of women. Even in the tragic aftermath of Calvary, Sarapha was the person who never lost faith due to her memory of the extraordinary events she had witnessed in Bethlehem when Jesus was born. The readings say Sarapha " . . . aided in sustaining those of the household that were beginning to feel that possibly the Mother, Mary, had misjudged. Yet the entity *knew* from her own experience, had not forgotten that choir before the celestial throne that sang, "Glory, *glory* in the highest—Peace—*peace* on earth, to all men of good will." (1152-3)

The agony was over and the first part of Jesus' mission now complete.

He had shown the world that God lived among them. For this was, is, " . . . the fulfillment of promise" states Cayce, " . . . the fulfillment of law, the fulfillment of man's estate. Else why did he put on flesh and come into the earth in the form of man, but to be one with the father to show to man *his* (man's) divinity, man's relationship to the Maker, to show to man that indeed the Father meant it when he said, 'if ye call I will hear. Even though ye be far away, even though ye be covered with sin, if ye be washed in the blood of the lamb ye may come back.'" (5749–6) Now would come the second phase of his work: to prove irrefutably that a human being is not merely the child of matter but the offspring of Spirit.

Chapter 12
Spirit Rising

For what meaneth the story of the
Christ, of the man, Jesus, that walked
in Galilee, without that resurrection
morn?   5749-6

Jesus was dead and his disciples were devastated. It seemed as if their leader's words and all their hopes had come to nothing. "We trusted that it should have been he which should have redeemed Israel . . . " a couple of them would say to a stranger in the days following the resurrection when unbeknownst to them they ran into the risen Master walking along the road to Emmaus. (Luke 24:21) Little did anyone realize during those mournful hours immediately following their teacher's passing that just as Jesus predicted when he claimed, "Destroy this temple, and in three days I will raise it up," (John 2:19) in the span of three short days the sacred temple of his body would be rebuilt, proving what he had told them was true.

A little before sunrise on the first day of the week, while it was still dark, several of Jesus' disciples arrive at his tomb to anoint the body with spices. The specific list of the people included in the grief-stricken party and the exact timing of subsequent events are not completely clear from the scriptures. The Cayce readings speak of a small group of friends and relatives comprised of " . . . His brethren with the faithful women, those that loved His mother, those that were her companions in sorrow, those that were making preparations that the law might be kept that even there might be no desecration of the ground about His tomb . . . " (5749-6) A second reading mentions some cousins who accompanied the group in a comment Cayce made to one individual who apparently had had the privilege of being " . . . among those with the mother, with the cousins, with Mary Magdala, and those that had come to anoint again the body, and find the dead Lord a risen Christ! . . . " (489-3) In another deviation from the biblical account, the readings also report an interesting new detail, which indicates the Master's " . . . friends, His loved ones, His brethren, saw the angels" at the tomb. (5749-6) The gospels' accounts imply that only two or three people, led by Mary Magdalene, were on site to see the massive stone rolled away, discover the empty sepulcher, and witness the presence of an angel proclaiming the remarkable news of Jesus' resurrection.

More than thirty-three years after an angelic being named Gabriel had appeared to Mary to announce the impending birth of the Christ gestating within her, angels took up residence around the burial chamber of her son, surprising the group of mourners both by their presence and their revelation. Matthew provides a powerful description of one of these supernatural messengers: "His countenance was like lightening, and his raiment white as snow. And for fear of him the keepers did shake, and became as dead men." (Matt. 28:3-4) Notably, the grounds-keepers on site are felled by a mighty jolt similar to an electrical shock. Not yet attuned to the raised vibrations of the Christ spirit and unable to handle the highly charged atmosphere around them, without warning the workers lose consciousness. One of the angels then proceeds to tell Mary Magdalene and the others that what they are seeking cannot be found in the deserted burial chamber. The Christ is risen and among the living, not entombed in a grave of dead matter. "He is not here, but is risen," records the Gospel of Luke. "Remember how he spake unto you when he was yet in Galilee, saying, The Son of man must be delivered into the hands of sinful men, and be crucified, and the third day rise again? And they remembered his words." (Luke 24:6-8)

The astonished witnesses at the tomb quickly disperse to run and tell the apostles and other disciples what they have seen and heard. Not surprisingly, no one believes them. " . . . Their words seemed to them as idle tales, and they believed them not," states Luke. (Luke 24:11) Upon hearing the reports, the apostle Peter is incredulous and heads to the sepulcher to see for himself what has happened. But once he arrives at the site, he has no idea what to think. "And stooping down, he beheld the linen clothes laid by themselves, and departed, wondering in himself at that which was come to pass." (Luke 24:12) The account in Matthew's gospel also references the bewildered guards assigned to the tomb who undoubtedly were upset about the missing body. The men soon leave their posts to report on the strange situation to the Jewish authorities. "Now when they were going, behold some of the watch came into the city, and shewed unto the chief priests all the things that were done. And when they were assembled with the elders, and had taken counsel, they gave large money unto the soldiers, saying, Say ye, His disciples came by night, and stole him away while we slept." Matthew makes note of the big lie the temple elders were perpetrating with this terse comment: " . . . And this saying is commonly reported among the Jews until this day." (Matt. 28:11-13; 15)

Three Days in a Tomb

There should be the reminding that—though He bowed under the burden of the Cross, though His blood was shed, though He entered into the tomb—through that power, that ability, that love as manifested in Himself among His fellow men He broke the bonds of death; proclaiming in that act that *there is no death* when the individual, the soul, has and does put its trust in Him.

5749-13

No greater mystery exists on earth than the mystery surrounding the resurrection of Jesus of Nazareth. The Edgar Cayce readings compare his breaking forth from the tomb to that of " . . . the bulb of the tree of nature itself breaking forth from the sleep that it may rise . . . " (5749-6) and describe how " . . . He, thy pattern, resurrected the body, *quickened* the body . . . " (262-88) When someone once asked Cayce to explain the meaning of the resurrection of the body and exactly which body it was, he replied "That Body thou hast taken in thine individuality to draw upon, from matter itself, to give it shadow or form, see?" (262-86) From the Cayce perspective, if we hope to catch the tiniest glimpse of how the resurrection may have occurred—and the effort it required of the Adam soul during those three difficult days working in the tomb—we must reacquaint ourselves with how spirit entered into the earth plane in the first place and man became a living soul. In other words, remember how it all began.

In one reading Cayce prefaces his approach to the subject with an assertion that the entire concept of the resurrection may be summed up in a single sentence: " . . . As in Adam all die, so in Christ all is made alive . . . " The earth and the universe, as it relates to man, came into being " . . . through the *mind—mind*—of the Maker . . . ," he asserts and as such, " . . . has its same being much as each atomic force multiplies in itself, or, as worlds are seen and being made . . . " today. The earth became " . . . an abode for man, man entered as man, through the *mind* of the Maker, see? in the form of flesh *man*; that which carnally might die, decay, become dust, entering into material conditions . . . " By the same token, Spirit is a gift of God so that man might be one with Him by making use of these same Creative Forces within a physical world. " . . . Man, in Adam (as a group; not as an individual), entered into the world (for he entered in five places at once . . . called Adam in one, see?) . . . ," and when he had reached the point where he " . . . walked not after the ways of the Spirit but after the desires of the flesh *sin* entered—that is, away from the Face of the Maker, see? and death then became man's portion, *spiritually*, see? for the physical death existed from the beginning; for to create one must die, see? . . . " (900-227)

According to the readings, " . . . The body, in the flesh, of the Christ, became perfect in the flesh, in the world . . . " And this body, which was " . . . the body laid aside on the Cross, in the tomb, the *physical* body . . . " moved away through what we know as dimensions. Spirit then was able " . . . to take hold of that Being . . . " in such a way that it reentered the body, allowing it to present itself again to people living at that time as well as today. (900–227) The information further explains that the resurrection was not a process of changing from physical flesh to a different type of flesh rather it was the body manifesting in its purest spiritualized form. "There is no mystery to the transmutation of the body of the Christ," professes Cayce. "For having attained in the physical consciousness the at-onement with the Father–Mother–God, the completeness was such that with the disintegration of the body—as indicated in the manner in which the shroud, the robe, the napkin lay—there was then the taking of the body–physical form. This was the manner. It was not a transmutation, as of changing from one to another." (2533–8)

In answer to a question about the specific changes required in order for the Master's physical form to become a glorified spiritual body, Cayce says it was the passing of the material life into the spiritual life which brought about his glorified body, " . . . enabling the *perfect* body to be materialized . . . —a *glorified* body made perfect!" (5749–10) Neither was the resurrection process the type of revivification we might normally associate with a near–death experience. Simply stated, the material body and spirit body are portions of every individual and Jesus was able to elevate both. " . . . He gave his physical blood that doubt and fear might be banished, so He overcame death; not only in the physical body but in the *spirit* body—that it may become as *one* with Him, even as on that resurrection morn—that ye call thy Eastertide." (5749–6)

And when asked why the Master told Mary Magdalene not to touch him when he appeared to her shortly after his resurrection, Edgar Cayce described the principle involved. "For the vibrations to which the glorified body was raised would have been the same as a physical body touching a high power current. Why do you say not touch the wire? If ye are in accord, or not in touch with the earth, it doesn't harm; otherwise, it's too bad!" (262–87) A fully spiritualized human body vibrates at a geometrically higher rate than the slower-moving vibrations of the material realm and as such is capable of harming anyone not yet in tune with that elevated frequency. The implication is that Jesus' resurrected body needed to completely merge with its infinite source before its re-attunement to a lower frequency more in harmony with the physical world might occur. Prior to this readjustment no one except those who had attained the same level of attunement or spiritualization the Master had achieved would be allowed to come in contact with his resurrected form.

The readings add, "As indicated in the spoken word to Mary in the garden, 'Touch me not, for I have not yet ascended to my Father.' The body (flesh) that formed that seen by the normal or carnal eye of Mary was such that it could not be handled until there had been the conscious union with the sources of all power, of all force. But afterward—when there had been the first, second, third, fourth and even the sixth meeting—He *then* said: 'Put forth thy hand and touch the nail prints in my hands, in my feet. Thrust thy hand into my side and *believe*.' This indicated the transformation." (2533-8)

Elsewhere in reading 262-88, however, Cayce explains that because the Father or Christ-Consciousness is present everywhere, the change that had to take place actually was in the consciousness of Mary rather than in the " . . . Body Himself . . . " The expression in the biblical story that she was not to touch Him is similar to using any expression that might attempt to interpret spiritual things from a material standpoint, or " . . . infinity brought down to the finite understanding . . . " The words " . . . I have not yet ascended to my Father . . . " could imply to some that heaven and the Father are somewhere else, " . . . a place of abode, the center about which all universal forces, all energies must turn . . . " But the idea of going "up" Cayce explains refers to the within—moving toward that to which each soul must become aware. He continues: " . . . For heaven is that place, that awareness where the Soul—with all its attributes, its Mind, its Body—becomes aware of being in the presence of the Creative Forces, or one with same. That is heaven."

Seeing and Believing

The period of resurrection—here we find that in which ye all *may glory. For without the fact of His overcoming death, the whole of the experience would have been as naught.*   5749-10

The gospel narrative and the Cayce readings agree that it was Mary Magdalene to whom " . . . the Master first appeared upon the resurrection morn . . . " (295-8) for she had been among those who initially discovered the stone rolled away and the empty tomb. The Cayce material further clarifies that it was the deep emotional impact the death of Jesus had had on Mary Magdalene, which caused her to mistake him for a caretaker when, upset and weeping, she first perceives her resurrected Lord. " . . . As visioned by that which is read, she thought he was the gardener. This indicated all the hopelessness, all the sorrow that is possible to be indicated in hopelessness . . . " (295-8)

Shortly thereafter the gospel scene shifts to the road to Emmaus where a small group of disciples will experience the risen Master for the first time. Some biblical scholars studying the origins of the word Emmaus have posited a theory that this was the same place Jacob, later called Israel, had slept using a rock as his pillow when during the night God visited him in a dream. They draw a parallel between the revelation of God to Jacob and the appearance of Jesus disclosing the risen Christ to his disciples. Following his supernatural experience the Old Testament patriarch had erected a pillar to mark the site, calling it the house of God. Fittingly Jacob's stone calls to mind the rock (*petros*) of truth upon which Jesus had told Simon Peter he would build his sacred community of believers.

In referencing the scene near Emmaus, the Cayce readings speak in some detail about a man named Philoas who was walking down the road that memorable day. Philoas was a Roman married to Jesus' sister Ruth and one aspect of his job was inspecting the activities around Emmaus and its environs. He happened to be on his way home that morning, traveling back from Rome to Jerusalem, with Cleopas, a tax collector, and Luke, the beloved physician, who accompanied him for a portion of the journey. Philoas had been absent from the holy city when the Master was killed, but the Crucifixion was fresh in the minds of all three men who understandably were dejected and confused about the recent turn of events. So when a stranger appears and starts walking with them and asks why they look so sad, Cleopas notes the man must not be from that area because that was the only way he could have missed the news. The tax collector tells the stranger about an innocent Jew named Jesus of Nazareth who had been condemned to death and executed, and how several women had astonished them with their tales of an empty tomb guarded by angelic beings. As they continue on their journey, the three travelers fail to realize they actually are speaking with the Master, whom, according to Edgar Cayce, Philoas should have been able to recognize. "And as there had been created in the heart and mind of the individual (*Philoas*), there was—as has been the promise ever—'Draw nigh to me and I, thy Lord, will draw nigh to thee.' And he came, and walked, and talked . . . " (1151-4) Yet he did not know him.

Because Philoas had been out of town during the tragic incident on Calvary, he asked his companions for more details about what had been happening " . . . and the conditions surrounding all of the conditions that arose—as to the opening of the graves, the rending of the veil of the temple, and the like . . . " (1151-4) During the course of their conversation, Jesus finally loses patience with his obtuse disciples and refers to them as "fools, and slow of heart to believe all that the prophets have spoken." (Luke 24:25) He then proceeds to give the men a lengthy discourse on the various prophecies concerning him beginning with Moses.

As evening approaches and the small group draws closer to the village of Emmaus, Jesus acts as if he is going to keep on walking, but his companions invite him to remain with them. So the Master agrees to tarry for a while ostensibly to sit down and share their dinner. "And it came to pass, as he sat at meat with them, he took bread and blessed it, and brake, and gave it to them. And their eyes were opened, and they knew him; and he vanished out of their sight." (Luke 24:30-31) Using the breaking of the bread, the same symbol he had presented to his followers at the Last Supper as the sign by which to remember his words and deeds, the Master opens the eyes of his disciples who are now able to clearly recognize the presence of the Christ among them. "Then as they sat at meat, as He brake the bread (that represents His broken body), there came the knowledge that they spoke with the Master." (1151-4) In the next instant Jesus vanishes from sight and the three immediately head toward Jerusalem to tell the apostles what had transpired. The sleeping Cayce's instructive comment to the individual who approached him in 1936 asking for guidance and who was told he had spent that previous lifetime as Philoas, was that the man had " . . . broke[en] bread with *life* itself! . . . " (1151-4)

Bethany
❧

. . . For as had been given, "Tarry ye in Jerusalem—in the upper
chamber—until *ye* be endued with power from on high." 2533-8

The readings maintain that in the immediate aftermath of the Crucifixion the eleven apostles along with some of the other disciples
gathered in Bethany at the home of Mary, Martha, and their brother
Lazarus whom Jesus had raised from the dead. "With the death and
separation of the Master from the disciples (as it may be called)," states
Cayce, "the home of Mary and Martha became—for the time—rather
the center from which most of the activities of the disciples took place
. . . " (295-8) The family's home would continue to serve as the nucleus
of the group's activities during this epochal period. The disciples were
lying low, fearful of what the Jewish and political authorities might try
to do next and unquestionably very cautious—and perplexed—by the
reports they had been hearing about their teacher.

One day while the group was gathered together in a second story
room discussing the various appearances of the Master, Jesus suddenly appeared in their midst through the closed doors. This particular
incident prompted the readings to delve a little more deeply into the
concept of the spiritualized body and its relation to physicality. Cayce
explains that Jesus' body–physical entered the upper chamber with
the doors closed " . . . not by being a part of the wood through which
the body passed but by forming from the ether waves . . . " that were
present in the room. (2533-8) This activity was made possible because
the meeting of his disciples had been prepared by faith.

Elsewhere the Cayce material expounds on the mystery of the regeneration of the body as a spiritualized physical form, which those in tune
with the higher energies or vibrations are capable of apprehending.
"For as indicated when the soul departs from a body (this is not being
spoken of the Christ you see), it has all of the form of the body from
which it has passed—yet it is not visible to the carnal mind unless that
mind has been, and is, attuned to the infinite. Then it appears, in the
infinite, as that which may be handled, with all the attributes of the
physical being . . . " And when Jesus asked for something to eat, Cayce

says it " . . . indicated to the disciples and the Apostles present that this was not transmutation but a regeneration, recreation of the atoms and cells of body that might, through desire, masticate material things—fish and honey (in the honeycomb) were given." (2533-8)

In an extraordinary statement tying the Master's appearance in the upper chamber to an activity manifesting throughout the universe, the readings compare the process of Jesus re-creating his material form to what happens to the soul when it takes up residence in other dimensions. The Cayce information emphasizes that rather than a transmutation of flesh the process was " . . . creation, in the pattern indicated," and likens it to what happens in various realms of the solar system where an " . . . entity may find itself when absent from the body . . . " In the course of experiencing these other realms the soul assumes " . . . not an earthly form but a pattern—conforming to the same dimensional elements of that individual planet or space." (2533-8)

After having made his presence known to the faith-filled company gathered in the upper chamber and eating the food they had provided, Jesus breathes upon his disciples with the words: "Receive ye the Holy Ghost." (John 20:22) Cayce attributes this act to the Master's desire to alleviate the doubt and fear, which had built up in their minds and hearts from all the phenomena they had observed. " . . . As the breath of life was breathed into the body of man, so breathed He that of love and hope into the experience of those who were to become witnesses of him in the material world," (5749-10) is the explanation the readings supply.

Sea of Tiberias
⤳⤲

The final chapter in the Gospel of John adds more detail to the chronicle of events associated with the resurrected Master. The gospel writer reports on several other interactions between Jesus and his disciples during the weeks following their experience in Lazarus' home. The account begins with an early morning encounter at the Sea of Tiberias where a small group had assembled to go fishing. "There were together Simon Peter, and Thomas called Didymus, and Nathaniel of Cana in Galilee, and the sons of Zebedee, and two other of his disciples."

(John 21:2) The men had spent a long night on Peter's boat but despite their best efforts had caught nothing. At daybreak the fishermen noticed a man standing on the shore but had no idea it was the Master. The stranger called out "Children, have ye any meat?" and they answer no, having nothing to show for their night's work. Then Jesus imparts a core truth. "Cast the net on the right side of the ship, and ye shall find," (John 21:5-6) he directs them. Following his instructions, soon the men are barely able to haul in the teeming nets because they are so heavy with fish.

The words their teacher used were a summary of his instructions to those he had spent three years preparing to shepherd in the Piscean Age. These fishers of men would draw in the multitudes to a realization of God-with-us not by searching in the darkness using material ways and means, but by following the guidance of something unrecognizable to the five physical senses. The voice of the Christ was what would lead them to cast their nets on the right side of truth—and reap an incalculable harvest.

The gospel narrative states that after hearing the stranger's speech, the apostle John excitedly tells Peter it is the Lord who is speaking to them. Impetuous as ever, Peter quickly grabs his fisher's coat to cover himself, then plunges into the sea to swim ashore. The Cayce readings describe the episode this way: "As also indicated later, when He stood by the sea and the disciples and Apostles who saw Him from the distance could not, in the early morning light, discern—but when He spoke, the voice made the impression upon the mind of the beloved disciple such that he spoke, 'It is the Lord!' The body had prepared fire upon the earth—fire, water, the elements that make for creation. For as the spirit is the beginning, water combined of elements is the mother of creation." (2533-8)

Jesus has prepared bread and fish over the coals and asks his friends to dine with him. Still a little bewildered about what is going on, the incredulous fishermen are hesitant to say anything. "And none of the disciples durst ask him, Who art thou? knowing that it was the Lord." (John 21:12) Then after sharing the meal together, Jesus quietly asks Simon Peter a confounding question. "Simon, son of Jonas, lovest thou me more than these?" Peter immediately answers, "Yes" and tells Jesus he knows perfectly well that he loves him. The Master responds with a cryptic phrase: "Feed my lambs." The rabbi then asks the boisterous apostle the same question about loving him twice more and with each inquiry Peter becomes increasingly unsettled, thinking his teacher does not believe what he is saying. The second and third times Peter assures Jesus of his devotion, the Master responds with the words, "Feed my sheep." (John 21:15-17)

Hidden within this esoteric conversation is a blessing for Peter, as Jesus is giving his apostle the opportunity on three separate occasions to declare out loud that he loves him—mirroring the precise number of times prior to the Crucifixion that Peter, overtaken with fear, had denied knowing his Lord. From the Master's perspective there is nothing to forgive, but with his pointed questions has allowed his disciple to profess his devotion and acknowledge the man Peter truly is. The Cayce readings also interpret this episode as heralding a fundamental message for every follower of the Christ way.

After Jesus had bidden them to come and eat, there came the question to Peter (as it comes to us all), "Simon, son of Jonas, lovest thou me more than these?" which soon leads to the Master's request to "Feed my lambs" and "Feed my sheep." (John 21:15-16)

Edgar Cayce goes on to clarify the symbolic difference between the two phrases. " . . . One represents that of the fold, and the other that seeking the fold. The sheep represent those that know of, and know, the way. The lambs represent those that seek, that would know, that would find the way, that would come if shown the tenderness expressed in 'The good shepherd feedeth the sheep; he tendeth the lambs.'" (262-51)

Those who have had the opportunity to be exposed to the Master's teachings and have learned to embrace the ways of Spirit have a work to do. Their purpose is to shine a light on the dark and lonely passage through this earth and help the lost sheep find their way home again. Just as each facet of a glittering diamond uniquely refracts the rays of the sun, so, too, must the children of God humbly expose their own inner radiance to illuminate the path for others. "To *all* it may be as this . . . ," Cayce insists. " . . . The time draweth near, the time is at hand when there is more and more seeking for the light and understanding. Let each, then, in your own way, in that which seemeth good in the light of that which has been presented thee, from day to day, so manifest that love that has been showered on thee . . . so live thine own life that it may be an ensample unto those that study . . . " No matter what kind of work we have chosen to do, the aim of this lifetime is to let our spirits bear witness that " . . . the Lord is in his holy temple, and the rod has not passed from those that call His name . . . " (262-51)

On to Glory

The readings report that until his ascension approximately seven weeks after the resurrection, Jesus walked and talked with his disciples, appearing to many in and around Galilee. They also indicate that on at least one occasion thousands were able to experience the risen Lord at the same time, telling one woman in 1940 that she had been " . . . present when there were about five thousand who saw and heard the words of the Master after the resurrection . . . " (1877-2) The gospels do not go into great detail in describing Jesus' ascension, but tell us he was "received" or "carried" up into heaven. In commenting on this extraordinary moment in the history of humanity, Edgar Cayce adds that five hundred people witnessed the sacred event.

The Bible fills out the story by reporting Jesus' final words when he tells his followers he will send "the promise of my Father upon you," asking them to "tarry . . . in the city of Jerusalem, until ye be endued with power from on high." According to the gospel account, Jesus then leads the group as far as Bethany, lifts up his hands and blesses them. "And it came to pass, while he blessed them, he was parted from them, and carried up into heaven." (Luke 24:49-51) Thus do we learn that the spirit of Jesus or the Adam soul, which along with his brothers and sisters at the dawn of history had become entranced with matter and then trapped in it, exits the world of form and illusion by ascending beyond the limits of human perception. The first son takes his spiritualized body and returns home to the celestial realms from which he had descended.

After the Master has disappeared from sight, the Cayce readings provide a rare glimpse into the lives of a few of the people he had left behind. "Hence we find, with the return from Galilee and the activities there upon the ascension (which was fifty days after the resurrection), Mary the mother of Christ became a dweller in the house or home of John—who joined with those in Bethany; for John, as may be well known, was the wealthiest of the disciples of the Christ. His estate would be counted in the present, in American money, as being near to a quarter of a million dollars; or to the state where he was a power with those in the Roman and Jewish power at the period." (295-8) According to Cayce, Mary, the sister of Martha, is said to have become closely associated with John during this period and his household became a center of activity for the disciples. "With the joining of the mother of the Christ in John's household (which was composed then of Mary Magdalene and Elois [?], or the sister of Mary that was the mother of James and John), these journeyed then to what would be called their *summer* home—or that portion on the lake of Gennesaret where the activities of those that came and went were supervised by those of the whole household." (295-8)

Second Coming
∽

As the hart panteth after the water brooks, so panteth my soul after thee, O God. Psalm 42:1

Once again it seems that Jesus has departed from the earth, yet his ascension presaged new hope for the human race. In his readings, Edgar Cayce signals the promise of the eventual return of our elder brother whom he says will manifest the same form he carried with him when he left. Hundreds " . . . beheld him as he entered into glory . . . ," declares Cayce, " . . . and saw the angels, heard their announcement of the event that must one day come to pass—and will only be to those who believe, who have faith, who look for and who expect to see Him as He is." (3615-1) The Son of Man has not vanished from this world forever, but is destined to walk with us again. So wrote Luke in the Acts of the Apostles: "Ye men of Galilee, why stand ye gazing up into heaven? this same Jesus, which is taken up from you into heaven, shall so come in like manner as ye have seen him go into heaven." (Acts 1:11)

The whole idea of the Master reappearing "as ye have seen him go," the subject of vehement debate throughout twenty-one centuries of religious history, is corroborated by the readings, which decree that Jesus indeed will "come in body to claim His own." (5749-5) They explain that the Master " . . . shall come as ye have seen Him go, in the *body* He occupied in Galilee. The body that He formed, that was crucified on the cross, that rose from the tomb, that walked by the sea, that appeared to Simon, that appeared to Phillip, that appeared to 'I, even John.'" (5749-4) Yet the information also adds a sober codicil to the widely accepted theories about the Second Coming. While Cayce indicates there will be a time in the future when Jesus will reappear, this event will occur only when the collective consciousness has risen to a level of awareness high enough to enable men and women to experience his presence in the earth.

And when asked if the Master might be manifesting on this plane in a different body right now, Edgar Cayce's response was that he is always available through those unseen forces that forever surround us. " . . . All power in heaven, in earth," proclaimed Cayce "is given to Him who overcame. Hence He is of Himself in space, in the force that impels through faith, through belief, in the individual entity. As a Spirit Entity. Hence not in a body in the earth, but may come to him who *wills* to be one with, and acts in love to make same possible." (5749-4) In other words, human beings do not have to wait for some future date and place to experience the Christ spirit, which manifested through the first begotten of God. It is available to us now. " . . . Is He abroad today in the earth? Yea, in those that cry unto Him from every corner; for He, the Father, hath not suffered His soul to see corruption . . . For, He *is* the Son of Light . . . And He comes again in the hearts and souls and minds of those that seek to know His ways." (5749-5) Those who call upon the Christ do not go away empty-handed.

Still the question of pinpointing the exact timing of Jesus' return in a bodily form persists. When? How soon before his coming? Such queries have been the constant cry of religious devotees since the days of the apostles. But "the time no one knows . . . ," Cayce reminds us. "Even as He gave, not even the Son Himself. *Only* the Father. Not until His enemies—and the earth—are wholly in subjection to His will, His powers." (5749-2) The second coming awaits a metamorphosis in us. "How soon? When those that are His have made the way clear, *passable*, for Him to come," (262-49) declares Cayce.

Spiritual transformation is both a promise and our duty. The great Teacher of teachers did not impart the truth of Immanuel for his own benefit but to place responsibility for the state of this world and timing of his reappearance directly in our hands. We, the children of a divine Father/Mother, have been entrusted with a sacred charge: to create a new Eden, a new dwelling place for the Adam soul in the earth. Now is the time to claim our divine heritage by rising up again into conscious union with our Source. And the first step toward arriving at that glorious future begins with the practice of meditation.

Chapter 13
Into the Silence: Meditation

Meditate, oft. Separate thyself for a season from the cares of the world. Get close to nature and *learn* from the lowliest of that which manifests in nature, in the earth; in the birds, in the trees, in the grass, in the flowers, in the bees; that the life of each is a manifesting, is a song of glory to its Maker. And do thou *likewise!*   1089-3

In the beginning, when souls fell into illusion and became enmeshed in matter, physicality began to dominate consciousness and obscure little by little any recollection of the celestial realms out of which they came. It was not until the first son, the Adam soul, reentered the earth during its penultimate incarnation as Jesus of Nazareth that the chains of mind and matter imprisoning the children of God in delusion would be severed and a new pattern established for the human race. In his role as the Messiah Jesus would carry the light deeper into the third dimension and illuminate the Way to lead the lost souls back home again.

The Son of Man had trod the earth in a fully human form yet, because he had made conscious contact with the divinity deep inside his innermost being, was able to manifest the glory of the Godhead at will. For three years people scattered across Judea had witnessed firsthand the divine presence at work in the human scene because the Master's consciousness had brought that reality with him into every situation he encountered. And once the story of the man-who-was-God came to its fateful conclusion on the cross at Calvary, our elder brother was resurrected; his attunement and total surrender to the will of the One complete. The deliverer who had broken the bonds of death allowed those with the eyes to see and to perceive a body walking among them in its glorified form—proof that the immortal spirit of man, "fallen" from the heavenly heights—had been released from its entombment in matter to dwell with the Creator again.

Edgar Cayce says that Jesus was the first man to fulfill the destiny of every soul and as such became the prototype who showed the human race a way out of its long captivity. The readings are quite clear about the reason the soul continues to work through the cycles of birth, death, and rebirth during untold sojourns on this planet. " . . . To know itself to be itself and yet one with, or one apart from, the infinite . . . " or God, the great "I am," (2533-8) they explain. The return to a state of conscious Oneness with our Source is both our fate and final destination. "God seeks all to be one with Him," declare the readings. "And as all things were made by Him, that which is the creative influence in every herb, mineral, vegetable, or individual activity *is* that same force ye call God—and *seeks* expression! Even as when God said, 'Let there be light,' and there was light. For, this is law, this is love." (294-202) Just as the first begotten soul in its lifetime as the humble Nazarene rabbi became a Christ or the complete expression of God on earth, so, too, are we here to awaken to the reality of God with us, consciously reunite with this omnipresent force, and manifest our own divine nature as radiantly as a flower—like the lilies of the field.

But the task is not an easy one. For most of us, surrendering identification with external forms, especially the physical body and its endless list of wants and needs, presents a formidable challenge. The siren call of materiality is hard to ignore and countless distractions seem to crop up whenever we try to plug back into those deeper levels of aware- ness where God is said to dwell. To reach this unseen being, much less submit to its will, requires enormous amounts of patience, humility, and faith along with an unwavering commitment to keep pressing forward despite the obstacles standing in our way. We consistently must keep the gaze aloft, fixed on an ideal, and compel the unruly mind to settle down and enter into that sacred domain beyond the limits of time, space, and the sensate world. That is what meditation allows us to do.

The Temple Within

> Yet *know* that thy body is the temple of the *living* God; *there* you may seek communion! There you may seek counsel as to the choices to be made, the directions to be taken!   622-6

In Spirit and in Truth
⤙⤚

The Gospel of John relates a story about Jesus sitting at Jacob's well in the city of Sychar and meeting a woman who is curious about what he is doing there. When she questions the Master by asking him how he is going to draw water without a bucket or a jar, her query opens the door to an extraordinary interchange. Jesus responds by telling the woman the Christ in man is the water of life and anyone who drinks from that fount will not thirst again. It is the source that never needs replenishing. During the course of their conversation, the rabbi goes on to explain how senseless it is to try to worship God on the sacred mountain venerated by the Samaritans or honor Yahweh in the Jewish temple in Jerusalem. "The hour cometh," he tells her, "and now is, when the true worshippers shall worship the Father in spirit and in truth: for the Father seeketh such to worship him. God is a Spirit: and they that worship him must worship him in spirit and in truth." (John 4:19–24) The Master was imparting the central truth of his entire ministry to this stranger who happened to cross his path while filling her water jars. She in turn comes to recognize just who is sitting beside her at the well, calling Jesus the man "which told me all things that I ever did" and identifying him as the manifestation of the Christ. (John 4:29)

The Master's message was unequivocal: God is spirit and we need nothing of a material nature in order to honor this divine being except ourselves. The Cayce material explains why. " . . . Not only God is God . . . " but " . . . self is a portion of that Oneness that may make itself a One . . . with the Whole," (900–181) the readings maintain. Elsewhere they articulate an equally powerful maxim: "Know thyself . . . as a corpuscle, as a facet, as a characteristic, as a love, in the body of God," (2533-7) assuring us that we are inseparable, individuated aspects of divinity. We house the holy of holies—the incarnating soul—within us, which makes the human body a temporary outward expression of the eternal, omnipresent Godhead. And every day becomes a Sabbath when we choose to enter in.

Even though Edgar Cayce was an active churchgoer his entire life, the readings are explicit about the need for a reorientation of thought around the concept of church. " . . . The church is within yourself and not in any pope nor preacher, nor any building but in self! . . ."(5125–1) They remind us that the body is the temple of the living God. Acknowledging the truth of Spirit and the body–temple is the reason Jesus adamantly refused his apostles' request to construct a visible tabernacle marking the spot where the transfiguration had occurred. The readings comment: " . . . And ye may *indeed* say, then, even as they, 'Let us make here a tabernacle.' What indeed is thy tabernacle? It is thy body, thy mind, thy soul! Present them, therefore, as things holy, acceptable unto Him who *is* the Giver of all good and perfect gifts!" (877–27) The Master repeatedly tried to impress upon his students not to regard God as some sort of untouchable, superhuman entity who insists on fancy rituals and soaring buildings to satisfy its needs. The divine spark or Christ spirit present in man is what must be celebrated and revered.

According to our elder brother we simply need gently knock at the door of this inner kingdom and it will open to us. Our Father/Mother God " . . . standeth at the door of thy heart" states Cayce, waiting, and has promised to meet us there. (281–41) He . . . "has promised, 'If ye will but open the door of thy consciousness, of thy heart, I will enter and abide with thee.' This is not a fancy, this is not hearsay. Ye may experience such. For it is the law, it is the way, it is *life* itself!" the readings advise. (1632–2) They also pledge that any effort made to reach the divine will not be made in vain: "' . . . I will not leave thee comfortless, but will come and *enjoin* thee in thy daily activities, thy daily service.' This is the promise to every soul. If ye would make that promise thine own, then seek and ye shall find, knock and it shall be opened unto thee . . . " (557–3)

A statement from the book entitled *A Search for God* based on principles from the Edgar Cayce readings reinforces this theme when it states "It is through meditation that we may become aware of the existence of the spiritual forces within, that we unlock the door between our physical and spiritual bodies. Through this door come impulses from the soul, seeking expression in the physical."[34] It also assures us that "The soul is always present, always willing to express its true purpose, its true relationship with the Creator. Through meditation we make this possible; we open the way."[35] The recognition and understanding that everything we may " . . . learn of the Father God, is already within self . . . " (5155–1), and " . . . it is within self that ye must find thy answer . . . " (3457–1) unleashes a seismic shift in our approach to the sacred mysteries. The readings encourage us to keep seeking within and promise we shall find, pointing out that meeting God in the inner temple of our own being will gain us the satisfaction of walking and talking with our Creator.

Invitation to the Feast
⤳

"My soul thirsteth for thee, my flesh longeth for thee in a dry and thirsty land. Psalm 63:1

We are not to tarry in the task but remain ever alert and ready to open the lines of communication with the divine. Jesus said as much in a parable from the book of Luke about accepting the loving invitation to enter in and commune with our God. A certain man had prepared a

---

[34] Edgar Cayce, *A Search for God, Book I*, comp. Study Group #1 of the Association for Research and Enlightenment (Virginia Beach, VA: A.R.E. Press, 1942), 12–13.
[35] *Ibid.*, 13.

great supper and bade many friends to come and dine with him. After the food is cooked and the table set, the host sends out his servant to tell the guests it is time to come to his home and enjoy the feast. But one by one the people he has invited begin to make excuses. The first wants to go visit some land he had purchased. Another one has to attend to his five yoke of oxen and a third asks the host to forgive his absence because he is newly married.

Frustrated and angry about by their lack of interest, the master of the house commands his servant to quickly go into the streets and lanes of the city and gather "the poor, the maimed, the halt, and the blind" to invite them to the table. But once the newly minted group of guests arrives and his servant indicates the dining room still is not full, the lord of the house asks him to "Go out into the highways and hedges, and compel them to come in, that my house may be filled." The story ends with the host announcing that those who refused his request to enter into his home had lost the opportunity to dine with him and would be left out, remarking that "none of those men which were bidden shall taste of my supper." (Luke 14:16–24) With his parable Jesus was counseling his students to make certain they did not ignore the invitation to enter into the holy feast by failing to take the time to make their inner contact. While many are called to partake of the divine communion, those who cannot bear to tear themselves away from the distractions and cares of the world will lose the chance to be spiritually fed in the household of the Father/Mother God.

Ten Virgins
⬥

In a similar vein, the Master related a story about ten virgins who took their lamps to go meet a bridegroom. Five of the virgins were wise and carried oil with them in their vessels while the other five were foolish and took no oil. Because the hour was late and the bridegroom delayed, everyone soon fell asleep waiting for him to appear. At midnight when the cry finally went up announcing the bridegroom's arrival, the ten virgins rose and trimmed their lamps. "And the foolish said unto the wise, Give us of your oil; for our lamps are gone out. But the wise answered, saying, Not so; lest there be not enough for us and you: but

go ye rather to them that sell, and buy for yourselves. And while they
went to buy, the bridegroom came; and they that were ready went
in with him to the marriage: and the door was shut." Sometime later
when the five foolish women return and plead to be let into the wedding feast, the bridegroom says he does not know them. Jesus ends his
parable with this statement: "Watch therefore, for ye know neither the
day nor the hour wherein the Son of man cometh." (Matt. 25:1-13) The
Master was reinforcing his admonition to anticipate and be ready (have
enough oil) to meet the bridegroom (Christ spirit) when it arrives. No
one else can make our internal preparations for us, and no one knows
the precise moment the bridegroom will suddenly appear to wake us
up to meet him. Only those who make the effort to prepare themselves
for his coming will be allowed to enter into his presence.

Using another vivid analogy, Jesus went on to describe the conscious
union of God and man—and what happens when we fail to set aside
self and make contact with our divine Source through meditation. "I
am the vine, ye are the branches," he declared. "He that abideth in me,
and I in him, the same bringeth forth much fruit: for without me ye can
do nothing." (John 15: 5) If we make no attempt to reach the ineffable "I
am" at the center of our being and connect with the Spirit found there,
we are like the branch of a tree that is cut off and withers and dies,
only to be cast into the oven and burned up in the fires of unfulfilled
potential. But if we turn within to touch the divine energy and begin
to live out the reality of our innermost Christ essence, we will forever
draw sustenance from the trunk of the living vine, rooted in its source,
and glorify our Creator by bearing spiritual fruitage for the world.

"Cease ye from man whose breath is in his nostrils: for wherein is
he to be accounted of?" entreats the book of Isaiah. (Is. 2:22) Stop seeing yourself merely as material—a human form solely dependent on
outside forces—and acknowledge the life force upwelling from within.
" . . . Let there be definite periods when ye look within self," Edgar Cayce
urges, "cleansing the mind, the body, in such ways and manners and
measures . . . as thine offering unto the holy experiences that may be
thine . . . " He continues by explaining " . . . he that expects nothing shall
not be disappointed, but he that expects much—if he lives and uses that
in hand day by day—shall be *full* to running over . . . " (557-3)

What Did Hinder You?
∽∾

> . . . for he that seeks the Lord must believe that He is, would they
> . . . find Him; for one doubting has already builded that barrier that
> prevents the proper understanding . . . for that in faith sought for
> shall be thine, even as was given, "Be my people and I will be your
> God."   459-1

If it is indeed true that all may directly approach the divine, the
question remains why for thousands of years human beings have
resolutely ignored this God that is as intimate as breathing. He is
" . . . within thine own self. He is nearer than thy hand, closer than thy
foot," states Cayce. (1992-1) The answer coming through the sleeping
prophet attributed much of the problem to confusion and fear. People
are puzzled as to why they were born in the first place and where they
are headed once this brief span of fourscore years has ended. For the
most part he explains that neither the body nor the mind appears to
be particularly beautiful or pure in our eyes or the estimation of our
neighbors, which makes it difficult to understand why the world is the
way it is. As a result, the overwhelming majority choose to care about
nothing more than outward appearances and material riches, leaving
little room for spiritual seeking. Such an attitude puts them at odds
with the innermost longings of the soul.

The readings make plain that if our ambitions are wholly " . . . set in
whether ye shall eat tomorrow, or as to wherewithal ye shall be clothed
. . . " (281-41), we will miss the opportunity to have a relationship with
our Maker. Yet they also emphasize the Creator has left the decision up
to us as to whether or not we choose to acknowledge our close kinship
with the divine. The physical body that the soul inhabits and uses to
function in the world contains the means by which we may approach
our God, but each individual must first have the desire to come to know
the sacred presence. Then that desire must be put into action by purging
body and mind of those things that are hindrances. Edgar Cayce likens
the process to the declaration Moses gave of old. " . . . It isn't who will
descend from heaven to bring you a message, nor who would come
from over the seas, but Lo, ye find Him within thine own heart, within

thine own consciousness! if ye will *meditate*, open thy heart, thy mind! Let thy body and mind be channels that *ye* may *do* the things ye ask God to do for you! Thus ye come to know Him." (281-41)

Fear enters into the picture when we start believing ourselves unworthy of communing with this omniscient, loving Spirit. Many mistakenly believe they are unable to speak to God and others are afraid to try, which prompts Cayce to ask, " . . . Why? Have ye gone so far astray that ye cannot approach Him who is all merciful? He knows thy desires and thy needs, and can only supply according to the purposes that ye would perform within thine own self." (281-41) In addition to fear, guilt may weigh heavily upon us if we have belittled the opportunities life has presented or defamed body and mind, making us ashamed to approach our Maker. The progenitor of our own soul stands ready to communicate with us, yet we turn away.

The good news is that our current conditions and personal histories with all their high drama and vexing problems do not matter. Just like rotating the dial on an old-fashioned radio to tune into a favorite station, we may choose at any moment to set aside doubt and fear, ignore outer distractions, and attune ourselves to the divine frequency to experience our God. The readings explain: " . . . For He is not past finding out; and if ye will know Him, tune in to Him; turn, look, hope, act in such a way that ye *expect* Him, thy God, to meet thee face to face. 'Be not afraid, it is I,' saith He that came to those seeking to know their relationship with their Maker . . . " (281-41) The Cayce information also suggests that just as the patriarchs and prophets of old received the law, the Lord would speak with us today in the same manner a father converses with his children. " . . . Has God changed? . . . " the readings ask. " . . . Know ye not that, as He has given, 'If ye will be my children, I will be thy God'? and 'Though ye wander far away, if ye will but call I will hear'?" (281-41)

Not surprisingly, Cayce confirms that those who continue to believe this type of communication with the Creator occurred only in ancient times will not be able to participate in nor gain from such knowledge today. Those who want to know God must be willing to take the time to learn how to approach the Almighty through the sanctuary of their own souls. Further, the readings promise that whenever anyone enters into the inner temple with the right attitude and ideal, he or she will be given the opportunity to carry the fruits of the spirit into the earth and in so doing help lift human consciousness to a higher level. After all, touching the innermost God source made an unknown Hebrew rabbi the light of the Christian world. "Hold fast ever to those truths, those tenets that ye gained in thine meditation, thine contemplation . . . ," (798-4) advises one poignant reading. The choice is always ours whether or not we will take the time to listen and heed the call.

The Language God Speaks

Be silent, O all flesh, before the Lord: for he is raised up out of his holy habitation. Zech. 2:13

A wise person once remarked that silence is the language God speaks; everything else is a bad translation.[36] Connecting with our Source requires moving the attention away from all the alluring circumstances of our external lives to penetrate the hidden depths where Spirit resides. " . . . *Silence,*" commands Cayce, "if ye would hear the Voice of thy Maker!" (281-29) God exists in the silence, and stillness is the key to unlocking the secret dwelling place of the Most High. Moreover, it is only through the stillness of meditation that the prodigal soul is able to discover the route for a safe return to the Father's house. What is stillness? It is not the superficial tranquility produced by merely blocking out all the noise and tumult of the outside world. Genuine stillness denotes complete attention on the now—a resting in an inner state devoid of any thought, word, or desire. It is the secluded closet Jesus asked us to enter when we wanted to pray—a portal into the infinite.

Stillness characterizes the incorporeal Spirit alive at the very center of us—the place where nothing else exists except who and what we really are. As we enter into the silence through the meditative experience and begin the process of awakening from the dream of a purely material existence, we catch glimpses of our true spiritual nature. "Be still, and know that I am God," states Psalm 46:10, using eight brief words to describe the reality of man's inmost being. A well-known saying from

---

[36] *See* Rumi, Thomas Keating

the Old Testament also references this undisturbed, transcendental state. "Thou wilt keep him in perfect peace, whose mind is stayed on thee," (Is. 26:3) the prophet Isaiah proclaimed, speaking of that soundless presence upholding the universe. Moving beyond every worldly form and the steady cascade of words and thoughts infiltrating the mind, we touch the vastness of limitless being, becoming a bridge between the un-manifested and the manifested world; between Spirit and physicality. In stillness, we enter the Promised Land.

Enter In

I am the door: by me if any man enter in, he shall be saved, and shall go in and out, and find pasture. John 10:9

Much like the members of the ancient Essene community who prepared physically, mentally, and spiritually for the birth of the foretold Savior, those who wish to enter into the stillness of meditation must prepare themselves to mindfully meet and welcome in the spirit of the Christ. The readings confirm that " . . . thy Father, thy God, will meet thee in thy holy temple . . . " but first we have to invite this honored guest into our home by fully accepting the sacred promise. The readings admonish us to " . . . Prepare self. Dedicate self . . . " by taking the necessary steps to approach meditation correctly. If we do, Cayce assures us " . . . there needs be little fear—*ever*—to enter . . . " But if we entertain doubts, our hesitation and mistrust will invite " . . . that which would bring corruption, dissension . . . " By contrast, anyone who enters the holy of holies with the conviction that the divine " . . . promises are true, the promises are thine *own* . . . ," is said to be " . . . insuring self and making secure." (877-2)

Meditation is akin to opening wide a gate along the straight and narrow path leading to the supernatural, which the Master warned few would attain without effort. Despite our heritage as spiritual beings, connecting the deeper soul-self to the infinite, universal mind of God no longer feels natural in the hurried, externally focused lives most of us lead. Yet it is imperative that we shut our eyes to this earthly human sphere for brief periods of time to disentangle from the personal sense of "I," which seems to exist separate and apart from our divine selves, in order to set our sights on what is real and eternal. "I and my Father are one," (John 10:30) is as true for us today as it was for Jesus—a connection just as vibrant and alive as an electric current. Yet this truth will affect our lives only to the degree we are able realize it.

Approaching the Throne

Let the words of my mouth, and the meditation of my heart, be acceptable in thy sight, O Lord . . . Psalm 19:14

In general there are two safe ways to enter the inner temple: through deep sleep and deep meditation. While the entryway via sleep is unconscious, our slumber regularly generates dreams, which often include messages from the higher self about the state of our spiritual progress. Edgar Cayce describes sleep as " . . . that period when the soul takes stock of that it has acted upon during one rest period to another . . . " (5754-2) Needless to say, the prevailing mindset in many Western cultures has been to dismiss as fanciful nonsense the signs, characters, and stories embellishing our nightly dreamtime episodes despite the fact that these symbols often convey much needed guidance. Meditation comprises the other entrée to the soul, but it works consciously. Meditation is not musing, daydreaming, or contemplating ideas and opinions about God; rather it is harmonizing the triune nature of the human being (body, mind, and spirit) with its Source. Through meditation we attune our mental and physical bodies to the divine and in the process create an opening in consciousness for the Almighty to disclose its presence.

In *A Search for God*, Edgar Cayce remarks on the curious distinction between approaching the divine through prayer versus approaching it through meditation. The readings refer to prayer as " . . . the concerted effort of the physical consciousness to become attuned to the consciousness of the Creator, either collectively or individually . . . " (281-13) It is the attunement of the conscious mind to the spiritual forces manifesting in a material world. Further, prayer frequently entails a cooperative experience among individuals or groups of people who single-mindedly come together in one accord to try to draw nearer to their God. Conversely, meditation involves *emptying* oneself of anything that might hinder the Creative Forces from rising along the natural channels of the body—anything that keeps the life energy from circulating through the sensitive spiritual centers populating our physical form. Simply put, in prayer we endeavor to speak to God; in meditation God speaks to us.

When properly done, meditation makes us stronger both mentally and physically. The readings call to mind two passages from the Bible referencing this provocative idea: He "went in the strength of that meat forty days and forty nights" (1Kings 19:8) and "I have meat to eat that ye know not of." (John 4:32) Cayce stresses that in the process of giving out of ourselves, the physical and mental resources become depleted. Yet by entering into the silence through meditation " . . . with a clean hand, a clean body, a clean mind . . . ," we receive " . . . that strength and power that fits each individual, each soul, for a greater activity in this material world." (281-13)

These ideas begin to make more sense when viewed through the lens of Cayce's comment about the soul. The readings state that although many claim to be completely unaware of possessing a soul, it is nonetheless evident in everyone and is a true reflection of God. " . . . Not thy body, no—not thy mind, but thy soul was in the image of thy Creator" states the Cayce information. (281-41) Going within to attune the mental and physical to the one divine life and seeking to experience the soul or Christ light eternally aflame inside the body temple comprise true meditation.

Chapter 14
Raising Up the Son of God

> For the mind is both spiritual and physi-
> cal in its attributes to the human body,
> and if ye feed thy body-mind upon
> worldly things, ye become worldly. If
> ye feed thy mind upon those things that
> are His, ye become His indeed. 1299-1

The human body is designed for both physical and metaphysical experiences. Our task is to make use of the body through meditation to bring the physical, mental, and spiritual into alignment, perceive the presence of God here and now, and start to unveil a new Eden in the earth. The meditative process begins by setting an ideal, which the Cayce information defines as " . . . That not made with hands; that that is eternal . . . " (24-4). The readings reiterate the importance of always keeping thought focused on something higher than the material domain and humdrum human condition if we wish to become conscious of the inner Christ. "First, find self. Know thine ideal. Know Who and What is thy purpose," (1849-2) they counsel. From the Cayce perspective, answering the question "What and where is your ideal?" is the central factor shaping our lives. The readings go so far as to say that everything we are at any given moment in time " . . . is the combined result[s] of what we have done about the ideals that we have set!" (1549-1)

The importance of setting a spiritual ideal before entering into medi-tation cannot be overstated. Without it, one might be considered the "thief and robber" Jesus censured in the gospels—someone attempting to reach higher levels of insight and awareness for purely selfish mo-tives. "The thief," the Master said, "cometh not, but for to steal, and to kill, and to destroy: I am come that they might have life, and that they might have it more abundantly." (John 10:10) Opening the inner self in meditation to the influx of the soul forces is a sacred activity, which must be undertaken with the utmost reverence and respect for our-selves and those who ultimately may benefit from the light we carry into the world. Humility is the catchword. "Purify thy body, thy mind. Consecrate thyselves in prayer, yes—but not as he that prayed 'I thank Thee I am not like other fellows.' Rather let there be in thy heart that humbleness, for ye must humble thyself if ye would know Him; and come with an open, seeking, contrite heart desirous of having the way shown to thee." (281-41)

When someone once requested advice from Edgar Cayce about how to develop spiritual powers, the answer supplied by the readings was to fill the mind with an ideal that would vibrate throughout every corner of the mental being. After closing off " . . . the desires of the fleshly self to conditions about same . . . ," the recommendation was to surround oneself with the consciousness of doing the will of God. *"Not my will but thine, O Lord, be done in and through me"* (1861-4) is the affirmation the readings proposed, counseling the person to feel this idea within the inmost recesses of the heart and to open every center of the body, from the lowest to the highest, by infusing them with that ideal. His advice closed with a few words of wisdom about the importance of maintain-ing the same mental attitude of submission to the will of God once the period of meditation had ended. Never desire to attain anything the readings warn, " . . . without *His* direction, but *with* His direction—who is the Maker, the Giver of life and light; as it is indeed in Him that we live and move and have our being." (1861-4)

On another occasion Cayce posited that the ideals ingested into the mind become actual third-dimensional realities. The fact of the matter is that we literally initiate a process of rebuilding the body temple atom by atom whenever we hold onto the right ideal. " . . . What one thinks continually, they become," the readings insist. "What one cherishes in their heart and mind they make a part of the pulsation of their heart, through their own blood cells, and build in their own physical {body} . . . " (3744-5) Thus, the Cayce philosophy maintains that the deep desires of our hearts can make every cell of the physical body vibrate with the consciousness of the Christ. Similarly, the readings refer to the ideal as an essential factor in helping to alleviate doubt and fear. They emphasize that if we know what we believe and have set as our ideal, " . . . when the darker days come, and when the shadows come that would make thee afraid . . . ," we will be able to turn within " . . . and have a good time at scaring the bogies away . . . " (815-2) Furthermore, on a very practical level, they also claim that by simply holding onto the proper ideal, life's problems will be solved more harmoniously and stumbling blocks turned into stepping stones.

Watch and Pray
ের

In thine seeking, my child, know that He is nigh unto thee . . .

272-8

Perhaps the most critical reason for setting a spiritual ideal is to assist the act of meditation itself due to the security it provides against discarnate entities seeking entrance through the spiritual centers now opening up inside the body. We must remain the ever-alert guardians of our inner space, for if the master of the house is not home, a lot of squatters and shady characters may try to take up residence there. The readings caution us to be careful as we enter into the inner temple to approach the unseen forces surrounding the throne of grace, beauty, and might, advising everyone who meditates to envelop themselves in the protective thought of the Christ. " . . . But never open self, my friend, without surrounding self with the spirit of the Christ, that ye may ever be guarded and guided by His forces!" (440–8) Cayce warns. The readings urge us to surround ourselves only with the loftiest aims and standards of perfection and never to " . . . seek the lower influences . . . ," which may become destructive or lead us astray. (2072–11)

Arguably some of the most impressive and soul–stirring passages found among the entire collection of 14,000+ readings in the Edgar Cayce archives are the affirmations he suggested to help align the physical and mental bodies and to achieve inner attunement by raising the highest possible vibrations through the use of an ideal. It would be difficult to find anywhere in the religious literature of the world more potent and awe–inspiring illustrations of the spiritual ideal than some of these messages Cayce gave to people who had come to him hoping to better understand their roles in manifesting the love of God and man in the earth. What follows are two examples out of the dozens conveyed via his unconscious mind over the course of his career—

> *Our Father, who art in heaven, may Thy kingdom come in earth through Thy presence in me, that the light of Thy word may shine unto those that I meet day by day. May Thy presence in my brother be such that I may glorify Thee. May I so conduct my own life that others may know Thy presence abides with me, and thus glorify Thee.*   262-30

and . . .

> *. . . Thy will, O Lord, be done in and through me as Thou seest I have need of for my soul development, and that I may through this development be the greater channel of blessing to my fellow man.*   288-37

An ideal requires courage asserts Cayce. We must " . . . dare to do the impossible," he declares. "For with God nothing is impossible . . . " (165–21) Our ideal is the steady beacon lighting the way as we move through the process of meditation and the landmark by which to chart our course in navigating the rough seas of daily life. In the final analysis there is only one true, infallible ideal. And it was manifested in the earth more than 2,100 year ago by the first begotten son, Jesus of Nazareth, who revealed the pattern of the Christ to the world. The readings categorically maintain that the life of the Master " . . . should be every entity's ideal—physically, mentally, materially." (2533-7)

Preparing the Vessel

. . . There is the necessity that the physical body be in as perfect accord with the Creative and Universal Forces as is possible . . .

5640-3

Contrary to myriad religious theories promulgated through the ages, many of them still in vogue today, we do not reach God by denigrating, punishing, or abandoning the physical body. Our bodies are the sacred vehicles by which the human touches the divine and spiritual transformation occurs. Devised not only for physical but also metaphysical activity, the Adamic body contains the roadmap back to the Father's house. And when, through the use of meditation, we choose to arouse the energy centers inside us until they begin to vibrate in tune with the infinite, the body is what takes us there. Traveling along internal pathways designed into the human form, the invisible life force coursing through us awakens our dormant spiritual centers (chakras) and infuses them with light. Thus do we become conscious of the presence of God.

The Cayce information highlights seven of these spiritual centers incorporated into the body's glandular system. The number seven is noteworthy in itself since cultures across the globe traditionally have regarded it as a sacred sum. The number appears frequently throughout the Bible: seven days of creation, Egypt's seven plenteous years and seven years of famine, the seven daughters of Midian, the seventh day deemed the Sabbath, encircling the city of Jericho seven times, seven loaves with seven baskets of fragments left over, casting out seven devils, forgiving seventy times seven, and the seven churches of the Book of Revelation to name several. Similarly, the individual act of raising the kundalini energy through the seven chakras also represents a sacred activity. The life force pulsating within us, tethered to the earth since the fall in Eden, awaits our recognition. And with each decision to draw it upward by elevating our consciousness in meditation, we lift up this divine energy to its original vibration level and rightful place of dignity and illumination, thereby reclaiming our birthright as the sons and daughters of God.

Ye Shall Know the Truth
༺ᑫᑋᕽ

> Few are able, even as the prophet of old, (I Kings 19:11-12) to
> see God in battle, in the shedding of blood, in the thunder, in the
> lightning, in the earthquake, in the various tumults in nature—but
> *all* may experience Him in the still small voice within! Do *thou*
> likewise . . . Rom. 12:1 and 341-31

In Eastern mystical teachings the process of successfully raising up the kundalini energy results in a state called enlightenment. Since ancient times spiritual masters in countries such as Egypt, China, and India were known to have imparted to their initiates the mystery of arousing the seven spiritual centers. Sadly, however, while the knowledge about the importance of elevating consciousness to a higher level of attunement was present in the earth for millennia, during most of the world's history it remained inaccessible to the masses. The truth lay hidden from public view behind the walls of isolated monasteries or in obscure religious texts. Here and there holy women and men who practiced and taught meditation were able to spread the word by passing down their esoteric wisdom to the small groups of initiates sitting at their feet. The discipline started to slowly mushroom as students of these solitary gurus began to teach others, until thousands of people, primarily residing in the East, had learned how to meditate and practiced it regularly.

It took much longer for the idea to penetrate occidental culture and a population wholly unaccustomed to settling down the physical body and reining in the frenzied mind. Only during the last half of the twentieth century did meditation and other contemplative practices, such as yoga, grab a firm hold on the other side of the globe, gaining mass popularity in areas such as Europe and the United States. Along with the more recent teachers—Paramahansa Yogananda, Joel Goldsmith, Eckhart Tolle, and others—Edgar Cayce has constituted one of the bright lights elucidating for Western audiences the truth about the power of the meditative process. The unique, multi-dimensional picture of spiritual development delineated in the Cayce readings has helped move meditation into the twenty-first century by reaffirming its value to every soul on earth. East or West, however, it is probably safe to say relatively few practitioners actually understand the deeper meaning and esoteric purpose of raising up the serpent energy still crawling in the dust.

Opening the Centers

And Jacob called the name of the place Peniel: for I have seen God face to face, and my life is preserved. Gen. 32:30

The portrait of meditation drawn by the Cayce material says the spiritual centers dispersed throughout the human form are points of contact between the physical organism and the soul—connections just as real as the nerve centers and fibers carrying impulses from the sense organs to the brain. Incredibly, quieting the corporal body and turning the mind inward fixed on an ideal, incites actual physical vibrations. These vibrations are said to occur when spiritual influences become active on the body's sensitive vibratory centers, stimulating the touch points between the soul and its material shell. Humanity's legacy since the time Adam and Eve first appeared on the scene—and still the reality today—is that the infrastructure necessary for making contact with our God is incorporated into the physical forms we carry around with us every day. Moreover, each man, woman, and child who desires to know more of this unseen presence may avail themselves of the opportunity to access it at any time. But first, just like any savvy traveler who must be equipped for the journey into uncharted territory, we, too, must make fitting provision for passage into the inner temple.

The entry process begins with the simple decision to sit down the outer self and meditate. Edgar Cayce describes human beings as miniature copies of the universe, possessing physical, mental, and spiritual bodies knit together so tightly that the impressions made on one have an effect on the other two. Thus the choice to stop what we are doing and gently subdue the fleshly body will react upon the mind, making our determination to "lay down my life" (John 10:15)—the exterior life we lead every day—the first step in preparing outer conditions for the inward journey. Meditation involves an attitude of waiting, of silence, of listening, to be able to hear the still small voice whisper within. When " . . . the physical is subjugated or laid aside," states Cayce, "we find the soul forces give the information, and the body is under subjugation of the soul or spirit forces." (3744-1) The mere act of ceasing all external activity helps the mind break free of its normal focus on mortal concerns and begin moving into a different state.

One reading compares this withdrawal and separation from superficial circumstances and our external surroundings to the Israelites walking across the Red Sea as they departed from Egypt. Cayce describes it this way: " . . . That as Moses and the children passed through the sea, they were baptized in the cloud, in the sea, as an example, as an omen, as a physical activity of a spiritual, a physical separation from that which had been builded in their experience as the sojourn in Egypt . . . " (262-60) We, too, must disassociate from all the pressing obligations of the day and ignore the psychic pull of past events in order to walk on solid ground through the formless watery depths of Spirit. The promise is that by choosing to disengage from the material world for brief periods of time in meditation, we, too, will emerge dry-shod into our freedom.

The Lord's Prayer
⚬ᴁ⚬

And in the morning, rising up a great while before day, he went out, and departed into a solitary place, and there prayed.
Mark 1:35

The readings' counsel on the subject of preparing to enter the inner temple also includes a unique perspective on what is perhaps the most famous prayer in history. The Cayce material redefines the intent and purpose of the Lord's Prayer, also known as the Our Father, by noting its utility as a tool in laying the foundation for the meditative experience. Traditional interpretations view this prayer as the inspirational words Jesus once piously uttered in order to teach his disciples how to speak to God. But closer inspection reveals a more profound meaning and motive for the Master's invocation—as a prescription meant for the ages. According to Edgar Cayce, Jesus constructed the Lord's Prayer to give his students the secret technique whereby they and future generations might prepare body and mind for the divine encounter in meditation.

When someone once asked Cayce how to use the Lord's Prayer, his answer was to feel the flow of the meaning of each phrase throughout the entire physical body because engaging with the words on that level would engender a corresponding response in the mental body. He further assures us that the prayer would unlock for those who employed it correctly the kinds of experiences Jesus of Nazareth had had and build " . . . into the physical body in the manner as He, thy Lord, thy Brother, so well expressed in, 'I have bread ye know not of.'" (281-29)

Every clause in the prayer has the power to influence one of the seven chakras and acts as a catalyst to start the flow of the life energy coursing through the body–temple, raising its vibration levels and spiritualizing those attributes specifically tied to each energy center along the way. Beginning with the highest center, the third eye or pituitary gland,[37] the Lord's Prayer moves the life force on a path around the inner body until it completes a circuit, which serves to stimulate the various points of contact between the soul and its physical casing. As we begin repeating the Master's powerful words, the kundalini energy migrates from the middle of the forehead up onto the top of the head where the crown chakra (pineal gland) resides. It then proceeds downward to rouse the lower chakras until the flow abruptly shifts direction a second time and starts climbing up the spinal column, returning to rest in the area of the pituitary again.

Once awakened, the third eye of the forehead becomes the eye that is single, referenced in the gospels (Matt. 6:22) and as David's cup that "runneth over" from the Psalm 23. For our raised consciousness, which has attracted the kundalini life force from its inferior place in the body and lifted it up to flood the highest spiritual centers, has become the

---

[37]Q. Medical Science calls the glands at the base of the brain Pituitary and 3rd eye Pineal. Why have these names been reversed? Please explain.
A. Their activity indicates that, from the angles of this study, these should be reversed. (281-54)

agent of change. This sacred energy is the deliverer or liberator that can revive in us whatever has died or lapsed into unconsciousness during the soul's descent into matter and a carnal life. In an extraordinary example of symmetry, the final movement of the life energy heavenward inside the body follows a route harking back to the very familiar metaphor of the shepherd, which appears repeatedly throughout the Old and New Testaments. The ascending life current traveling straight up the spine, then arching over the top of the head down toward the forehead is said to resemble a shepherd's crook. The Christ spirit, now risen within us and activating the holiest centers of the body–temple, is indeed the good shepherd who will lead his flock to green pastures.

Lord's Prayer[38]

Phrase	Spiritual Center/ [Location]	Spiritualized Attribute
Our Father, which art in **heaven,**	Pituitary [Third eye in center of forehead]	Love
Hallowed be thy **name.**	Pineal [Top of the head]	Light
Thy kingdom come, thy **will** be done on earth as it is in heaven.	Thyroid [Lower front part of the neck]	Life
Give us this day our daily **bread,**	Gonads—Male and Female [Testes and ovaries]	Sustenance

[38]The information for this chart came from the book by Meredith Puryear, *Healing through Meditation and Prayer* (Virginia Beach, VA: A.R.E. Press, 1978), 10–11.

And forgive us our **debts,** as we forgive our debtors.	Adrenal [Solar plexus]	Self-preservation
And lead us not into **temptation,**	Cells of Leydig [Testicles]	Propagation of species
But deliver us from **evil.**	Thymus [Behind the sternum and in front of the heart]	Self-gratification
For thine is the **kingdom,**	Thyroid [Lower front part of the neck]	Life
And the **power,**	Pineal [Top of the head]	Light
And the **glory,** forever. Amen.	Pituitary [Third eye in center of forehead	Love

Preparing one's consciousness appears to be the single most important activity mentioned in the Edgar Cayce readings for those seeking admittance to the inner temple. And making use of the Lord's Prayer in concert with a personal ideal sets the stage for correctly enlivening the seven spiritual centers as we attempt to approach the throne of God. Unlike many of the more rigid religious sects, the Cayce philosophy indicates that performing special ceremonies or exercises before entering into meditation is never as important as the commitment and sincere attitude a seeker brings with him or her into the process.

External Environment
⮜

In presenting self, then, as has been given, come to the altar of
truth within thine own self . . .   262-77

Because the Master Jesus gave no credence to the idea that people
needed outward observances to gain access to the divine, preparation
for meditation does not require any formal rites or ritualized behavior.
On the other hand, Edgar Cayce concludes that if certain tones, music,
hues, or other aspects of one's physical surroundings will enhance our
ability to take the reins of the mind and steer it in the right direction,
we need not forego these supports.

Because human beings consist of three elements—body, mind, and
spirit—the readings mention several factors that might assist us in
tuning into the divine. At the same time Cayce explains that each soul
must come to recognize for itself the most satisfying and constructive
activities. For some it may be cleansing the body with pure water within
and without. Others may be drawn to fasting, burning incense, or surrounding themselves with special fragrances or colors they find calming. The readings' instructions are always to search out whatever might
be conducive to our own individual development and heed the answers
obtained from within. " . . . Not only the hearer but rather the doer
gains," they declare, "in its seeking through to the Infinite forces and
influences. Hence, whether it is desired from the experience to abstain
from this, that or the other influence to obtain the better conditions in
self, seek to know these—for *thou* art not dumb, my brother!" (440-12)

The important point to remember is that the body is not the enemy;
it is the vehicle. And while the fact remains that in times past and even
now amazing Eastern masters have been capable of meditating for long
stretches under extremely harsh conditions—some enduring years of
living in cold, rocky caves—no one is asking us to subdue our bodies
in such a radical manner. We need only settle down in a comfortable
position, seated with the spine straight if possible, so the external "vehicle" does not distract us from the interior reality.

The approach to meditation detailed in the readings also includes
some general advice about the benefits of using certain tones or chants

to help release our association with the body and begin vibrating with the light to achieve inner attunement. (281-25) Human beings are on a homeward journey and one of the most effective chants Edgar Cayce suggested was to employ a sound infused with the idea of returning home. He told one woman seeking assistance to chant the word "ohm." The inference was that the prodigal soul would benefit by intoning this sound when seeking entrance into the inner temple because that particular tone calls to mind its original celestial dwelling place. The woman's reading summed up its reasoning this way: " . . . from the longings within, a home—*home*—with all its deeper, inner meanings, is a portion of the entity's desire; to know, to experience, to have the 'feel' of, to have the surroundings of that implied by the word *home*! Is it any wonder then that in all of thy meditations 'Ohm—O-h-m—mmmmm' has ever been, is ever a portion of that which raises self to the highest influence and the highest vibrations throughout its whole being that may be experienced by the entity?" (1286-1)

Additional suggestions about the best way to prepare for the meditation session include establishing a routine such as setting aside a particular spot in the house—the corner of a room or other quiet space—and instituting a regular time for the practice. In several cases Edgar Cayce recommended rising in the middle of the night around 2:00 a.m. to meditate. This peaceful interval during the deepest part of the night when the world is hushed and outside activities have ceased creates an atmosphere highly conducive to quieting the mind and entering into a meditative state. But as always, the readings' primary focus remains on the interior attitude and not the external conditions. Although in many cases ready access to a favorite spot may make it a little easier for us to meditate, finding the perfect location is not a prerequisite for success nor should the lack of a dedicated space ever become a deterrent. It is important to resist the temptation to create a new "church" for ourselves. Neither special devotional activities nor the belief that meditation must always occur at a certain time and place can obstruct our entry into the temple unless we allow them to do so. The Master was able to center himself even in the middle of the Garden of Gethsemane after having taken leave of his beloved disciples following the Last Supper and psychically aware of all the horrors that awaited him during the upcoming Crucifixion.

Nature's Gate
ल्ल

... One that fills the mind, the very being, with an expectancy of
God will see His movement, His manifestation, in the wind, the
sun, the earth, the flowers, the inhabitant *of* the earth ... 341-31

Jesus' interlude in the Garden of Gethsemane, significant for many,
many reasons, points squarely at a related topic addressed by the Edgar
Cayce readings and of great potential value to anyone seeking to make
contact with the divine. The Master's brief retreat into the garden before the events on Calvary is one of several occasions mentioned in the
gospels where Jesus appears to have removed himself from the chaos
of his outer circumstances by withdrawing to a tranquil natural area.
"And he withdrew himself into the wilderness, and prayed," states the
gospel of Luke. (Luke 5:16) Interestingly the readings provide unique
insight into the process of growing closer to God in consciousness using
the portal of the natural world. Cayce speaks movingly about the value
of staying close to nature in the pursuit of higher awareness because
plants and animals are guileless transparencies of the infinite invisible
in the earth. "Know the first principles: There is good in all that is alive
... ," states one cogent reading. (2537-1) Proximity to the natural world
strengthens our connection to the still presence, the spirit of God, because this spirit is evident everywhere in nature, lying just beneath the
surface radiating through the wild. As the sublime epic poem of ancient
India, the *Bhagavad-Gita*, attests—

> Who sees his Lord
> Within every creature,
> Deathlessly dwelling
> Amidst the mortal:
> That man sees truly.[39]

The readings shed more light on the principle of tapping into the
divine dwelling in all things by explaining that anyone able to re-

[39]Swami Prabhavananda and Christopher Isherwood, trans., *The Song of God: Bhagavad-
Gita* (New York: New American Library, Inc., 1951), 104.

member a sunset or the harmony in the song of a bird's call already is experiencing the Creative Forces, and " . . . if they are a part of thyself, they bring you closer and closer to God." (1431-1) In fact, he told one seeker who in a past life had witnessed the natural phenomena surrounding the birth of Jesus that it " . . . awoke within the entity that as may be found in the present, how all nature—the face in the water, the dew upon the grass, the tint and the beauty of the rose, the song of the stars, the mourn of the wind, all proclaim—*now*—the mighty words of a merciful, a loving God." (587-6)

The readings also explicitly advised another individual to avoid becoming immersed in the strife and turmoil of the city surrounded by " . . . those forces that bespeak of the commercial life . . . ," but rather to seek out the soul's relationship with nature. For what is as " . . . beautiful and joyous as the music in the rain or in the babbling brook or in the moonlight or in the noonday sun or in the beauty of the rose or the smile of the child! . . . " they exclaim. These blessings are seen as demonstrations of the " . . . greater expressions of the love of a merciful heavenly Father . . . " And whenever we breathe in the wonders of the natural world, we are inhaling the sweetness and " . . . promise of the rest of a home . . . with Him." (1286-1)

The single most important caveat among the series of recommendations found in the readings on preparing for an encounter with the divine, either immediately prior to a meditation session or as we go about our daily business, is to refrain from falling in love with the places and personal observances used to set the stage. There exists no infallible handbook for entering into the meditative state, and the unruly mind is clever. Left to its own devices, it will try to convince us the moment is never right. The brain also has a tendency to cling to what is familiar and may soon begin to substitute the words and rituals meant to direct us toward the door of the sanctuary for the sanctuary itself. In the end we must find the peace Isaiah promised to those whose "mind is stayed on Thee" (Is. 26:3) by moving beyond the need for any proscribed techniques. Eventually we will learn to meditate whenever the impulse arises—day or night—and wherever we find ourselves, even if it is only for two or three minutes, by just making the decision to close the eyes and enter into the interior closet, retreating into the stillness to tabernacle with our God.

Chapter 15
Holy Union

Surrendering the Mind

For how does one cleanse the mind?
By the pouring out, the forgetting, the
laying aside of those things that easily
beset and *filling* same with pure, fresh
water that is of eternal life, that is of the
eternal goodness as may be found in Him
who *is* the light, the way, the truth, the
vine, the bread of life and the water of
life. These things are those influences
that purify.   1620-1

Regardless of how it may look from the outside, lifting up the ret-rograded life force is not a thought–based activity nor will we ever reach a state of paradise through the mind alone. Rather the process of moving the divine energy upward is a doing—a deliberate recalibration of body, mind, and spirit to their original celestial vibrations. This attunement may be compared to adjusting a musical instrument. Improperly tuning a violin to strum it like a banjo produces a discordant sound, but correctly tuning the same instrument so the oscillating strings resonate in accordance with what the violin was created to be can intone the harmonies of heaven. Jesus, the pattern, had kept his vibrations in perfect alignment with the Creative Forces such that his inner attunement was a fully conscious, uninterrupted state of "at-One-ment" with his Source. The Master did not merely *think* about God; he experienced divinity, then chose to stay in tune with that sublime reality. Thus did the Christ release a flawless transcendent melody into the earth.

The purpose of seeking inner attunement through meditation is always to lift consciousness nearer to its original Edenic state. It was the deliberate choice by Adam and Eve in the garden to turn their backs and ignore the voice of their Creator that was the soul's undoing. Once the two had set up an idol in their minds and had started lusting after something outside of themselves in order to feel powerful and whole and also once they had become invested in personal desire which slowed down the frequency of their godlike vibrations in order to grab at the forbidden fruit—the "apple" of their eye—our progenitors found themselves firmly ensnared in a web of material thinking. And because both halves of the soul, male and female, had disassociated from their own inner knowingness, convincing each other of the mistaken notion that they needed more than they already were in order to be divine, the outcome was fixed.

Adam and Eve's ill-advised decision had rejected the original divine plan whereby the children of God would eternally exist in a heavenly estate, cognizant of the absolute Oneness of all being. Instead they accepted a belief in duality—good and evil—and in doing so set the human race on its star-crossed course. The tempter had laid claim to the mind and dragged it down to a lower level of consciousness. Considered from this perspective, the lesson implanted at the center of the Genesis story begins to make more sense as a cautionary tale. The unrestrained human mind generating an unending stream of self-conscious ideas and bent on manipulating the kundalini life force to its own ends is the viper that continues to beguile the human race and alienate it from the truth of its own divinity.

Mind of the Christ
ॐ

Jesus said unto him, Thou shalt love the Lord thy God with all thy
heart, and with all thy soul, and with all thy mind. Matt. 22:37

Now the captive soul unwittingly keeps looking to this same mind to
set it free from its fleshly woes. But thinking cannot serve as the escape
hatch from the conundrum of an earthly existence because thought
was the passage into this sphere in the first place. What mystics of all
ages have taught is that gaining freedom from the clutches of a material
world is possible only when we are able to subdue the restive mind by
achieving a state of stillness. The general process might be compared
to asking someone to think of an apple. The thought-apple is not real
in the sense of having a third-dimensional existence in time and space
because the piece of fruit does not really exist anywhere except in the
thinker's head. Attempting to get rid of the apple by trying to imagine
it away presents both a frustrating dilemma and an impossible task.
Only in the *absence* of thought, in the silence, will it disappear.

The lust for material possessions, fame, glory, and private gain turns
the gaze outward toward a kingdom that is temporary, destined to
crumble to dust, and gone in the twinkling of an eye. While the many
tantalizing objects and conditions forever vying for our attention present a formidable test of our commitment to the Way, an even greater
challenge confronts us on the journey homeward. Arguably the subtlest
and most difficult stumbling block we need to overcome is the constant
stream of uncontrolled thought, which creates such desires in the first
place. Like the horrifying mass of writhing snakes that sprang forth
from the head of the mythological figure Medusa, an endless parade
of cognitive distractions—mental games, secret obsessions, embryonic
thought-forms, personal opinions, byzantine theories, and old memo-
ries—continuously crop up to excite the brain and captivate the psyche.
We have to quiet the incessant racket coming from the playground of
the mind.

Throughout history sincere spiritual seekers everywhere have attempted to reach God through the mind by holding onto good thoughts, analyzing complex theological precepts, and repeating long litanies of fervent prayers. But those approaches invariably fail because the unquestioned dominance of the human mind with all its noise-making activity is the foremost obstacle to attaining higher awareness. Humanity is adrift in a sea of time–bound forms, trapped in the illusion of a conceptual reality where solid walls of thought generated by intellects constantly in motion—building mental constructs, taking positions, making comparisons—block out the sacred dimension. Unbridled thinking is so seductive that it will misguide us until we have completely lost sight of our original destination and purpose. The *Bhagavad-Gita* observes that even a soul aware of the path can be dragged away from it. Only he who controls the senses, reins in the mind, and "fixes it on me" is said to be headed in the right direction and illumined.

> The uncontrolled mind
> Does not guess that the Atman is present:
> How can it meditate?
> Without meditation, where is peace?
> Without peace, where is happiness?[40]

Those able to attain the new state of consciousness Jesus described to his students will have overcome something far greater than merely forsaking a few material possessions. By subduing the overpowering urge to amuse themselves with unrestrained thinking, the "reborn" will have let go of all those thought-forms and deeply held prejudices and beliefs that separate man from man—and man from God.

Taking the Reins
⌇

Therefore I say unto you, Take no thought . . . Matt. 6:25

---
[40]Swami Prabhavananda and Christopher Isherwood, trans., *The Song of God: Bhagavad-Gita* (New York: New American Library, Inc., 1951), 43.

Lost in thought and inflated with a personal sense of ego, we have no choice but to look beyond the distractions of our own mental formations to touch the invisible reality lying behind the physical form. Man's ways are not the ways of God, Jesus explained to his disciples. A concept of God is not God, and the divine force permeating every atom of the universe is unknowable except through the stillness found in the inmost recesses of the soul. The excitable intellect, the monkey–mind, engrossed in an endless array of riveting ideas and opinions will never be able to plumb the mysterious depths of Spirit, which is infinitely vaster than any concept a reasoning brain might conjure up. Myths and fables from around the globe recount enchanting tales of humanity's struggle to find the Holy Grail of its God–self again and reclaim the divine state of Oneness lost so long ago. Yet mystics throughout time have pointed to a single solution to that eternal quest. The secret key to reopening the gates to the garden of paradise guarding the Tree of Life is to reach a level of consciousness beyond the limitations of the mortal mind.

Shutting ourselves away from the cares of the world, calming the waves of thought rippling across the turbulent brain, and purging the mental self of past conditioning help move us into a timeless dimension devoid of any conceptual projections about who and what we are. This is the process of carrying the Christ–babe down to Egypt—keeping it safe from every plot, plan, idle musing, mental image, hope, wish, or scheme that might snuff out the life of the holy child. Such is the path of true monasticism, which neither evades nor represses the desire to engage with and judge this world but is able to rise above all the pairs of opposites and alluring mental images that tie the soul to mortality. The *Bhagavad-Gita* bears witness to the need for the seeker not to flee from the cravings of the mind but simply to leave thinking behind—

> The abstinent run away from what they desire
> But carry their desires with them:
> When a man enters Reality,
> He leaves his desires behind him.[41]

---

[41] Swami Prabhavananda and Christopher Isherwood, trans., *The Song of God: Bhagavad-Gita* (New York: New American Library, Inc., 1951), 42.

and . . .
> Not shaken by adversity,
> Not hankering after happiness;
> Free from fear, free from anger,
> Free from the things of desire.
> I call him a seer, and illumined.[42]

The Wedding Garment
ᚲᚫᚱ

Empty thy minds, *empty* thy hearts of all that thou hast held that is of a secular nature, if ye would know the *true* Knowledge of thy God.   262-96

A well-known parable from the Gospel of Matthew set at a wedding feast contains a warning from the Master about trying to bring our mind-generated prejudices and thoughts with us as we enter into the divine presence. In this story Jesus compared the kingdom of heaven to a certain ruler who had made a marriage for his son. But when the king sends out his servants to call the people he had invited to his home, they refuse to come. So he dispatches a second group of servants to remind his guests the oxen and fatlings have been killed and the wedding feast is ready. Yet even these exhortations do not convince the people to attend. After making light of the invitation they go on their way, one to his farm and another to take care of his merchandise. Worse, the group treats the king's servants spitefully and kills them. Angry about their crimes and refusal to sup with him, the king decides to deploy an army to destroy the murderers and burn down their town.

He then informs his servants that the ones who originally were bidden to join him at his table were not worthy and sends out footmen into the highways to ask whomever they can find to attend the marriage festivities. These servants proceed to gather together a large collection of strangers (both good and bad according to the gospel account) until the party is fully furnished with guests. But when the host

---

[42]Swami Prabhavananda and Christopher Isherwood, trans., *The Song of God: Bhagavad-Gita* (New York: New American Library, Inc., 1951), 42.

enters the room to welcome the new arrivals, he notices one man who is not wearing a suitable wedding garment. "And he saith unto him, Friend, how camest thou in hither not having a wedding garment? And he was speechless. Then said the king to the servants, Bind him hand and foot, and take him away, and cast him into outer darkness, there shall be weeping and gnashing of teeth. For many are called, but few are chosen." (Matt. 22:9–14)

Jesus was imparting two fundamental spiritual lessons with his brief parable. We can refuse the divine invitation to be a guest of the king, but if and when we do, we are destined to live life merely as human beings vulnerable to all the problems and pain inherent in an earthly existence subject to the laws of cause and effect. Conversely, we may choose to answer the king's invitation to come and be welcomed into his dwelling place—no longer as strangers but as honored guests taking their rightful place in the royal household. But only a soul wearing the unblemished garments of someone fully prepared to witness the sacred union of God and man may remain in the divine presence and share in the ineffable joy. If our consciousness is clothed in the garb of egoistic material concerns or soiled by the mud of dissent, desire, and dissatisfaction, we are not properly dressed and will be cast out before experiencing the foretold marriage. Cayce sums up this core principle with one straightforward piece of advice: "Then let us purify our bodies, our minds, and consecrate ourselves in prayer. Let us put away from us hate, greed, and malice, and replace them with love and mercy. Let there be in our hearts humbleness, for we must humble ourselves if we would know Him. Let us come with an open, seeking contrite heart desiring to have the way shown us. Then let us seek to enter."[43]

Harnessing mind and heart by placing them under the yoke of meditation is in itself a humbling experience. The self-abasement traditionally extolled by some faith traditions, such as beating the breast, kneeling for hours on a cold floor, dressing in nondescript clothing, or as in ancient biblical times, wearing sackcloth and ashes, is merely the outward show when the demand is always for an inner submission—the meekness of a mind chastened by yielding itself to a higher Source and

---

[43]Edgar Cayce, *A Search for God, Book I*, comp Study Group #1 of the Association for Research and Enlightenment (Virginia Beach, VA: A.R.E. Press, 1942), 12.

will. This is the meekness of a Moses or a Jesus Christ who made no pretenses about their status as holy men but, having set aside all mind-generated hopes and desires, entered into the stillness to listen for the still small voice of divine guidance and reassurance. The Cayce readings remind us that those the Lord would exalt, " . . . He first brings low that they may know the strength is of the Lord—and not in hosts but the still small voice that beareth witness with thy soul . . . " (165-26)

Setting aside all mind formations and living on the knife edge of the now, moving from the inner to the outer and back again, we sit in a state of alert, aware presence immersed in a pool of limitless being and possibility. This is the space where we finally begin to shake off the shackles of mortality and enter into immortality. And as we reunite with fathomless divinity, our consciousness, previously rigid and unyield-ing, becomes more compliant, submissive, and open to the influx of metaphysical wisdom. After donning the garments of pure spirituality and opening the third eye, we are able to see through the false sense of existence and touch what is real. "Before Abraham was, I am," (John 8:58) the Master Jesus had declared to his disciples. Before the created universe, the universe of the mind, emerged from the void, Spirit, the great I am, was ever present, awaiting our recognition. Now we have begun to penetrate its depths.

Many Mansions

In my Father's house are many mansions {*states of consciousness*}: if it were not so, I would have told you. I go to prepare a place for you . . . that where I am {*in consciousness*}, there ye may be also {*in consciousness*}. John 14:2-3

There comes a moment in our meditation practice when we sit on the cusp of making God contact. The Cayce readings tell us that by letting the soul take over, we will soon reach a state of silence and light unlike anything ever experienced before. This is the jumping off point—the place where our encounter with the divine begins, cleansing us from within. Hatred and self-pity disappear, and a sudden knowing of the nature of things begins to develop.

The meditative state does not involve a loss of consciousness, but rather a heightening of awareness, which includes a sense of awe upon entering the presence of something indescribable, far beyond the boundaries of the feeble time-bound self. And along with this inner state of knowing, an understanding grows about what we must do, what we may have left undone in terms of our interpersonal relationships, and what we still need to complete in order to fulfill our purpose in the earth. But gaining such insight assumes we began our inward journey with a clean slate. "Therefore if thou bring thy gift to the altar, and there rememberest that thy brother hath ought against thee," the Master cautioned, "leave there thy gift before the altar, and go thy way; first be reconciled to thy brother, and then come and offer thy gift." (Matt. 5:23-24) Only a soul unencumbered by the weight of its debts to other people and situations, released from the chains of rancor and conceit, is free to reach out and make contact with the divine.

While the promise of reunification with our Source is a given, Jesus also explained that the timing of the arrival of the bridegroom or Christ in consciousness is not entirely up to us. We have no say as to precisely when this union will occur or how the experience might reveal itself. "Take ye heed, watch and pray: for ye know not when the time is," he admonished his students in Mark. It is essential to remain vigilant, open, and available to the unexpected moment of reunion. The Master described this attitude by comparing it to a man who was preparing to take a far journey. But before the man left home, he gave authority to his servants and assigned each of them a job best suited to his particular skills. Then the lord of the house commanded the porter to watch. Watch, he said, because you do not know when your master might return. He could arrive at any time: during the day, in the evening, near midnight, or perhaps when the cock crows at daybreak. You do not want him to find you sleeping [unconscious] he reminded the man. "And what I say unto you I say unto all, Watch." (Mark 13: 33-37)

The Bridegroom Arrives

... know that the way is open to thee to approach the throne of God; not as an excuse, not as a justification, but rather in love, in harmony, in that which brings hope for a sin-sick world. 5749-12

In a moment that we know not, in a moment that we think not, the bridegroom comes, and spiritual realization dawns. The great "I am" asserts itself, and God is revealed as the center and circumference of our being. Such a "conversion" reassures us that whether we mount up to heaven or "make my bed in hell" (Psalm 139:8), the spirit of God is ever present. Many believe such a reunion with their Creator impossible given the low estate the human race seems to occupy in the earth, but the Master promised the reward of divine awareness to anyone willing to take the time sincerely to seek it.

To that end, Jesus spoke a parable about the man who knocked on the door of his neighbor's house at midnight, asking for three loaves of bread because he had nothing to offer a guest visiting his home. But the neighbor immediately tries to run the man off for disturbing him saying it is too late; his door is shut for the night. The petitioner keeps "importuning" his friend, however, until eventually he receives the bread he had requested. Jesus ends his story by commenting that the man's success was not due to their friendship but because he had never stopped asking. "And I say unto you, Ask, and it shall be given you; seek, and ye shall find; knock, and it shall be opened unto you," the Master told his students. "For every one that asketh receiveth; and he that seeketh findeth; and to him that knocketh it shall be opened." Then the rabbi posed a few rhetorical questions to reinforce his point. If a son asks for bread, would a father give him a stone? Would he offer his child a serpent for a fish or give him a scorpion instead of an egg? "If ye then, being evil, know how to give good gifts unto your children: how much more shall your heavenly Father give the Holy Spirit to them that ask him?" (Luke 11: 5-13) Jesus inquired. The commitment on our parts to keep knocking at the door of the inner temple with a meek and contrite heart virtually will unlock the doors to heaven.

Child of a King

The Master also explained that in equal proportion to the energy we expend in the effort to return to our Father's house are we renewed and fit to wear the princely robes of a child of the king. The metaphor of a king and his kingdom is a thematic thread woven throughout the teachings of Jesus as recorded in the four gospels. It even shows up during the final hours of the Master's life when the Roman soldiers, in a brutal attempt to vilify their prisoner, force a crown of thorns onto his head and later post a sign at the top of the cross identifying him as the now-dead King of the Jews.

Interestingly the crown of gold, which has adorned the heads of royalty since ancient times, endures to this day as an outward symbol of the inward process of divine reunification—the kingdom the Master was heralding to his followers. The jeweled uprights or stanchions encircling the metal ring mimic in visible form the beams of light radiating out from the head or highest chakras of the body when an individual has achieved conscious union with the Source. In experiencing the divine marriage we, too, become members of a royal family—anointed to that elevated status by the sacred oil of truth. And just as the cruse of oil the Old Testament prophet Elijah presented to the poor widow contained an inexhaustible supply, the oil of our divine contact will never run dry or fail us. (I Kings 17:14-16) Those who find their Oneness with God are royal sovereigns entrusted with the welfare of a new kingdom of the Christ established in the earth.

Ye Are the Light
cᐯ

The Lord is my light and my salvation; whom shall I fear? the Lord is the strength of my life; of whom shall I be afraid? Psalm 27:1

Due to the quickening vibrations and spiritual centers newly energized in us from raising up the kundalini energy through meditation, it sometimes appears as if a light is illuminating the body. This is the fulfillment of the Master's declaration, "Ye are the light of the world. A city that is set on an hill cannot be hid." Our inner radiance is the candle Jesus exhorted his followers never to hide under a bushel but allow to shine openly and cast its warmth on everyone in the household. "Let your light so shine before men," he instructed, "that they may see your good works, and glorify your Father which is in heaven." (Matt. 5:14-16) In addition, the Master denotes the eye as the light of the body and maintains that whenever the gaze single-mindedly is focused on God, "thy whole body shall be full of light." (Matt. 6:22) The Cayce readings echo his words in referencing the interior temple. "Consider all of those things given of old in comparison to that taught by the master . . . that it is not from without where there may be visions, voices or what not, but it is the light that comes from within." (877-27)

Not surprisingly Edgar Cayce also asserts that the purpose for which each soul enters a material experience is that it may be as a light unto others. Then he directs us to watch and pray because as " . . . light bearers for Him" (262-26), we are called upon to use whatever degree of wisdom we have attained to help dispel the darkness in the earth. The readings also exhort us not to approach our assignment in a boastful way, feeling self-important or proud of our unique mental and physical abilities. (641-6) The goal of time spent on this planet is to convey hope to our brothers and sisters and " . . . a smile again to those whose face and heart are bathed in tears and in woe . . . " Adding a modicum of light and joy to the lives of people experiencing difficulties or are steeped in sorrow is " . . . making that divine love *shine—shine*—in thy own soul," counsels Cayce, and testifies to the fact that " . . . the day of the Lord is at hand." (987-4) Fanning the divine spark aglow inside us ignites a flame of love, and its incandescence—shining through each soul—is the light of the world burning bright.

Chapter 16
Ark of the Divine

Who shall ascend into the hill of the
Lord? or who shall stand in his holy
place? Psalm 24:3

E ver since the first involution of spirit in the earth when souls,
entranced with the idea of playing with matter, chose to separate
from the whole and pushed the life force into individual projections
of the mind, confusion has reigned. Slowly, over umpteen millennia,
the memory of humanity's origins as expressions of the divine moved
deeper and deeper into the subconscious until the children of God
began to identify themselves solely as terrestrial beings. The proof lay
in the dense physical bodies that encased us. Tricked into believing we
never were celestial beings born of pure spirit but simply creatures of
the flesh worth little more than a pile of dust, we fell asleep pursuing
the myriad delights of sensual gratification that had been seducing
souls since before the fall in Eden. Here and there clues about our sa-

cred ancestry and incorporeal past would pop up in dreams, but more often than not, trying to remember that bygone era felt like chasing a shadow. The memory of our godlike heritage lay buried deep beneath the sands of time, returning only as a faint whisper lingering somewhere in the dim recesses of the mind.

As time relentlessly marched forward, the earthbound souls began to feel increasingly vulnerable. It was as if they had been left to fend for themselves in some alien country governed by irrational laws of decay and death. In despair and determined to find answers to the suffering experienced on a mass scale every day, women and men sought help from various man-made deities and tried hard to appease the gods whose ire could spell their doom. They offered sacrifices, bowed their heads in supplication, and pleaded for help from any higher being who might save them from their plight. Periodically new religions would spring up to formalize the efforts to placate these supernatural forces that seemed to hold all the power, but no one really understood. The stubborn belief—and ardent hope—of devotees was that by embracing certain dogmas and devoutly observing rituals the priests called holy, life might finally begin to work out the way it should. Surely fulfilling all their sacred obligations would be enough to save the human race from the chaotic, hardscrabble world it inhabited. Remnants of these earliest attempts to construct a theology of rescue and redemption form the basis of most religious traditions to this day.

The fragrance of smoldering incense still fills our temples and churches, wafting toward heaven representing the prayers of an abject people ascending toward an almighty God. So, too, do we continue to raise our arms in benediction and send songs of exaltation skyward, carefully entreating the Supreme Being from whom we seek blessings and comfort. Yet sadly even the most ostentatious invocations and sincerest attempts at influencing the deity which believers have imagined more often than not prove futile. Because God is spirit, and it is impossible to affect an incorporeal being with physical sacrifices, smoke projected into the ethers, or words strung together in a formula called prayer. Grandiose promises, man-made objects, and ceremonial rites have no effect on the limitless presence infusing the cosmos, for they reach no further than the human minds which created them.

The unalloyed message found repeatedly throughout the Holy Scriptures bespeaks a truth that humankind has overlooked and forgotten. All that is holy dwells inside us and the spark of divinity burning bright within each soul—the silent, unseen life principle animating every cell of the body—is the only God we will ever reach. It is impossible for the sons and daughters of Spirit to think or talk their way back into the celestial realms from which they descended. No, to make contact with divinity we must do the hard work of raising up the fallen life force again. Only through the practice of meditation, only by migrating to higher ground in consciousness—attaining a state of awareness beyond the limitations of mental constructs and material forms—can the lost souls reconnect with the Creator and regain their foothold in heaven.

Look Up!
❧

And when these things begin to come to pass, then look up, and lift up your heads; for your redemption draweth nigh. Luke 21:28

Raising one's consciousness is the foremost answer to the eternal question of life. The analogy of going higher, elevating our awareness, is a recurring motif telegraphed through some of the most renowned stories from the Bible, starting with Genesis when Noah's Ark lands at the top of Mount Ararat and running through Jesus' transfiguration on a mountainside and his ascension into heaven. Mounts and other types of lofty locations have always symbolized the spiritual imperative to move out of the ordinary terrestrial state of consciousness and scale higher—to reach that holy place where God has promised to meet us.

"And no man hath ascended up to heaven, but he that came down from heaven, even the Son of man," Jesus declared in the Gospel of John. [John 3:13]. And no one on this plane will achieve the heights of a Christ without first ascending in consciousness to reunite with the Source. Running throughout the text of the New Testament are tales of people gathering in second-story rooms, moving from lower to higher vantage points, and hearing truth or experiencing otherworldly events on hilltops and mountainsides. These descriptions hint at a theme found frequently in the Jesus narrative illustrating the need to raise up the God force within in order to manifest divinity in the without.

The metaphor of going up to the mount or gathering in an elevated location where the spirit of God is revealed provides one small clue to unraveling the mystery of why the Master's words still persist more than 2,100 years after he uttered them.

The symbol of attaining a heightened state of awareness presented itself even before Jesus' ministry officially began when Satan took him up into "an exceeding high mountain," to display the glory of all the kingdoms of the world in a moment in time. (Matt. 4:8) We see the Master resist this devil, the temptation to use his spiritual awareness and newfound abilities to control physical objects, inflate his ego, or acquire personal wealth and power. The potential for world domination had entered the realm of possibility once Jesus had risen high enough in consciousness to achieve complete reunification with the universal forces. But he steps back from that precipice.

Throughout his lifetime, this Master will enter into the stillness whenever he is led to withdraw from earthly pursuits and reunite with his God. The "high place" within him is where he finds the strength and renewal to continue on his mission. "And when he had sent the multitudes away," records the Gospel of Matthew, "he went up into a mountain apart to pray: and when the evening was come, he was there alone." (Matt. 14:23) Similarly, Luke reveals that Jesus "went out into a mountain to pray, and continued all night in prayer to God." (Luke 6:12) Matthew also comments in another chapter that " . . . seeing the multitudes, he went up into a mountain: and when he was set, his disciples came unto him," (Matt. 5:1) while Mark describes the scene this way: "And he goeth up into a mountain and calleth unto him whom he would: and they came unto him." (Mark 3:13)

It appears that Jesus, the master teacher, is meditating in preparation to receive his students. So, too, does he go "up" into the silence before carrying his sacred message to the masses below, which enthusiastically respond to the spiritual ardor his teachings exude. "When he was come down from the mountain, great multitudes followed him," states the gospel text. (Matt. 8:1) We also observe the Master withdrawing into quiet contemplation whenever an unforeseen temptation enters the picture. John's gospel recounts a moment in the immediate aftermath of the miracle of the loaves and fishes when the crowds became so excited about the possibility that this rabbi was the long-awaited prophet

God had sent into the world, they start to hail him as their ruler. But he escapes that trap too. "When Jesus therefore perceived that they would come and take him by force, to make him a king, he departed again into a mountain himself alone." (John 6:15)

Of the many heights mentioned in the Bible, one of the most celebrated is the mountain where Jesus brings his three apostles for the transfiguration. "And after six days Jesus taketh with him Peter, and James, and John, and leadeth them up into an high mountain apart by themselves; and he was transfigured before them." (Mark 9:2) During this supernatural incident the veil separating the physical and nonmaterial realms drops away and the disciples not only see Moses and Elias [Elijah] but also glimpse the Master's Christhood in all its effulgence. " . . . And his face did shine as the sun, and his raiment was white as the light," (Matt. 17:2) reports Matthew's account. The rapturous experience of the transfiguration the three men witnessed no doubt was made possible by the elevated state of consciousness their teacher had attained.

Unfortunately, while the imperative to raise our consciousness is fundamental to the message Jesus imparted, it consistently has gotten lost under the endless layers of theological constructs churches have devised and piled onto the four gospels. A quote favored by many a preacher in the pulpit is Jesus' proclamation, "And as Moses lifted up the serpent in the wilderness, even so must the Son of man be lifted up: That whosoever believeth in him should not perish, but have eternal life." (John 3:14-16) The tendency is to translate the Master's words literally by conflating the raising of the serpent energy/Son with the raising of the cross on Golgotha when in reality the act of lifting up the divine Son is an interior, mystical process.

The Christ spirit lifted up and realized in the man Jesus enabled him to perform miracles and allowed the people around him to directly experience Immanuel (God-with-us). And the "eternal life" he promised refers to the uninterrupted, boundless God force, which permeates the universe and to which we have access once we have reconnected with our Source. During the course of his three-year ministry, Jesus will teach his students that this same spirit of God, the indwelling Christ, is present and available to everyone. But they would not be able to recognize the truth of God-in-man unless and until they chose to view life from a different perspective—by going higher.

A brief story in Luke's gospel about a wealthy publican named Zac-chaeus alludes to this seminal teaching of the Master's. Zacchaeus " . . . sought to see Jesus who he was; and could not for the press, because he was little of stature. And he ran before, and climbed up into a sycomore tree to see him: for he was to pass that way. And when Jesus came to the place, he looked up, and saw him, and said unto him, Zacchaeus, make haste, and come down; for today I must abide at thy house." (Luke 19:3–5) Zacchaeus was not able to see the Christ until he rose higher in his awareness. Once he does, the spirit of God promises to enter his household that very day and abide with him. We also learn from Luke that this "person of little stature" whom many Jews considered a sin-ner, in reality was someone already living his life in alignment with the Christ principle. Jesus acknowledges as much when he calls Zacchaeus a member of the family of the chosen people: "And Zacchaeus stood, and said unto the Lord: Behold, Lord, the half of my goods I give to the poor; and if I have taken any thing from any man by false accusation, I restore him fourfold. And Jesus said unto him, This day is salvation come to this house, forsomuch as he also is a son of Abraham." (Luke 19:8–9)

State of Elevation
ᗄᗃ

Look unto the heavens, and see; and behold the clouds which are higher than thou. Job 35:5

One of the most soul–stirring lectures the Master ever gave describes him speaking from a high place. The Sermon on the Mount refers both to a heightened physical location, which would have allowed his pupils to see their teacher as he spoke, and the internal mount—the "hill" lo-cated between the top of the head and forehead. This is the area where the ascending life force connects with the highest spiritual centers or chakras found in the body. Other episodes scattered throughout the New Testament provide additional, subtle hints about the way esoteric truth reaches humankind and how those who attain an elevated state of consciousness are capable of perceiving it.

The Mount of Olives is the setting for any number of significant conversations and incidents during the course of Jesus' lifetime, including his painful interior struggle in the Garden of Gethsemane prior to the events on Calvary. The guiltless rabbi seems to retreat to that particular "high place" fairly regularly. "And in the day time he was teaching in the temple; and at night he went out, and abode in the mount that is called the mount of Olives," states Luke. (Luke 21:37) This mount is also where the Master will impart confidential information only his closest adherents are supposed to hear. "And as he sat upon the mount of Olives, the disciples came unto him privately, saying, Tell us, when shall these things be? and what shall be the sign of thy coming, and of the end of the world?" (Matt. 24:3) Jesus then proceeds to prophesy about the upcoming spiritual transformation.

Similarly, an upper chamber is the backdrop for the Last Supper and the site where the apostles and other disciples decide to gather immediately following the Crucifixion. While congregating together in a second-story room in the home of Lazarus and his sisters, the group sees their "dead" Master appear after entering the space through a closed door. They will also hear Jesus speak and watch him eat real food, proving that what they are experiencing in that heightened state of awareness is not a specter but their resurrected Lord.

According to the Cayce material, we, too, may rise in awareness to directly experience our God. " . . . If ye would know Him at all, . . . he is not past finding out . . . " the readings explain. Even in those times of greatest trial, He is not far from us, they tell us. He is closer than our right hand. He stands at the door of our hearts. Will we bid Him enter, or will we turn Him away? (281–41) Step by step our perception of this immanent divine presence will unveil itself as we hold up the standard of an ideal before the mind and maintain the "altitude" of prayer, as we take the time to go higher and tabernacle with our God.

I Am That I Am

He that dwelleth in the secret place of the most High shall abide under the shadow of the Almighty. Psalm 91:1

"I will lift up mine eyes unto the hills, from whence cometh my help," declared the Old Testament psalmist (Psalm 121:1) in describing the upward movement of the kundalini life force inside the body temple with its energy rising ever higher toward the third eye. This is the secret place of the Most High—the fortress and high tower human beings must ascend in order to make contact with the divine and realize the peace and security Spirit bestows. In meditation we defy the gravitational pull of earth by calming the frantic mind and dropping the heavy burden of material desires to sit humbly and unencumbered in the presence of our God. And after making our connection, we are transformed.

The religious leader and prophet Moses was one such seeker. Jettisoned from his former life in the palaces of Egypt, he found his God by choosing the quiet contemplative life of a nomad who followed the seasons, leading his father-in-law's sheep from pasture to pasture. The days and nights spent watching a flock of animals were a 180 degree shift from the role he had played as the powerful prince of a wealthy nation with all its tumult and pageantry. Somehow the spiritual hunger inside of him was so insistent and close to the surface that it propelled him forward through a series of strange yet miraculous events to meet his messianic destiny.

Moses' inner compulsion to find his God allowed him to cross an impossibly vast desert with no sustenance, stripped of every external prop he had counted on in the past. Outcast, without a home, and caught in a desperate situation, he eventually accepts shelter with a group of fellow wanderers, embracing a way of life radically different from the one he had known in the past. This former "master of the world" becomes a solitary shepherd sitting on a hillside with long periods of time to retreat within himself. It is not too difficult to imagine the herdsman spending his days pondering the mysterious, unseen power, which had saved him from death during his agonizing march across a desert wasteland, while gazing up in wonder at the nearby mountaintop where the locals claimed "He-who-has-no-name" resided.

According to the biblical account, after months spent in such a meditative state, one day Moses decides to lead his flock to the back side of the desert toward Mount Horeb near the place where God is said to dwell. Here he sees an angel standing in the midst of a flaming bush, and here is where he meets his Creator. In symbolic terms, the shepherd had raised his consciousness to the degree where he was able to make contact with the holy fire flickering at the altar of his inner temple. Moses' moment of enlightenment is the burning bush of Exodus—a bush engulfed by a blaze that will never consume it. The interior spark of illumination had inflamed the synapses and pathways of his brain with a light that promised to glow forever. And later, when the barefoot shepherd is overwhelmed by the thought of challenging a powerful Pharaoh to demand the release of the Hebrews and asks to know the name of this God who would send him on such a hopeless mission, the answer breathed into his ears is the words "I am that I am." (Exod. 3:14) Moses has perceived the divinity within his own being and now understands the very place whereon he stands is holy ground. No longer the Moses of old, he is a new man whose life from that day forward belongs to the great "I am."

The Exodus story testifies to the fact that the slightest contact with the absolute, animating principle of the universe is utterly transformative. Moses' experience changed a simple sheep herder, whose personal history began in the royal household ruling over the material domain, into the leader of a nation of spiritual seekers and a savior to the people of Israel. Yet on the heels of Moses accepting his new role, temptation quickly rears its ugly head. As soon as the inner voice instructs him to return to Egypt to guide the Israelites out of their bondage, a powerful symbol from Genesis reappears to confront the reluctant shepherd/savior: the serpent. After the still small voice tells Moses to throw down his rod and it suddenly turns into a snake, he immediately flees from the noxious creature. As was the case with Adam and Eve, the serpent crawling on its belly on the ground symbolizes an aspect of the man himself—the temptation to fear the capabilities of his own soul. Soon, however, compelled by an inner directive, Moses picks up the snake by the tail—raises the kundalini life force—until the previously unrestrained serpent energy undergoes a metamorphosis and becomes the staff upon which he will lean to carry out his sacred commission.

"And thou shalt take this rod in thine hand, wherewith thou shalt do signs," (Exod. 4:17) is the message he receives from his God. Moses' staff of divine understanding is what will sustain the Israelites for forty years through the trials and tribulations of a desert passage, with manna delivered every morning and a cloud by day and pillar of fire by night to faithfully guide their path through the wilderness. Lit by

the spark of his own inner divinity, Moses becomes the deliverer who
leads a group of Jewish slaves held captive to an existence mired in
materiality to the land flowing with milk and honey—a place imbued
with the nectar of heaven—promised to the children of God. The Edgar
Cayce readings interject that due to his God-inspired leadership, Moses
also became the lawgiver to the world. (5367-1)

Sacred Refuge

For, before *that* the entity was that one to whom was entrusted
man's advent into the world—Noah.   2547-1

To enter meditation is to enter the vessel that will safely carry us
through the turbulent waters of a material world. The story of Noah
and his ark, which on its surface appears to have little to do with the
personal journey toward God awareness, nevertheless foreshadows the
idea of the meditative experience and its relevance to the ages. According to Edgar Cayce the catastrophic inundation described in Genesis
and recounted by cultures across the globe was real. "The deluge was
not a myth . . . ," the readings say, " . . . but a period when man had so
belittled himself with the cares of the world, with the deceitfulness of
his own knowledge and power, as to require that there be a return to
his dependence wholly—physically and mentally—upon the Creative
Forces." (3653-1) Indeed sometime in the distant past much of the planet
must have experienced a monumental flood, which profoundly affected
the collective psyche. And the Cayce information directly associates this
deluge with humanity's mindset at the time. Evidently there is much
more to the story of Noah than its horrifying images of tidal waves
rushing over the land to drown a stiff-necked people. At the core of
the thrilling tale lies a vital soul message wrapped in an allegorical
truth: like Noah we are called upon to transport the children of God to
safety—in the ark of our own God awareness.

During the period immediately prior to the deluge, human beings
had lost their way and no longer paid attention to the inner promptings of the soul. Disregarding divine direction and worshipping only
sensual pleasures, the spark of God light within them had dimmed to
the point where darkness had enveloped the earth. Simply put, sin and

corruption were rampant and chaos reigned. Conditions continued to deteriorate until the situation reached a climactic turning point and divine order finally reentered the scene. "And God saw that the wickedness of man was great in the earth, and that every imagination of the thoughts of his heart was only evil continually," states the biblical text. (Gen. 6:5) In fact, circumstances were so dire that the book of Genesis portrays a God grieving over having created the human race in the first place. "And the LORD said, I will destroy man whom I have created from the face of the earth; both man, and beast, and the creeping thing, and the fowls of the air; for it repenteth me that I have made them." (Gen. 6:7) But one faithful soul still connected to his Source, a servant of God by the name of Noah (a moniker meaning rest and comfort), was said to have found grace in the eyes of the Lord. He would change the course of history.

By remaining centered on the divine and thus connected to the whole, Noah intuitively knew floodwaters were headed their way and that nothing material could survive such a massive disaster without help. Spiritually speaking, the raging storms of material thinking and the deep waters of unconsciousness were on the verge of overwhelming the human race and destroying the last vestiges of the third-dimensional world souls had inhabited up to that point. Recognizing the looming clouds of darkness (unconsciousness) gathering on the horizon, Noah defies conventional wisdom and responds to a call from within. He steps up to the plate to assist in creating the conditions whereby the natural processes necessary to sustaining the family of man formed from the dust of the earth would survive into the future. Fully in tune with the will of the One, Noah understood that the panorama of the divine plan did not dictate a complete annihilation of matter. His willingness to accept his God-inspired mission meant that out-of-control egos engulfed in the depths of their own ignorance would not lay waste to the sensate world. Creation would have another chance.

A Great Flood
☙

The biblical account of the great flood presents a moving portrait of one individual's journey of faith. We watch Noah as he obeys the voice of supernatural guidance to secure the fate of plants, animals, and people in an ark designed to exacting specifications, built physically from pieces of gopher wood and spiritually from the planks of his own inner work and contact with the divine. The shipbuilder constructs a massive sanctuary from the floodwaters to house his immediate family, and hewing to the tenets of material law, two of every beast and creeping thing populating the earth. Genesis reports that it rained nonstop for forty days and forty nights with the flood tides prevailing upon the land for one hundred–fifty days. The waters kept rising until the deluge covered the mountaintops and " . . . all flesh died that moved upon the earth, both of fowl, and of cattle, and of beast, and of every creeping thing that creepeth upon the earth, and every man: All in whose nostrils was the breath of life, of all that was in the dry land, died." (Gen. 7:21–22)

Noah and his companions are said to have been floating in the ark until the seventeenth day of the seventh month when the "fountains also of the deep and the windows of heaven were stopped, and the rain from heaven was restrained." Once the rain ends and the colossal inundation starts to recede, their boat comes to rest on Mount Ararat. According to the biblical timeline, it was not until the tenth month that mountaintops finally started to surface again. Soon Noah releases a raven to see if the waters "were abated from off the face of the ground," but the bird just keeps going and never returns. Then he sends out a dove, which comes back to him empty–handed, having "found no rest for the sole of her foot." Seven days later the bird flies off again, but this time it returns carrying a leaf plucked from an olive tree, which convinces the patriarch the teeming waters have subsided and dry land has appeared. Directed once more by the inner compass of the still small voice, he proceeds to step foot onto the solid ground of the earth, exiting the ark and entering the collective consciousness. For Noah has emerged from his passage a savior. Through unwavering obedience to the will of the One, he has become the vehicle by which man is reconciled to God, and human beings are given a new opportunity to evolve in understanding. (Gen. 8:2–11)

Grateful for his survival, Noah builds an altar and makes burnt offerings to the omnipotent, unseen power that has saved him and his family. This God in turn is said to be pleased with the fragrance of his servant's sacrifices and pledges in his heart never again to " . . . curse the ground any more for man's sake; for the imagination of man's heart is evil from his youth; neither will I again smite any more every thing living, as I have done. While the earth remaineth, seedtime and harvest, and cold and heat, and summer and winter, and day and night shall not cease." (Gen. 8:21–22) Never again would creation be subject to annihilation by cataclysmic floodwaters, mirroring the deluge of spiritual unconsciousness that had befallen humanity, such that the climb out of matter would have to "start over." The material world and its laws of cause and effect would continue to exist for the benefit of the soul and the expansion of consciousness in every living creature on the planet. And the totality of creation would abide under the protection of the same supernatural force that had preserved Noah. Furthermore, the eternal sign of God's promise to humanity would be the rainbow—symbol of the unbreakable bond between heaven and earth.

Sanctuary
ౡ

Keep that faith which has prompted the self to set thy ark to the port of the higher calling as found in Him . . .   420-6

The spiritual lesson at the core of the tale of Noah and his extraordinary achievement speaks to the soul's responsibility to stay connected with its Source and thus contribute to the upward movement of consciousness in the third dimension. While the rising floodwaters of insensitivity and unawareness may threaten to overwhelm our world, those who walk with God, transmitting their spiritual lights into the dark corners of the earth, are fated to become its deliverers. In the story of the great flood, only the few aligned with Noah's higher state of attunement were able to escape the murky waters of death. Conversely, those who deliberately chose to remain oblivious to the toxic environment they had created for themselves were doomed. Caught up in waves of selfishness and swept away by the flood tides of sensuality, the egoistic and greedy were dragged down by the waters and lost; their personal histories wiped clean, and material possessions shattered. The catastrophic flood literally had forced them to die to the physical sense of life in order to awaken to a spiritual reality.

In meditation each of us is a Noah taking leave of the past to embark upon a journey of deliverance. And as we prepare to enter the inner sanctuary, quieting the flow of thought-forms rippling across the mind and fearlessly plunge into the bottomless depths of an incorporeal reality, we also are carrying the world with us. For the magnetic field of divine energy infusing the universe has irrevocably bound us to every other living being. The ark of our God awareness is a Noah refuge riding above the waves of life with its precious cargo—humanity and the planet—safely sheltered inside. And as we disembark from the voyage and are anchored back in physicality again, we emerge from the watery depths of Spirit not only purified but also endowed with new perspective, purged of former failings and ready to scatter the seeds of higher understanding in the earth. Inwardly a multihued rainbow appears to mark the event formed by the seven colors of the seven chakras. The kundalini life force has reawakened inside the body signaling the eternal promise that our world, individually and collectively, is both purposeful and blessed.

Ark of the Covenant
ﻌ

> . . . Do stay close to the Ark of the Covenant which is within thee; knowing the Father, the Son, the Holy Ghost must move within and through thee if ye would bring thyself closer to the fullness of thy purposes in the earth.   5177-1

A second historically significant ark with an outsized influence on humanity's spiritual destiny also represents the interior movement toward our God. Since the time of Moses, the legendary Ark of the Covenant with its tablets of chiseled stone has intrigued historians and scholars and given birth to a majority of the dominant Judeo-Christian beliefs and traditions still followed today. Constructed by way of divine guidance to house the Ten Commandments, this precious vessel carried on poles and veiled from sight by a special tent made of skins and cloth, led the wayfaring Hebrews through the desert for forty years.

The Ark of the Covenant's somewhat fractured history in the Old

Testament depicts it moving from place to place until finally coming to rest at the Holy of Holies in Solomon's temple. There it remains until the Babylonian conquest when an unidentified abductor seizes the sacred object and it disappears from history. While many still search the world over for the remains of a tangible ark (and there is little doubt the celebrated container described in Exodus did exist), its spiritual meaning extends far beyond any material value the item might convey as a religious icon. The ancient box constructed according to sacred principles and numbers, two cubits long and built of shittim wood overlaid with gold, is a totem for what lives inside of us. In fact, during one reading Edgar Cayce rhetorically asked why upon the return of the Hebrews to Jerusalem from exile so little consideration was given to the location of the Ark of the Covenant, especially since it was supposed to have been housed in the Holy of Holies forever. His take on the subject suggests the need for a radical reorientation of thought about the subject. " . . . It had *not* been destroyed, and was not destroyed, nor removed, until the Prince of Peace came, wherein there was the declaration that 'neither in this city nor in this mountain, but in the hearts of men' will there be the meeting in the Holy of Holies," (1000–14) affirms Cayce.

Carried down from the mountaintop transporting the word of God, the Ark of the Covenant embodied a supernatural unseen power and served as the vehicle that would guide the Israelites to their freedom. So, too, do the promptings received from the holy mount of our raised consciousness create an ark of the sacred word, leading the lost souls wandering a desert of materiality into the promised land of illumination and spiritual harmony. As we sit in a state of alert presence, having left the Egypt of earthly concerns behind and enter the sacred space of the inner holy of holies, we find it there, fulfilling a promise made thousands of years ago. " . . . I will put my law in their inward parts, and write it in their hearts; and will be their God, and they shall be my people," (Jer. 31:33) pronounced the prophet Jeremiah who had predicted the demise of the visible Ark of the Covenant. "They shall say no more, The ark of the covenant of the Lord: neither shall it come to mind: neither shall they remember it; neither shall they visit it; neither shall that be done any more." (Jer. 3:16) Jeremiah was describing the new covenant between Yahweh and His people, created "not according to the covenant that I made with their fathers in the day that I took them by the hand to bring them out of the land of Egypt," (Jer. 31:32) but the placement of divine law in the intangible ark of the soul.

While the idea of someday discovering the actual Ark of the Covenant is fascinating and it no doubt would be thrilling to exhume what is left of the ancient wood, feeling its rough splinters graze our hands, even such a momentous find could not bring us any closer to God than we already are. As significant as the celebrated box may be as an archeological treasure and religious symbol venerated by millions of devout believers everywhere, the material Ark has been supplanted by its spiritual counterpart: the spirit of God housed within. And through the act of meditation we, too, become members of the tribe of Levi, donning the unspotted robes of that ancient priestly caste charged with bearing up the sacred tabernacle of the hallowed word and whose sole inheritance is the Lord God of Israel. (Deut. 18:2)

Chapter 17
Nations Shall Be Blessed

And I will make thy seed to multiply as the stars of heaven, and will give unto thy seed all these countries; and in thy seed shall all the nations of the earth be blessed. Gen. 26:4

As we move from object consciousness to space consciousness in meditation, attuning ourselves to the divine and activating the Christ pattern imprinted on the soul, we are merging with the universal Creative Forces. Edgar Cayce describes this reunification of soul to Source as similar to a beam of light, which radiates from the sun but by its very nature remains a feature of the daystar out of which it emanated. Like a hologram the gleaming ray embodies all the attributes of the entire sun due to its indivisibility with its source. " . . . Not only God is God . . . ," the readings tell us " . . . for self is a portion of that Oneness . . . " (900-181) This defines our true nature: as a light that does not end but " . . . lives on and on, until it becomes one in essence with the source of light . . . " (136–83)

The idea gains even more credence when considered from the standpoint of the limitless soul. "The entity knows innately the *relationship* of the soul . . . with infinity; the relationship of infinity to each entity . . . ," the Cayce material explains. " . . . For every spark of light, whether in the spiritual, the mental, or the material sense, must have its inception in infinity." (877-26) Moreover, Reading 136–83 asserts that the repercussions of a single soul moving from " . . . sphere to sphere . . . " seeking its way home via the humble act of meditation—"to the face of the Creator, . . . the first cause, the all infusible force as is manifest . . . "—are cosmic in their proportions. God contact not only transforms us, it transforms the world.

The effects of one touch of the Christ, one moment of contact with our Source, are incalculable. For this flowering of human consciousness will spread the seeds of spiritual understanding far and wide until they bless every nation and corner of the globe. Whenever we touch the ineffable Spirit housed inside the body–temple and open out a way for the "imprisoned splendor [to] escape,"[44] a tiny grain of God awareness takes root and begins to blossom in the sensate world, ordaining the illumined soul " . . . a song of glory to its maker . . . " (1089-3) Such was the experience of the virgin mother who, when the seed of divinity implanted within her quickened and she conceived of the Christ idea, exclaimed, "My soul doth magnify the Lord, and my spirit hath rejoiced in God my Saviour." (Luke 1:46–47) Paradoxically the savior she lauded was not something separate and apart from herself but a hidden aspect of Mary's own being. Her realization of the invisible Christ spirit was going to gestate and blossom forth from the inmost recesses of her soul. Eventually its fruitage would multiply to cover the earth.

Just like Moses coming face to face with the divine fire, when we awaken to our true identity in the realization "I am that I am" we are re-formed. The "I" in the midst of us is the eternal principle the Master disclosed when he said before Abraham was "I am" had existed. (John 8:58) It is the wisdom King Solomon revealed—the mysterious, forbidden password whispered into the ears of initiates and spoken

---

[44]Robert Browning, *Paracelsus.*

aloud only by the temple high priests. The presence of God within, the divine "I," is the wellspring of freedom, joy, and healing Jesus the Christ revealed to the suffering masses enslaved by their fleshly ills and limited perspectives. "I" will not leave you comfortless he had told his followers because the Spirit of God is ever present and available to all. The Master's enigmatic aphorism, "I am with you always, even unto the end of the world," (Matt. 28:20) spoke to the omnipresence of this "I," the Christ-self, which will never leave nor forsake the children of God because it is the essence of their very being.

Promised Land
⊰⊱

Behold my servant, whom I uphold; mine elect, in whom my soul delighteth; I have put my spirit upon him. Is. 42:1

The experience of reuniting with our Source is both a touchstone and the catalyst for a substantially different way of living. God contact restores the lost years of the locust and rebuilds lives, allowing the prodigal soul debased by years of eating with the swine to begin anew washed clean in the fountain of living waters Jesus had promised would never run dry. Recognition of the sacred "I am" means we can stop the desperate search for security in dollars and armaments and realize our protection flows out from an inner source fed from the wellspring of Spirit. "Not by might, nor by power, but by my spirit saith the Lord of hosts" to the prophet Zechariah. (Zech. 4:6) "Put up thy sword," (John 18:11) be still and trust, repeated the Master to his disciples reinforcing his instructions to keep relying on the same unseen presence and inner storehouse he accessed every day. God in the midst of us is the pole star by which the lost souls will safely navigate the shoals of life and find their way home again.

Once we finally grab hold of this concept and no longer feel the need to act out the role of petulant children roving a troubled world living by the sweat of our brow, we become a blessing rather than a burden to others. A life sustained by an inner connection to the Source is lived at a higher frequency where the soul assumes ascendancy and wisdom reigns. The readings explain that " . . . the more and more each is impelled by that which is intuitive, or the relying upon the soul force within, the greater, the farther, the deeper, the broader, the more constructive may be the result." (792-2) Not only does an individual gain remarkable insight by staying plugged into this galvanizing current of divine energy, he or she also manifests a deep-seated sense of harmony. The Cayce information reiterates that true harmony can come only with the knowledge of His peace abiding ever with us; " . . . for with His peace there comes contentment, no matter what may be the vicissitudes of life . . . " And though trials may arise in both the mental and material conditions to test us, " . . . all is well with those who have made Him the ideal . . . " (451-2)

In addition, making our contact unveils heretofore unknown realms before our eyes. A land as far as the spiritual eye can see is now ours, fulfilling a promise made to Moses in the book of Exodus: "And I will bring you in unto the land, concerning the which I did swear to give it to Abraham, to Isaac, and to Jacob; and I will give it you for an heritage: I am the Lord." (Exod. 6:8) This statement, the nucleus of untold problems among warring factions in the Middle East, represents much more than a divine impartation to the Hebrew people permitting them to put their stake in the ground by seizing a piece of real estate. Lost among the centuries of zealous pronouncements about ownership rights and bloody military campaigns to lay claim to God's special acreage is the deeper esoteric meaning and intent of the message Moses received.

Attaining God's Promised Land was never intended as merely securing the deed to an unstable clump of dirt vulnerable to occupying invaders and natural disasters that could swallow it up in the twinkling of an eye. No, it reflects a profoundly spiritual idea. True fulfillment of the divine promise to provide a holy landing site for the people of God refers to an unseen estate and eternal domain. For the avowed land "flowing with milk and honey" refers to a new state of consciousness, and the covenant made with the Israelites, the people of God, the promise to lay a kingdom of spiritual treasures at their feet.

Spiritual Bounty
ﰦ

Blessed is the nation whose God is the Lord; and the people whom he hath chosen for his own inheritance. Psalm 33:12

The riches harvested from this Promised Land are the fruits of the spirit. And the Tree of Life flourishing in the soil of an enlightened consciousness is what yields this bounty. A feeling of the presence of power, beauty, patience, and kindness identifies the holy landscape Yahweh bequeathed to his people according to the Cayce information, " . . . and, as the complement to same, brotherly love, understanding, the awareness of strength, the awareness of continuity of thought, of life, of hope . . . " (2533-7) The attributes of a Christ bloom in abundance in the land we inherited from our forefathers Abraham, Isaac, and Jacob who first marked the boundaries of a new nation of believers in the one God.

Further, Edgar Cayce calls these fruits of the spirit ready evidence of a divine energy and intelligence continuously infiltrating the third dimension, which is the terrain the children of God now occupy. He explains that whenever we manifest those qualities or recognize them in another, we are witnessing the infinite " . . . penetrating, or inter-penetrating the activities of all forces of matter . . . " The eternal animating principle of life is forever pushing into this plane of existence, and as it does " . . . the finite becomes conscious of same," (262-52) confirming the promise made in Leviticus: "And I will walk among you, and will be your God, and ye shall be my people." (Lev. 26:12) The same Spirit, which provided direction and sustenance for forty years to a motley group of Hebraic nomads roaming the wilderness of their own unknowingness, permeates the earth today. And just as Moses opened up the way for life-giving waters to bubble up from a desert rock, we, too, may tap into this vital force to quench the spiritual thirst of a waiting world.

Spirit is nigh and eternally available to all, and the Cayce readings encourage us to go through life paying close attention to that invisible reality. For it takes only one tiny David's pebble of spiritual understanding to cause a towering giant of material thinking to fall. This is how we slay the Goliath of duality that has frightened us into believing brute physical force is always more powerful than the shadowy presence of a silent, intangible Spirit. The readings' advice is to depend more upon the intuitive forces welling up from inside the soul rather than hew to outside influences. "Learn to trust the still small voice within," they instruct, for it will not lead you astray. Remember the lesson the prophet Elijah learned. God was not in the storm or the lightening or in any noise or external distraction, but in a stir as hushed as a butterfly's wing. Whispers from the divine are what should impel all of our human endeavors.

Again and again the readings reiterate that one's outer life and immediate circumstances, high or low, carry little weight in the grand scheme of the universe. From the perspective of the Cayce philosophy success " . . . is not those who seek to do some great deed, or to arouse some throng to such an activity as to revolutionize . . . ," (2173-1) but those who stay mindful of what the soul discloses. For that is staying close to God. Maintaining a listening attitude and open ear is the magnetic needle that will keep us on track tirelessly advancing toward the true north of our spiritual ideal. Cayce notes that by taking this tack we will not become " . . . one as adrift, pulled hither and yon by the various calls and cries of those who would give of this world's pleasure in fame, fortune, or what not . . . " (239-1) The readings encourage us never to allow celebrity, material riches, or any other earthly trifle to become our raison d'être, but to let those tokens be the outcome of time spent heeding the divine impulses from within.

Saint or Frankenstein

For, know that each soul constantly meets its own self. No problem may be run away from. *Meet it now!*   1204-3

Those who have touched the presence of God are remolded, and something far greater than the mundane constructs of the human mind now guides them. These are the faithful stewards Jesus predicted the lord of the house would make rulers over all he had. (Luke 12:42–44) Cayce asserts that as we trust in the divinity found within, " . . . there may be given thee those things that have been thy experience from the foundations of the earth." (1286-1) God in the midst of us is mighty and a conscious realization of one's unity with this Creative Force can lift a person to unimagined heights. The humble are exalted and the least among us become the greatest. But those who receive divine impartations and develop psychic powers also bear an enormous responsibility and have a critical choice to make. They can apply their gifts to assist others—become a saint—or use them for purely selfish motives and turn into a Frankenstein.

Whether human beings realize it or not, we are, as the poets allege, made of stardust, born of cosmic forces and integral components of the universal divine purpose and plan. Edgar Cayce urges us to keep in mind that we are part and parcel of the eternal consciousness of God and as such are a portion of everything held within that omnipresent awareness, including the stars, the planets, the sun, and the moon. " . . . Do ye rule them or they rule thee? . . . " the readings ask, before proceeding to assure us that these " . . . were made for thy own use, as an individual—yea, that is the part, the thought thy Maker, thy Father–God thinks of thee." (2794-3) Spirit recognizes each soul as itself, meaning every individual has boundless potential locked up inside him or her. And we are the ones responsible for opening the floodgates to release this dammed-up capacity by interacting with our neighbors either as a blessing or a curse. The purpose of attaining an enlightened state of consciousness is to never pursue selfish ends. Worshipping the false god of egoism by placing self between the sun of the soul and others obstructs the light of God and casts a shadow, which prevents the healing warmth of the "Son" from reaching a world trembling in pain and darkness.

Since the beginning of time the misuse of one's spiritual gifts for personal gain has left a trail of human suffering on a massive scale. Experience has shown that people whose sole desire is to devour and dominate rather than humbly honor the divinity extant in all creation carry the DNA of potential monsters. The history books are filled with the names of notorious despots fueled by hate, greed, and lust who misused their lights to manipulate, grab at power, and subdue others. Oppressing the weak and brutally forcing events to go their way, these tyrants have tortured and killed millions. The poet Shakespeare regularly evoked this theme in his dramas by portraying the tragic consequences of clever people who perverted their soul faculties in order to feed mad ambition. On a smaller but no less horrifying scale, charismatic but corrupt religious leaders continue to profane the divine fire of illumination by using it to inflate both their egos and their bank accounts. Unbridled self-seeking has turned these "pastors" into autocrats who seduce the naïve, wield the law like a cudgel, and defile innocent victims through sadistic cults and mind control. And they do it all in the name of God.

Choose Ye This Day
ᢙᢀ

> For as thoughts are things, and as their currents run into the ex-
> perience of individuals, they shape lives and activities so that they
> become miracles or crimes in the experiences of others as they
> mete them in their associations with their fellow men.   1472-1

As within, so without, the mystics aver. And the greatest among them, Jesus of Nazareth, went even further with these words in the Gospel of Mark: "That which cometh out of the man, that defileth the man." (Mark 7:20) What emanates from inside us matters mightily, and every thought we think and action we perform weighs heavily on the soul because it is either helping or hindering the process of spiritual evolution. Nothing that occurs in the universe is lost or goes unnoticed, and one with God is a majority. The choices made daily about whether to use our soul faculties in service to the good of the whole (that which is holy) or indulge in a personal sense of self have sweeping consequences, which ultimately affect the totality of the created world, including ourselves.

"Choose you this day whom ye will serve," proclaims the book of Joshua 24:15, confirming a core religious tenet. Again and again the Cayce readings assert that it behooves us to choose wisely, for success in life is going to be gauged against the standard of love and not calculated by material measures. "It is not that which causes the uprising or the tumult or the shout, nor the voice of the trumpets for the mighty, that brings accomplishment within one's own self . . . ," they proclaim. (1641-1) Luckily the readings also mention that any honest attempt on our parts to try to do the right thing is sufficient: "For we grow in grace by applying grace and mercy—and in understanding as we try to understand. For it is the try, the attempt, that is the righteousness of man . . . " (1598-1) The admonition is to hold fast to our ideal and bear in mind that whatever esoteric knowledge is brought to our remembrance arrives there purely for the purposes of soul development. It is given to us so that we may glorify the Father through the Son.

We are the sons and daughters now, yet have no right to assume the status of legitimate offspring of a benevolent Father/Mother God—heir to all the heavenly riches—and at the same time use our portion of that spiritual birthright to harm other members of the divine family. Some of our brothers and sisters truly are innocents, unschooled, or mentally incapable of understanding and thus are unaware of the deeper spiritual truths. Neophytes and the ignorant, who, through no fault of their own, remain fast asleep and "know not what they do" (Luke 23:34), are blameless. But those who have caught even the tiniest glimpse of the light, no matter how dim, no longer can feign ignorance. "All knowledge is to be used in the manner that will give help and assistance to others, and the desire is that the laws of the Creator be manifested in the physical world . . . ," states one pointed reading. (254-17) We, the illuminated ones, are responsible for what is sown in this earth with our divine potential and are destined to reap the harvest of good or ill germinated from the seeds we have planted lifetime after lifetime.

Incredulously the good news is that at this moment we have access to all the wisdom necessary not only to avoid turning into a Frankenstein but to also become another Christ light to the world. Deep down we know who we are. The spirit of God, the Messiah, was established in us in the beginning, and through inner discernment we have the ability to release this deliverer. Such knowledge is not far off, neither is it hidden away from anyone who sincerely desires to find it states Deuteronomy 30—a favorite chapter of the Bible frequently recommended by Edgar Cayce:

> It is not in heaven, that thou shouldest say, Who shall go up for us to heaven, and bring it unto us, that we may hear it, and do it? Neither is it beyond the sea, that thou shouldest say, Who shall go over the sea for us, and bring it unto us, that we may hear it, and do it? But the word is very nigh unto thee, in thy mouth, and in thy heart, that thou mayest do it. See, I have set before thee this day life and good, and death and evil; In that I command thee this day to love the LORD thy God, to walk in his ways, and to keep

his commandments and his statutes and his judgments, that thou mayest live and multiply: and the Lᴏʀᴅ thy God shall bless thee in the land whither thou goest to possess it. Deut. 30:12-16

Out of Many, One

I and my Father are one. John 10:30

The big lie of the ego, the lie of duality, is that each one of us is locked up inside a world of our own, detached from everyone else experiencing this plane of existence. But dualism and separation are not the reality; Oneness is. The revelation of man's indivisible unity with the Almighty first revealed to Moses is still intoned by Jews everywhere in the words of their daily prayer, the Shema Yisrael, which expresses it this way: "Hear, O Israel: The Lord our God is one Lord." (Deut. 6:4) There is but one omnipresent divine force moving in and through every fractal of the universe. The entire cosmos is a web of interconnectedness and this earthly experience but a single aspect of an integrated spiritual "ecosystem" where each element is fulfilling its unique role and function in the expansion of consciousness. The process will continue to unfold and advance in an ascending spiral as the soul on its journey homeward rises ever higher in awareness until it closes the circuit broken in Eden and becomes a fitting companion to the Creator.

Oneness is the constant shibboleth of the Edgar Cayce philosophy. The readings emphasize a collective purpose for the human race and speak to the unbreakable bonds binding us together soul to soul. We are unique facets of the divine totality, and like dropping a pebble into a calm lake, whatever we think and do—whatever is released into the all-pervasive energy field we occupy—moves outward from the soul in an uninterrupted stream of ever-widening circles of influence to affect the universe of souls. The people with whom we regularly interact during the course of our day will probably feel its impact most acutely. But no meeting is by chance according to the readings. In reality every person who shows up in our lives has arrived there for a predetermined metaphysical purpose—no matter how insignificant the particular incident may appear at the time. They point out that " . . . the relationships, the meetings with others in whatever form or manner, such are not coincidental but are rather as purposeful experiences." (1722-1)

Included among that cross section of purposeful experiences are the close friendships we have formed and nurtured. The readings emphasize that friendships are actually the renewing of former purposes and ideals, (2946-2) and further define these relationships as " . . . necessary in the experiences of others, though they may not always use their opportunities in a spiritual way or manner." (2751-1) In response to a question someone posed about what friends are, Cayce indicated that such associations exist to help the soul progress through " . . . the testing of our own abilities, as to that application of truth related to the divine and to mental reaction in relationship one to another." (2772-5)

During the span of a single lifetime, some people who cross our paths we will love dearly and long to see again; others we may be hard-pressed to tolerate. Those predisposed to physical and emotional brutality may choose to inflict pain, wreaking violence on us and collateral damage on the unsuspecting bystanders. A host of colorful characters appears on stage with us during the unfolding drama of our life stories, and each of these actors plays a unique role in our awakening. The readings maintain that the primary reason we find ourselves mired in a specific set of circumstances with any other individual is to achieve the mutually agreed-upon goal of soul growth—a compact made by both parties before incarnating together at this juncture in time.

My Brother's Keeper
ശ

> In the urges, then keep in that way ever of being a channel through which the greater amount of good may come to all, being—as the Master Himself—all things to all people; tempted in all points like each soul and yet without offense to any.   3395-2

"Am I my brother's keeper?" Cain asked his God in the book of Genesis 4:9. The answer was yes because the foundational connection Cain shared with his sibling Abel was much closer and more impenetrable than any blood tie. The children of the Most High, created of God stuff, collectively constitute an indivisible spiritual unity—the body of the Christ. This makes each of us explicitly accountable for the attitudes we project and the actions we take, which affect that body. Trying to make excuses or justify our deeds is pointless because the Law of One is perpetually in operation and dwarfs every other rule. This law rigorously applies even when we are unaware of having physically, mentally, or emotionally touched another person because the moment of contact passed so swiftly it never registered on the mind. " . . . And ye change each soul ye contact, literally or mentally—insofar as ye, as an individual entity, are a witness for or against the Lord, thy God . . . ," affirms Cayce. He then goes on to say that " . . . No soul may come in contact with the entity without being changed, either in body, in mind or in purpose. And purpose is, of course, of the soul." (2794-3)

Oneness is why the Master taught us to pray for our enemies because within the framework of the whole there can be no enemies, and why Edgar Cayce maintains that peace will finally flourish in the earth. Peace and harmony flow out from the inner pool of tranquility reached through our meditation practice, and those healing waters, fed from an inexhaustible inner supply, sooner or later must spill out into the world. The choice is always ours whether or not we will add peace to human affairs. The readings elaborate with this clear directive. " . . . Peace must begin within self before there may be the activity or the application of self in such a manner as to bring peace in thy own household, in thine own heart, in thine own vicinity, in thine own state or nation . . . " (3976-28) The transmission of spiritual energy communicates instantaneously over a network faster than the Internet and in a language more formidable than words.

Edgar Cayce insists that consciousness is the key and everything expressed by or through us is building the world we experience and share together. " . . . When there is trouble, doubt or fear," he suggests, "the greater portion lies within thy own consciousness. If you would have others show themselves lovely, be lovely yourself! If you would have friends, be friendly! . . . " The readings contend that for us to engender more harmony in any phase of this earthly existence it must first be lived, conceived, born, and reared within our own consciousness (1002-1) for that is the cardinal factor in determining the authority we project and effect we have on those around us. "Thus there may be light; not by preaching in thy experience, not by the lording over others, but rather by *being* that which has been indicated in the experiences of each," (2533-7) the readings counsel.

If the quality of our consciousness is what creates our experiences and governs our interpersonal relationships, then it is imperative to pay close attention to the intangible energies we are continuously broadcasting outward. In one instance Cayce commented on the duty of every soul to take responsibility for its conduct and bearing while speaking with a client who carried the vibrations of the planet Jupiter about her. Referencing how much sway the woman could have on others, he said it would not matter whether she ended up working as a secretary, keeping a home, or traveling around the world, her mere presence would affect untold numbers of people. "For *all* are changed by contacting the entity. Hence it behooves the entity to realize the influence it has upon those even it meets in passing." (1669-1) Thus do we also—daily and powerfully—impact family, friend, and so-called foe.

The reverse side of the coin and reason for genuine optimism is that those who make the concerted effort to know God aright and succeed in achieving their spiritual freedom, attain it for the world. Cayce exhorts each of us to do our part, for all are destined to enter the heavenly estate on the arm of someone they have helped along the way. " . . . For if the Lord is One and ye are one with Him," the readings explain, "then it is as the current runs; or thy oneness with Him, as to the extent of thy ability to guide, direct, or to encourage those who are weak or lost in confusion of the times . . . " (792-2) Likewise, the truth of Oneness means that no one can be "saved" or freed from the consequences of Adam and Eve's descent into the illusion of duality until the totality of creation has been rescued. And we are intrinsic pieces in solving that puzzle.

The readings are very clear about why we are in our current situation having a human experience: to help every soul find the way back to its Source by becoming a savior of some other soul. (1472-3) " . . . *He* came, the Master, in flesh and blood, even as thou didst come in flesh and blood . . . ," states Cayce, adding that the Son of Man proclaimed that the ability to become illumined with power from on high is " . . . *within* thine own body to will! . . . " (1152-1) The Master has chosen us as messengers and lights so that in the hours of disturbance and stress " . . . ye may give that strength, that blessing to others in His name. For, remember, as has been given, 'Jesus we know. Paul we know. Who are ye, speaking in the name of?'" (2533-7)

Happily the Master also assured us that although fulfilling the role
of liberator demands unwavering vigilance and dedication—following
the straight and narrow way—it is well within our reach. But according
to Edgar Cayce, the process of finding and staying on the path to freedom also demands enormous amounts of patience on our parts. " . . .
Let thy light shine where ye are! Be ye not impatient . . . ," advises one
insightful reading. (254-85) The new consciousness taking root from the
invisible seed of God contact matures gradually with every small step
forward, line upon line and precept upon precept, until it ripens to bear
fruitage for the world. Pilgrims on the pathway home make the greatest
strides by inexorably placing one foot in front of the other and calmly
picking themselves up to try again whenever they falter or fall during
the uphill climb. With boundless fortitude and unfailing patience, the
true seeker will overcome inner resistance and the gravitational pull of
heavy, earthbound thinking to ascend the heights and awaken.

A Little Leaven
ﾟ

> *Lord, Let me fill that place in the lives of others as thou hast given and do*
> *give the opportunity in such measures and such manners that others may*
> *come to know that life is of thee, in thee.*   1823-1

The message Jesus disclosed during the days he spent on earth as a
spiritual mentor and teacher was one of unbridled hope and promise
about the prospects of human beings achieving their freedom to redeem not only themselves but also their brothers and sisters. A brief
parable found in the Gospel of Matthew confirms his understanding of
the common destiny of humanity. "The kingdom of heaven is like unto
leaven, which a woman took, and hid in three measures of meal, till the
whole was leavened," he told his disciples. (Matt. 13:33) One tiny trace
of the Christ released from its entombment in matter and added to the
mix metathesizes to transform the whole. Be as perfect as I am perfect
was the exhortation this great teacher left behind for his students since
they, too, had the capacity to become a Christ light to others. The Cayce
information comments further on the part we all play in the advance-
ment of consciousness: "It is as the leaven, as He gave. Not that there

is to be sounded a cymbal or a drum, or a laudation of any character, but rather in meekness, in gentleness, *live* that influence! . . . Let that leaven as of the Father-God manifested in the Christ work in the heart, the mind, of those ye meet day by day!" (2533-7)

God is of no avail to the human race except where God is realized, and in the end what matters most is the degree to which the Christ spirit has risen in us. Through inner attunement and the power of the Christ consciousness active in our lives, we, too, can begin to know a love and peace passing all understanding. And while for many this idea may strike them as only a myth or impossible dream—something aspirational and merely hoped for but well out of reach—for those who have " . . . tasted of the joys of the personal contact with those influences within the soul, it may come to be His power working within." (255-12) Spirit is moving in the earth; the promise of freedom beckons and the power of divine grace and mercy is ours. It is up to us to determine how we will use it.

Chapter 18
Servant of All:
Application

He that findeth his life shall lose it: and
he that loseth his life for my sake shall
find it. Matt. 10:39

One of the central tenets of the Edgar Cayce readings is that every soul is expected to *do* something with the knowledge it has acquired. We are not supposed to rest on our spiritual laurels, content with how much we think we understand. The mandate is to utilize whatever we have received in order to manifest one fundamental truth: God with us. " . . . For it is, as He has given, not the knowledge alone but the practical application—in thine daily experience with thy fellow man—that counts . . .," instructs one incisive reading. (922-1) In a related text Cayce maintains that the purpose of life is " . . . not the gratifying of appetites nor of any selfish desires, but it is that the entity, the soul, may make the earth, where the entity finds its consciousness, a better place in which to live" (4047-2) Further, the assertion is that until we are willing to lose ourselves in service, " . . . ye may not indeed know that peace which He has promised to give—to all." (1599-1)

The summons to act is the message Jesus conveyed when at the tender age of twelve he asked his parents, "How is it that ye sought me? wist ye not that I must be about my Father's business?" (Luke 2:49) According to the Cayce material, there are no shortcuts to knowledge, wisdom, and understanding; these must be *lived* and experienced by each and every soul. The directive is to get up and do. " . . . Nothing grows, nothing remains alone unless dead. A mind, a body that sits alone and considers the outside and never turning that within to the out, nor that without from within, soon finds *drosses* setting up in the system; for development is change . . . ," explains Cayce, adding that change is the activity of knowledge from within. " . . . Learn to *live*! Then there *is* no death, save the transition, when desired . . . " (900-465)

The unceasing demand is to keep developing for as long as we draw breath; keep pressing forward by applying the knowledge we have gained to contribute to the welfare of the whole. The readings describe application as indispensable to successfully fulfilling the purpose for which a soul enters the material plane. The basic rule of thumb is that the application of self through the influence of the will is the deter-minative factor by which the children of God either " . . . develop or retard in the earthly experience." (97-2) "Hear, O Israel, The Lord our God is one . . . " (Deut. 6:4) was the divine invocation imparted to the Hebrews. Accepting this omnipresent, unifying force as our sole reality means we are walking together on the path back to the heavenly estate, and as Edgar Cayce so emphatically points out, will reenter paradise on the arm of someone we have helped along the way. Never be afraid of giving self in a service the readings decree. If the purpose of serving is to allow " . . . the glory of truth . . . " to manifest, *"spend it all*—whether self, mind, body, or the worldly means—whether in labor or in the coin of the realm . . . " (1957-1)

Do Thou Likewise
༒

. . . For the greater individual is the one who is the servant to all.
And to conquer self is greater than taking many cities . . . 3253-2

During the Last Supper when Jesus stooped down and kneeled before his disciples to wash their feet, he marked the dawning of a new
age in the spiritual evolution of humankind. This simple act represented
a sublime moment and crowning achievement in the Master's ministry
as he mirrored for his closest circle of students—the ones who had followed him up and down the dusty roads of Judea for three eventful
years—one final, unmistakable lesson about the absolute relationship
between God and man. Edgar Cayce comments on the far-reaching implications of Jesus' actions and demeanor that evening: "The next period
we find in the upper chamber with the disciples, and the humbleness
that was manifested. Though He was their leader, their prophet, their
Lord, their Master, He signified—through the humbleness of the act—the
attitude to which each would come if he would know that true relationship with his God, his fellow man." (5749-10)

The meekness and quiet diligence of the Master in performing his
task signaled once and for all that the God human beings had long
revered as a deity located somewhere out in the cosmos actually was
close at hand. And it would present itself to them in the faces of their
brothers and sisters, including those who held even the lowliest of sta-
tions. Worship of the Almighty no longer meant complying with the
external trappings and hierarchical structures of religious sects and
institutions or making loud demonstrations of prayer and praise, but
humble service to others—by honoring the God *in* man.

The Gospel of John depicts the apostle Peter, outspoken as always,
seated at the table and adamantly refusing the ministrations of his
Lord, whom by that time he surely must have considered a god. "Then
cometh he to Simon Peter: and Peter saith unto him, Lord, dost thou
wash my feet? Jesus answered and said unto him, What I do thou
knowest not now; but thou shalt know hereafter. Peter saith unto him,
Thou shalt never wash my feet. Jesus answered him, If I wash thee not,
thou hast no part with me. Simon Peter saith unto him, Lord, not my
feet only, but also my hands and my head." (John 13:6-9) Much like
the impetuous disciple, we, too, at first may resist the silent approach
of the Christ. But in meekness and gratitude not only have a right but
also the duty to accept its cleansing waters and immerse ourselves in
them with the abandon of a Peter. Then in the same spirit the Master exemplified, humbly pour out whatever we have received for the

care and solace of others.

Once Jesus finishes his task, he asks the group if they understand what he has done. "Ye call me Master and Lord: and ye say well; for so I am," he noted. "If I then, your Lord and Master, have washed your feet; ye also ought to wash one another's feet. For I have given you an example that ye should do as I have done to you." He concludes the lesson by reminding his initiates that although they may receive divine impartations and someday be able to demonstrate enough mastery over the physical realm to rule material forces as he did, they were to keep their egos in check and simply continue serving. "The servant is not greater than his lord; neither he that is sent greater than he that sent him. If ye know these things, happy are ye if ye do them," Jesus instructed. (John 13:13–17)

The themes of humility and loving service had cropped up many times during the weeks and months the Master and his followers roamed the countryside together. In one instance the rabbi and his apostles were on their way to Capernaum when Jesus heard the men arguing amongst themselves. Once the group had reached its destination, he inquired of the twelve, "What was it that ye disputed among yourselves by the way?" Embarrassed, the disciples initially hold their peace because " . . . they had disputed among themselves, who should be the greatest," recounts the Gospel of Mark. "And he sat down, and called the twelve, and saith unto them, If any man desire to be first, the same shall be last of all, and servant of all." (Mark 9:33–35)

Ripening Fields

> Then, be up and doing; knowing that the day approaches when there must be given that opportunity for a service in His name . . .
>
> 2673-1

The approach to service promulgated by the Edgar Cayce readings parallels Jesus' appeal to his disciples when he called upon them to labor in the fields and gather in the heavenly harvest, bringing hope and comfort to the lost sheep. Matthew's gospel tells the story. "But when he saw the multitudes, he was moved with compassion on them, because they fainted, and were scattered abroad, as sheep having no shepherd. Then saith he unto his disciples, The harvest truly is plenteous, but the labourers are few; Pray ye therefore the Lord of the harvest, that he will send forth labourers into his harvest." (Matt. 9:36-38) Contrary to many popular religious interpretations of this particular biblical passage, the Master's words were not meant as a license for pious zealots to start proselytizing about their personal religious convictions. Jesus was not out to recruit believers either in the cult of his personality or in a new theology; he was out to recruit workers. And the job requirements were strenuous. He was asking a dedicated number to accept responsibility for raising their consciousness and living life in an entirely different manner from previous modes of thinking and acting. These were the elect he was counting on to remake the earth "as it is in heaven." (Matt. 6:10)

Their teacher was turning over to his students the task of sustaining and sanctifying every element of the created world. And adherents of his Word would glean the spiritual harvest he envisioned with each decision made to love and unite instead of divide. "Take what you have learned from me and use it" was the message of the Christ and such was its challenge—a challenge to this day most people still refuse to fully embrace. Because by accepting responsibility for one's innate divinity and the moral imperative to become stewards of the whole requires living a life that no longer belongs to us. It is the will of the One alone that matters and must be done.

By Their Fruits
☙

> ... Give unto self that worthy, acceptable period of service, for in service to others is lending to that Creative Energy that makes or destroys lives ...   2497-3

Several times during Jesus' three-year ministry the lowly fig tree took the spotlight and on at least two occasions he used it as a metaphor to convey an important rule of living to his students. They must give back. Edgar Cayce articulated the principle this way: " ... Learn, or teach, or train the body—not only to be good, but be good *for* something ... " (53-

1) The Master had employed the analogy of a fruit tree to underscore a central precept of his teaching: Give. Generously offer the spiritual bounty germinated in the sacred soil of your own consciousness to nourish a waiting world.

One morning Jesus was hungry and noticed a fig tree growing by the side of the road. Yet upon moving closer he realized that although leaves sprouted from the branches, no figs were growing on it. Not one to let a teachable moment pass by, the rabbi quickly denounced the unproductive tree. "Let no fruit grow on thee henceforward for ever. And presently the fig tree withered away. And when the disciples saw it, they marvelled, saying, How soon is the fig tree withered away!" (Matt. 21:18–20) On a separate occasion recorded in the Gospel of Luke, the Master delivered a parable about a man who had planted fig tree in the midst of his vineyard. But when the owner returned sometime later seeking fruit from the tree, found none. So the man went to the vine dresser and complained, declaring that since for three long years they had tried to get figs from his tree and it had not yielded any fruit, they should chop it down. Why encumber the ground with something barren? he asks. The worker importunes his employer, however, to request a little more time. He would like another year to be able to dig around the plant and fertilize it with dung. If the tree remained fruitless after all his efforts, then they would get rid of it. (Luke 13:6–9)

Jesus was imparting a vital spiritual lesson to his disciples pointing to evidence found in the natural world. Like the scorned and sterile fig tree, which satisfies no one's hunger, if they are unproductive and provide nothing of value to others during their lifetimes, the experience on earth is not worth the life energy coursing through them. The spirit of God is of no benefit when the children of the Most High abnegate the duty to bear spiritual fruitage for the world. Souls will not be uprooted or have the circumstances necessary to their growth removed prematurely—women and men will always be afforded the means to develop spiritually—but the divine Creative Forces present and available within each soul must be released and given back. A refusal to offer up something of ourselves to the greater good means the brief span of time spent on this plane might as well be cursed. An opportunity lost.

You shall know the true followers of the Christ by their fruitage, the

Master had told his disciples. "Do men gather grapes of thorns, or figs of thistles?" he asked. (Matt. 7:16) In other words, do not look to gather the fruits of the spirit where they cannot be found. Only a consciousness lifted toward the higher realms is able to water the Tree of Life planted in the midst of the inner garden and produce a spiritual harvest. Jesus goes on to characterize two distinct varieties of trees. "Even so every good tree bringeth forth good fruit; but a corrupt tree bringeth forth evil fruit. A good tree cannot bring forth evil fruit, neither can a corrupt tree bring forth good fruit. Every tree that bringeth not forth good fruit is hewn down, and cast into the fire. Wherefore by their fruits ye shall know them. Not every one that saith unto me, Lord, Lord, shall enter into the kingdom of heaven; but he that doeth the will of my Father which is in heaven." (Matt. 7:17–21)

The fruit from a tree cultivated in an awakened consciousness turned toward the light of the "Son" ripens to multiply good in the earth. The product of a corrupt tree—a consciousness fertilized with self-centered-ness and hate—cannot surrender anything of lasting value and is as useless as a dead piece of wood, chopped down and burnt to ashes. Jesus amplified his message by adding that no one will enter his new kingdom simply by asking to be let in. Admission is predicated on personal application by faithfully following the internal promptings of the still small voice of the soul.

With What Measure
ᶜᵅᵉ⁓

> For it is not altogether true that knowledge is power, but the *ap-plication* of knowledge within the self's experience is power.
>
> 1908-1

Jesus was also referencing the idea of application during an episode related in a couple of the gospels when the sons of Zebedee, James and John, entreat him to give them the choicest seats directly at his right and left hands as he sat in his glory. The men's indiscreet request induces the Master to explain his definition of hierarchy, success, and the honor that accrues from an authentic association with the Christ. "But whosoever will be great among you, shall be your minister: And whosoever of you will be the chiefest, shall be servant of all. For even the Son of man came not to be ministered unto, but to minister, and to give his life a ransom for many." (Mark 10:43–45) Even their teacher Jesus who had overcome every limitation of the corporeal world did not trod this planet just to collect accolades. The Adam soul had incarnated to offer the best of himself to others through service. And while the promised reward was not a high-ranking seat on the fanciful holy throne of heaven, it was greater than anything even his closest disciples could possibly imagine.

"If any man have ears to hear, let him hear," the Master had announced one day to catch his listeners' attention before hammering home a truth about the critical importance of application to the law. " . . . With what measure ye mete, it shall be measured to you: and unto you that hear shall more be given. For he that hath, to him shall be given: and he that hath not, from him shall be taken even that which he hath." (Mark 4:23–25) As we allow the surge of spirit to flow through us and begin fulfilling our unique role and function in the universe, we are riding a wave of harmony. In addition our capabilities increase, reflecting a consciousness drawing substance from its invisible Source.

But when we fail to release the divine energy locked up inside us by obstructing its movement outward into the world, life starts to resemble a stagnant pool severed from the crystalline inlet that once replenished it. Without regular refreshment the water turns brackish until sunlight no longer is able to penetrate the surface and a death spiral begins. All too soon the profusion of living forms inhabiting the pool will begin to die off, erasing every benefit they might have provided the world. With his statement, "from him shall be taken" the Master was signifying that those, who have heard his words (the spiritually affluent who "hath much") yet choose to dam up the life-giving waters of the inner Christ behind a logjam of unoffered gifts, are bound to lose the spiritual faculties they had depended upon. Detached from the fount of life, their creativity will atrophy only to dry up and disappear.

By contrast, serving the Christ in man releases an energy boundless in its potential. Much as the wind which "bloweth where it listeth, and thou hearest the sound thereof, but canst not tell whence it cometh, and whither it goeth . . . ," (John 3:8) the transcendental power hidden behind every act of loving service, while imperceptible to the senses, is nonetheless real. Contact with this invisible force has a multiplier effect, which will manifest in the material world as palpably as the morsels of food the five thousand ate from the five loaves and two small fishes. Jesus was calling attention to the generative impact of this spiritual energy when he remarked, "Verily I say unto you, There is no man that hath left house, or brethren, or sisters, or father, or mother, or wife, or children, or lands, for my sake, and the gospel's, But he shall receive an hundredfold now in this time, houses, and brethren, and sisters, and mothers, and children, and lands." (Mark 10:29-30) Offering others the benefits of what we have received opens up space for more to return to us—heaped up, pressed down, and running over.

Thy Servant
ᬭ

In any field of service where thy hands find work to do, serve—as a message to those that may not justify but glorify God in the Christ.   3292-1

The Edgar Cayce readings clearly articulate the value of application to the progress of every soul on earth and repeatedly draw attention to the fact that there is ample opportunity each day to attend to the needs of those walking alongside us on the road back to the Father's house. Moreover, the unremitting expectation is that the children of God will brighten the circumstances of their divine siblings by lending a helping hand. "What is the choice?" Cayce asks, "That as creates love, hope, faith, patience, kindness, gentleness in the experience . . . " (1992-1)

The readings are emphatic: Manifesting the Christ spirit in order to help illuminate the way for others is the key to a life well spent. Over and over again Cayce reiterates that unless and until a soul, through its words and activities, makes " . . . that corner or place of the world a little better, a little bit more hopeful, a little bit more patient, showing a little more of brotherly love, a little more of kindness, a little more of longsuffering . . . ," the life is a failure, especially as far as growth is concerned. Though we may gain the whole world he contends, " . . . how little ye must think of thyself if ye lose the purpose for which the soul entered this particular sojourn!" (3420-1) Happily one of the primary offshoots of a genuine commitment to the way of life the Master preached is a greater ability to assist those who are stumbling. " . . . Some blindly, some gropingly, some discouraged, some overanxious, some overzealous of their own peculiar twist or turn; yet all seeking—seeking the light." (1301-1)

Granted a life of service is no picnic. It commits one to listening and contentedly following the innermost promptings of the soul—and never doing it for personal gain. Rather true service is an emptying of oneself of all selfish aims and ambitions with a plea to aid others. *"Create within me a perfect mind, O God!"* begins one poignant reading, *"with the desire and the purpose to use my life, my talents, my gifts, in Thy Service!"* (308-6) According to the Cayce material it does not matter whether we are preaching a sermon, working in a factory, entertaining an audience, caring for a family, or leading a nation, each activity should be conducted " . . . with an eye-singleness of *service*, of *joy*, of helpfulness to thy fellow man." (887-3) The great Teacher of teachers provided the pattern and the tools but has left us with the assignment to spend our lives uplifting human consciousness in whatever capacity we may find ourselves.

Not surprisingly the readings also point out that the process of personal application should begin with an honest look inside. Cayce insists that whatever we have to offer must first be found within ourselves before it may be given to others. (3253-2) Equally important is withdrawing any sense of personal judgment by leaving the ego behind and recognizing that the spark of light we carry is not ours but only the tiniest reflection of something much, much greater. No doubt, at some time in the past we also squandered the opportunity to see the light, faltered, and lost our way. As Jesus remarked in the Garden of Gethsemane, the spirit is willing but the flesh is weak. Cayce concedes that even though the divine forces are ever-present working through human circumstances, no one ever completely eludes the siren call of temptation. The blindness of pride and self-indulgence are our constant companions and stand ready to lead us astray. In fact, even the Master who had put on flesh to better understand its desires and urges was confronted with a series of temptations he had to overcome. As we take up our work day by day, the readings caution us to stay alert and remember the strength, influence, force, and power necessary for true service comes by keeping " . . . that trust, that faith in Him . . ." (1301-1)

As children of the one Creative, Living Force we have free will and by virtue of that fact are not robots, but embody the capacity to choose whether or not we will live for self alone or expend our energies doing that which is constructive to the greater good. Cayce alleges that each soul is going to one day " . . . stand as He . . . " before the throne with the deeds done in body and mind " . . . presenting the body–spiritual before that throne of mercy, before that throne of the Maker, the Creator, the God." (5749–6) Thus the constant command is to "Give of thy best to Him" (262-2) by opening heart and mind to the manifold opportunities and glories now awaiting us if we choose to accept them. As we commit to a life of ministering to others, we are taking up the mantle of the Old Testament hero Joshua who confidently declared, "But as for me and my household, we will serve the Lord." (Josh. 24:15)

Individual Purpose

> . . . Each entity enters a material experience for a purpose; not accidentally, not by chance. But life and its expression are purposeful . . .
>   1792-2

The gospels include a parable where Jesus compared the kingdom of heaven to a man preparing to travel to a far country. But before the householder leaves on his trip, he calls together his servants to put a portion of his property into their hands for safekeeping while he is away. The man entrusts five talents to one of his servants, two to another, and a single talent to the third, disbursing them to "every man according to his several ability." Then he departs on his journey. During their master's absence, the servant allotted the five talents uses them to trade and ends up earning five more. Likewise the second servant who had received two talents puts his coins to work and secures another two. But the third servant does something different. The story says he "went and digged in the earth, and hid his lord's money," leaving it underground until the lord of the house returned to square the accounts. (Matt. 25:14-18)

When the servant who received the five talents reports a profit of 100% to his employer, the master commends him saying, "Well done, thou good and faithful servant: thou hast been faithful over a few things, I will make thee ruler over many things: enter thou into the joy of thy lord." The second servant who likewise had doubled his money elicits a similar response. But when the third servant explains that fear had made him hide his lone talent in the ground to avoid losing it, the lord of the house becomes angry, calling the man wicked and slothful. "Thou knewest that I reap where I sowed not, and gather where I have not strawed: Thou oughtest therefore to have put my money to the exchangers, and then at my coming I should have received mine own with usury," the owner scolds. Because the overly cautious servant had done nothing to increase the good he had received, his master proceeds to take his one talent away and present it to the loyal worker who already had ten. Jesus ends his parable with a stinging message. "For unto every one that hath shall be given, and he shall have abundance: but from him that hath not shall be taken away even that which he hath. And cast ye the unprofitable servant into outer darkness: there shall be weeping and gnashing of teeth." (Matt. 25:19–30)

Just as his authoritative words had withered the barren fig tree, the Master once again was warning his students to stay alert to the temptation to stay focused solely on themselves and paralyzed by fear of what they might lose in giving their all. The followers of the Christ way were not to cover up or hoard the spiritual gold—the talents—they had received. They were to increase what had been entrusted to them by faithfully applying it in this dimension. The spirit of God is vibrantly alive in us, and our chief responsibility is to use all the faculties at our disposal both individually and collectively to magnify its presence in the earth. Thus did the readings once warn a seeker that " . . . so great are the abilities of the entity to make of this experience a *glory* for the living God that to fail would be indeed calamitous in the experience of this soul!" (1362-1)

Cayce continually reminds us that we are here on earth for a reason: "Know that the purpose for which each soul enters a material experience is that it may be as a light unto others . . . " As the reading continues, he then confirms that as we sow the seeds of the Spirit through our daily activities, we need never worry about their growth for " . . . *God* giveth the increase. Hence be not weary in well–doing." (641-6) " . . . Man looks upon the things of the day but God looks upon the heart . . . ," state the readings, and whatever we help build in the minds and hearts of others " . . . grows and grows and grows . . . " (3253-2) In sum, if the primary purpose for inhabiting this plane is to serve as a light to our brothers and sisters, we have no business burying that light—or our heads—in the sand.

Lord, Use Me
✎

> To some are given to be teachers, to some are given to be healers, to some are given to be interpreters. Let each, then, do *their* job and their part *well*, *in* the manner as is given *to* them, knowing—in the forces as manifest through them—they become, then, a light in *their* own respective action and field of endeavor . . .   262-1

Every atom in the universe has a reason for being and so do we. " . . . Each soul . . . has a definite job to do. But ye alone may find and do that job!" (2823-1) the readings observe, exhorting us to get in touch with our Source through meditation and determine where our talents lie. They insist that each person must be free to choose the course he or she will pursue in life and that any enterprise we undertake should express the greatest coordination of body, mind, and soul. (2540-1) Cayce implores everyone to do much more than just find a decent job in order to accumulate wealth and build a temporal empire—gaining earthly riches but losing the soul. He once summarized the principle by telling a man to avoid spending " . . . self in making money . . . ," rather to spend money " . . . in making self." (257-13) Another recipient of Cayce's advice heard this powerful affirmation for aligning her consciousness with her soul's sacred mission—

> . . . Let me bear in my body those conditions, circumstances, physical *and* mental, that will bring me wholly closer to an understanding of the purposes for which I came into being; without censure to anyone, without censure to myself, but *use* me as *Thou* seest fit!
> 5640-3

Interestingly the readings also mention that throughout history there have been periods " . . . requiring an individual to be raised up for special service. Many individuals might have filled those positions, yet apparently those individuals and no other . . . " (3183-1) While Cayce acknowledges that these are trying times, he also assure us " . . . there is no one in authority that has not been raised to same by the grace of Creative Forces . . . " By virtue of their abilities as leaders the individuals so selected have been presented with a unique opportunity to express their divine purpose through their relationships and dealings with their fellow man. By the same token it does us no good to spend time comparing our purpose or vocation to what others may be called upon to do. The command to each is to do " . . . that *thou knowest* to be the constructive experience in thy field, and trouble not thy mind or heart as to others. For the very thought of there becoming turmoil is *opening* the way *for* turmoil." (816-10)

Similarly the readings advise us to bear in mind that God is not a respecter of persons as persons, for as the Master once proclaimed, " . . . whosoever shall do the will of my Father which is in heaven, the same is my brother, and sister, and mother." (Matt. 12:50) Because the soul is one with God, our very essence embodies infinite potential and the intrinsic ability to know the truth that " . . . shall set men free, not only from the burdens of the spiritual and the mental but also the material . . . "(3183-1) In Cayce's view, the reason we are present in any phase of activity is to " . . . meet the various problems that have been and are the part of an entity's experience throughout its sojourns in a material consciousness" (3183-1)—and turn those stumbling blocks into the stepping stones to freedom for ourselves and others.

The readings also urge us not to lose heart, professing that while there may be discouragements and periods of anxiety within any given experience, " . . . the very fact that ye are conscious of being in the earth life . . . " indicates that we are in the thought and mind of the Creative Forces. (3333-1) Do not be " . . . too easily discouraged. Brace up! . . . " is their injunction. " . . . *Know* in what ye have believed and do believe, but know *who* is also the *author* of such. For life *is* real, life *is* earnest, and the grave is *not* the goal!" (1792-2) The Cayce philosophy insists we have the ability to accomplish whatever we set our minds to doing as long as we do not place our trust in our own abilities but in " . . . His grace, His power, His might . . . " And while it may be possible to achieve success in this dimension using the talents and wisdom we innately possess, the charge is to act as a channel through which " . . . He, God, the Father, may manifest His power . . . " in whatever enterprise we choose to undertake. (3183–1)

Divine Opportunity

> Know that ye are going through a period of testing. Remain true
> to all that has been committed to thee, and know that each day is
> an opportunity, and an experience . . .   3245-1

We are the sons and daughters of God now, and today presents us with the occasion to act and apply what we know. The readings maintain that no soul enters into this sphere without opportunities. " . . . And the choice is ever latent within self and the power, the ability to do things, be things, to accept things, is with the entity." (3226–1) Cayce continually reminds us that the sojourn on earth is the natural outgrowth of the soul's evolution, and our mandate is to recognize in every soul, as well as in ourselves, those possibilities, opportunities, duties, and obligations " . . . that are a portion of each soul–entity's manifesting in a material plane." (2271–1) The philosophy laid out in the readings goes so far as to proclaim that we should count it as a gift of a merciful Father that there are opportunities in the present to have this experience despite any hardships or disappointments we may endure. (1709–3) Speaking in a similar vein to another seeker, Cayce delivered a brief pep talk about the importance of the times in which we live while sending the woman on her way to labor in the fields of the Lord. "Be *glad* you have the opportunity to be alive at this time," he counseled, "and to be a part of that preparation for the coming influences of a spiritual nature that *must* rule the world. These are indicated, and these are part of thy experience. Be happy of it, and give thanks daily for it." (2376–3)

Now is the moment to make use of the conditions at work in our lives to satisfy the reason our souls came into the earth: " . . . to manifest to the glory of God and to the honor of self." (3333–1) Our entrance was not by chance; not for fortune, fame, self-indulgence or self-glorification, but to help fulfill " . . . His promises to each soul . . . " and make the world—materially—more and more aware of man's relationship to the Creative Forces. (1957-1) The children of God are here to serve and in so doing amplify the spirit of the Christ within this dimension. That alone constitutes the inner and outer purpose of our lives. And it does not matter where or how we embark upon the task, we must begin it now.

Chapter 19
Your Names Are Writ in Heaven

. . . And each individual has the choice, which no one has the right to super-sede—even God does not!   254-102

In a parable from Matthew's gospel about a vineyard owner and his sons, Jesus directs us to be resolute in choosing whom and what we will serve. The story describes a certain man who has two sons and approaches the first one asking the young man to leave without delay to go work in his vineyard. His son refuses, but a short time later repents the decision and goes. The owner then reaches out to his other son to make the same request. The second son responds by telling his father that he will go into the vineyard, but never does. "Whether of them twain did the will of his father?" Jesus inquires of his disciples who correctly answer it was the first one. The Master ends his story with this statement: "Verily I say unto you, That the publicans and the harlots go into the kingdom of God before you. For John came unto you in the way of righteousness, and ye believed him not: but the publicans and the harlots believed him: and ye, when ye had seen it, repented not afterward, that ye might believe him." (Matt. 21:28–32)

The crux of the Master's lesson was a reproof to the spiritually dishonest and lazy as well as a warning to his students about their obligation to see beyond appearances. It is never enough to pretend to be faithful but do nothing practical to help advance the divine kingdom. The son, who initially refused to go into his father's vineyard, the publicans, and harlots were considered reprobates yet in the end they were the ones who acted on the self-awareness they had gained. Jesus' story confirmed that it is not the roles we play, how devoted we appear to be at first glance, or what we claim with the words escaping from our lips. It is what we **do** that counts.

According to the Cayce material, choosing to answer the Master's call to service satisfies a debt to that which brought the soul into existence in the first place. "Show due consideration as to how much ye owe the world, rather than as to how much the world owes you!" is the injunction from the readings. From their perspective "the world owes every individual *only* an opportunity to express itself and its ideal of the Creative Forces—which will find expression in the manner we treat our fellow men." (2172-1) In a separate instance Cayce makes this terse statement: "Do not worry as to whether you are fat or thin. Worry rather as to whether you use your body, mentally and physically, as an expression of thy ideal." (308-8) The readings also intimate that we cannot afford to be wishy-washy in our efforts. For as the Book of Revelation warns, "I will spue thee out of my mouth," (Rev. 3:16) referencing those people who are neither hot nor cold but only lukewarm in their commitment to the Christ way.

Time spent in this sphere has enormous significance to the progress of the soul, and Edgar Cayce enjoins us to remember that " . . . *every* experience is a conditional one. For, choice must be made daily." (2034-1) Lives are as worlds he explains, each one comprised of the same material out of which the universe is and was created. And certain conditions will enter into every life, which we alone have the power to transform into miracles or crimes. (2497-3) The choice is ours.

Free Will
⤟

Man alone is given that birthright of free will. He alone may defy
his God!   5757-1

The readings contend that until we become as a savior to help some
soul that has lost hope or lost its way, we do not fully comprehend
the God within and without. And the single biggest impediment to
knowing our God aright is the human will. Cayce is adamant about the
unassailable power of man's will. " . . . There is no urge in the astrological, in the vocational, in the hereditary or the environmental which
surpasses the will or determination of the entity. For the entity finds
that it is true there is nothing in heaven or hell that may separate the
entity from the knowledge or from the love of the Creative Force called
God, but self . . . " (5023-2)

Day by day each soul has a choice to make according to the readings. One may lead to happiness and joy while the reverse may result
in disturbances, confusion, evil, and self-condemnation. Their assertion
is that the *will* to go one way or the other is wholly ours. If this were
not the case, we would not be children " . . . of the Creative and Living Force or God that ye are; but as an automaton." (1538-1) Another
especially incisive reading reveals that as we look into the infinity of
space and time realizing there is a force and influence aware of our
needs, we also will detect " . . . that will, that choice given to the souls
of men that they may be used, that they may be one . . . " Ultimately
the decision as to whether or not in our own " . . . feeble, weak ways
. . . " we will agree to serve as instruments of spiritual evolution rests
entirely with us. (1158-14)

In a related passage on the subject, Edgar Cayce observed that as
children of God, " . . . we *can*, as God, say Yea to this, Nay to that . . . ,"
ordering one thing or another in our experience by virtue of the divine
gifts appointed to our keeping. Indeed that which women and men
freely choose to do with the manifold opportunities presented to them
daily is so salient every thought, word, and deed has been catalogued in
a universal record. The Cayce material reveals a strange but significant
fact about the enduring nature of our lives and decisions in noting that

" . . . as we have moved through the realms of His kingdom, we have left our mark upon same." (1567-2) Likewise, in discussing the source of the information his unconscious mind was able to tap into, the sleeping Cayce once remarked that "in giving these descriptions, these are as those that made impressions—as it were—upon the skein of time and space . . . " (540-4) or " . . . upon the Akashic records—as sometimes termed . . . " (2791-1) Later he would personally confirm the existence of these soul histories in a statement recounted in his memoirs: "Don't think that your life isn't being written in the Book of Life. I found it! I have seen it! It is being written. *You* are the writer!"[45]

While the priceless gift of free will engenders unfathomable benefits, it also imposes enormous amounts of responsibility. We have work to do. Countless numbers around the globe await the return of the Master, vividly imagining the Second Coming when Jesus will re-appear riding in on a big white cloud to finish what he started. But the Son of Man had made it clear that the work he had left undone was ours to do. He was counting on those who had heard his words to freely and enthusiastically choose to help build his new kingdom in the earth. And though like little children waiting for Santa Claus to climb down the chimney, we may hope and expect someone else to show up and take responsibility for the state of our world; that was never the plan. "Ye are the salt of the earth," the Master had informed his disciples, "but if the salt have lost his savour, wherewith shall it be salted? it is thenceforth good for nothing, but to be cast out, and to be trodden under foot of men." (Matt. 5:13) The spirit of the Christ has seasoned us, and it is our duty to add the salt of truth to a world hungry for spiritual meat. Jesus' analogy directs us to take whatever we have in hand and start using it now. Because stockpiling truth and doing nothing with it will make our gifts lose their potency—until life becomes utterly unpalatable.

The Cayce readings endorse the Master's perspective, asserting that "all knowledge is to be used in the manner that will give help and assistance to others, and the desire is that the laws of the Creator be manifested in the physical world . . . " (254-17) But such a directive is meaningless if the followers of the Christ way decide to wallow in a

---

[45]A. Robert Smith, *The Lost Memoirs of Edgar Cayce* (Virginia Beach, VA: A.R.E. Press, 1997), 229.

slough of inadequacy, professing themselves too weak or small to heed the divine command to become transformed and serve. The human will is like a muscle; it must be exercised or it will waste away.

Eleventh Hour
ᘓᴁᗐ

Study that thou sayest, that thou doest, and reserve *nothing*—in strength of body or mind—in service to others, *that is* a reflection of that He would have thee do, as thou knowest how . . . 262-12

For centuries one of the most baffling parables in the Bible has puzzled readers across the spectrum. In his sermon Jesus tells the story of a group of laborers who at the end of a very long workday are confounded by the wages they receive. "The kingdom of heaven is like unto a man that is an householder, which went out early in the morning to hire labourers into his vineyard," commences the Master. After the vineyard owner chances upon several men for hire and agrees to pay them a penny for the day, they head over to his vineyard to start working. A few hours later when the householder is in the marketplace he sees several more laborers standing idle and tells them to go into his vineyard too, promising "whatsoever is right I will give you. And they went their way." The landowner subsequently goes out near the sixth and ninth hours and does the same thing. Finally, at approximately the eleventh hour he discovers still more unoccupied workers, and asks, "Why stand ye here all the day idle?" When they reply it was because no one had hired them, the man says, "Go ye also into the vineyard; and whatsoever is right, that shall ye receive." (Matt. 20:1-7)

When evening comes, the lord of the vineyard asks his steward to call together all the laborers and pay them starting from the last hired to the first. The workers who began at the eleventh hour each receive a penny. But when the laborers hired in the morning approach the steward to collect their pay, expecting more money for having worked an entire day, they each also receive a penny. This affront causes them to murmur "against the goodman of the house, saying, These last have wrought but one hour, and thou hast made them equal unto us, which have borne the burden and heat of the day." The owner responds to one of the disgruntled workers with this statement, "Friend, I do thee no wrong: didst not thou agree with me for a penny?" He tells the worker to take what is his and go his way for it is the master's prerogative to give to the last as much as he has given to those who were with him from the beginning. "Is it not lawful for me to do what I will with mine own?" he asks. "Is thine eye evil, because I am good? So the last shall be first, and the first last: for many be called, but few chosen." (Matt. 20:8–16)

With his parable Jesus was asking his students to perceive life from a higher vantage point than their normal narrow views of what constituted fairness. "Judge not according to the appearance, but judge righteous judgment," (John 7:24) he had instructed them in the Gospel of John in calling attention to the fact that God's ways are of an entirely different order than the methods employed by man. The divine promise to each soul is the same no matter when it accepts the invitation to leave spiritual inertia behind and start toiling in the vineyards of the Lord. Those who answered the call to service in the beginning and have labored mightily for the entire day are due their just recompense. In the divine domain, however, the laborers who started early—be it a single moment or many centuries prior as mortals count time—are due no more than those who came to the harvest late. The lord of the heavenly vineyard makes no distinction among his workers by offering one more than the other. Nor does he fault the "latecomers" who waited patiently for someone to engage them but were overlooked and thus lacked the opportunity to enter into the holy estate until the final hour. A worker delayed deserves no less than what has been pledged to all.

Many Are Called
ۅ

> For, we are joint heirs with that universal force we call God—if we seek to do His biddings.   5755-2

Only the spiritual egoist believes he or she is the one who began toiling at daybreak when in truth most of us have stood idly by for eons, showing up only at the last minute to finally get to work. And during all the lost days and years while we procrastinated, the pure of heart had been in the fields since first light humbly laboring under a sweltering sun. Jesus was wrapping a potent message about spiritual pride around his parable of the dayworkers by denouncing the narcissists who believe they are doing more to help build the spiritual kingdom because they comply with human ideas about what constitutes holiness.

Just as the laborers initially hired felt more deserving than those who had entered the vineyard at the eleventh hour, so, too, do these self-serving moralists feel superior to the people who do not embrace their particular brand of religiosity. Pride causes them to piously dismiss the nonbelievers as laggards unsuitable for a place among the spiritually elite and wholly unworthy of an equal portion of the divine reward. In their puffed-up estimation the apostate who comes late or, even worse, never arrives at their way of thinking or the "sinner" who fails to appear inside the church, synagogue, or mosque, has not earned the right to enjoy the benefits and special corner of heaven promised to the upright. But Jesus took the opposite view. He never exalted lifelong devotion to man-made systems and institutions but was concerned about the state of the heart. The Master understood that every sincere effort to help gather in the Father's spiritual harvest would be counted as righteousness.

Despite Jesus' clear rejection of the conventional beliefs about divine justice, it is probably safe to say a majority of religious believers today still harbor grave doubts that their particular God is going to end up treating everyone the same. Since most spiritual traditions profess only a favored few, usually those church members who usher the "unsaved" to the altar of its belief system, will be rewarded with heaven. The portrait Jesus painted of a Father who loved all of his children equally contrasted sharply with the traditional image of a self-absorbed deity who valued one soul over another. The Master recognized each individual as divinely appointed to contribute something to the whole and receive precisely what had been promised to all: God awareness. Further, the rabbi's story ends with a robust warning to his students about forming opinions as to the reward or punishment their neighbor deserves. The Cayce readings concur, decreeing that we have no right to condemn ourselves or judge others in terms of their work or progress along the spiritual path. " . . . Each soul has a mission in the earth, and is in expression a manifestation of the thought of God, of the First Cause . . . ," they proclaim. " . . . Thus all stand upon an equal basis before Him." (2683-1)

Do not grow faint in well doing is the summons from Edgar Cayce. Just keep at it. " . . . For in the knowledge that there is a mission—yea, that a star hath risen for thee—*work, diligently!* in spirit, in mind, in body! . . . " (2533-7) he urges. In the divine computation it does not matter how long we have tarried before answering the call to contribute our talents or what type of activity we undertake to express a spiritual ideal. Those who have stepped up to help are first in the eyes of God. Many are called but few chosen because only a small number will genuinely give their all without seeking personal gain but to fulfill His purposes. The readings press home the point that our every thought and act either " . . . adds to the bringing about of His Kingdom in the earth, or adds to that which prevents it from becoming manifest in this material plane . . . " (911-6) So we must " . . . work like thunder! . . . " (99-7) And as we begin to take up our life's mission, they offer this simple prayer—

> *Have thine own way, Lord. I give praise and glory to thee for that thou has done in my body, my mind. My soul is in thy keeping. Guide thou me in every way that I should go. And let me ever be, Father, joyous and glad in the service that I may render to my fellow man.* 272-8

Take My Yoke

Take my yoke upon you, and learn of me; for I am meek and lowly in heart: and ye shall find rest unto your souls. For my yoke is easy, and my burden is light. Matt. 11:29-30

The Cayce readings magnify the principles the Master taught by offering any number of very specific, eminently practical ideas about how the adherents of the Christ way will function in this world. First, they stay busy. "Ever be a worker, as the bee . . . ," advocates Cayce, " . . . but in that way in which it is ever a contribution to making thy portion of the earth a more beautiful place for men to live in." (3374-1) His guidance is to expend one's abilities whether in body, purse, mind, or spirit to help heal the disturbing conditions which arise among groups and individuals. (1662-2) Calm and steadfast, we must attempt with all our might to do " . . . what thy hand finds to do today . . . "(254-71) using whatever means is at our disposal because whether we realize it or not the " . . . *ground* whereon thou standest is holy! . . . " (262-13) The readings continually urge us to keep pushing forward, realizing that this instant we are " . . . the very representative{s} in flesh of Him . . . Not in the future, not of the past! For in the eternal *now* is He *active* in thee." (683-2)

The key to success, however, is maintaining a sense of balance. Cayce insists that " . . . He that contributes only to his own welfare soon finds little to work for. He that contributes only to the welfare of others soon finds too much of others . . . ." (3478-2) Regrettably, this kind of imbalance signifies the surest way to lose appreciation for ourselves and our ideals. Do not overdo or waste your strength is the recommendation from the readings rather budget " . . . the time for work, for recreation, for enlightenment in all its phases . . . " (2012-1) In similar fashion, they offer this solid piece of advice: "Keep self, then, well balanced. Budget thy time more . . . For he that makes material gains at the expense of home or of opportunities and obligations with his own family does so to his own undoing." (1901-1)

As we take up our work day by day to fulfill our life's purpose, the prescription is to approach each project or activity with a spirit of cooperation. In reading after reading Cayce stressed the theme of cooperation because maintaining a collaborative attitude is the truest reflection of Oneness and tends to bring out the best from everyone involved. The readings define the concept of becoming a channel for Spirit as cooperation and call serving as a blessing to the world " . . . cooperation in action . . . " Individuals representing different states of consciousness regularly will enter our lives and when they do, we are supposed to meet them where they are and " . . . *lift* up, look up—and *this* is cooperation." (262-3)

To that end Cayce urges us to always look beyond the façade in dealing with our brothers and sisters to recognize the pure and good dwelling inside everyone. His view is that " . . . until ye are able to see within the life and activities of those ye have come to hate the most, *something* ye would worship in thy Creator, ye haven't begun to think straight." (1776-1) Rather than arrogantly standing back trying to appraise the state of someone else's spiritual progress, the readings beckon us to " . . . judge not as to this or that activity of another; rather pray that the light may shine even in *their* lives as it *has* in thine . . . " (2112-1) The universal law governing this frame of mind is both fixed and just: As we forgive, we are forgiven and as we condemn others, we ourselves are condemned. " . . . Thus in patience condemn not, neither find fault; not condoning, not agreeing, but let thine own life so shine that others, seeing thy patience, knowing thy understanding, comprehending thy peace, may take hope . . . " (3459-1) Otherwise as Jesus once cautioned his disciples, we are like the blind leading the blind who both fall into the ditch. (Luke 6:38-39)

As the children of God move out into the world holding high the light, they will temper their egos and remember every soul has the right to walk its own path and advance according to the pace it has chosen. God does not compel anyone to return home who is not ready. Those who serve as guides and companions along the sacred journey back to the Father's house must remain mindful that it is not up to them to hound the stragglers, demanding others conform to their idea of how things should proceed. A good shepherd gently moves his flock forward and does not resort to anger or violence to frighten the sheep into submission. The readings also include a stern warning against trying to subdue other people by quashing the hallowed gift of free will. "Then—in correcting the entity—*do not* ever break the entity's will! . . . " they command. The directive is to reason with our siblings and resist the temptation to pressure anyone into yielding to our point of view. " . . . For the mental ability and aspects will incline to make the entity become stubborn, if there is the attempt to force or to cause the entity to act in any direction or manner 'just because.' Tell {*the person*} why! . . . " (2308-1)

Carefully tracking the markers left behind by the Master, we will speak kindly and gently to those who falter because no one really knows the temptations they face or how much they have understood. " . . . Smile upon those that are downhearted and sad; lift the load from those that find theirs too heavy to bear . . . ," the readings instruct. (272-8) Similarly, Cayce explains that if we hold grudges or rail against people who neglect, mistreat, or take advantage of us, we are creating poisons within our own systems. " . . . But if ye do not rail on them, it turns upon *them*! . . . " (1311-1) he insists. The readings beseech us never to act in any manner that might lead to regret. " . . . Let the moves and the discourteousness, the unkindness, all come from the other . . .," they advise, for " . . . it is better to be abased . . . and have the peace within!" Irrespective of what anyone else says or does, if we continually act in the manner we wish to be acted upon, " . . . the peace that has been promised . . . " is certain to be ours. (1183-3)

Karma Unveiled

> If the experiences are ever used for self-indulgence, self-aggran-
> dizement, self-exaltation, each entity does so to its own undoing,
> or creates for self that as has been termed or called karma—and
> must be met . . .   1224-1

Jesus' instructions about giving of ourselves and getting back did not represent the old way of the Mosaic law with its code of justice invoking an "eye for an eye and a tooth for a tooth." (Matt. 5:37-39) He was insti-tuting a new covenant between God and man in which compassion and for-"give"-ness reigned supreme. The redeemer had come to liberate the world from its entrapment in matter and worshipful subjugation to the vengeful God human beings had created for themselves—an almighty being who presided over his wanton children with an iron fist and showed his displeasure by punishing anyone who deviated from the law. Instead the Master had drawn a fundamentally different picture of a deity whom he identified as a tender parent forever concerned about the welfare of its offspring. The Son of Man had come to refute the time-honored systems religious believers had embraced for thousands of years by introducing a new paradigm: the law of grace. This law, the law of the Christ, nullified the need for karmic retribution.

Prior to Jesus' canon of love arriving on the scene, justice meant get-ting even and the unyielding force known as karma, that great equaliz-ing principle in the game of life, left little room for mercy. Mystics across the ages had claimed it impossible to escape the long arm of karmic law, which hounded human beings during the inexorable cycles of birth and death on the eternal wheel of life. Under karma, whether a situation had occurred millennia ago or just this morning, every action was added to a universal account. And sooner or later we were fated to settle those obligations by paying the very personal price of experiencing a situation equal in intensity and outcome to the precipitating event. Only then did the scales of justice move back into balance again. It was as if the effect of any decision, good or bad, was suspended in the cosmos somewhere until like a boomerang it could return to reward or punish the unsuspecting actor. Even the more spiritually advanced among us dreaded the repercussions of karmic law, too often disregarding their own positive deeds but fully expecting to reap harsh penalties for any missteps or transgressions along the way.

Endless Mercy
ᴐℛ

From what may *anyone* be saved? Only from themselves! That is, their individual hell; they dig it with their own desires!   262-40

By discarding the onerous eye-for-an-eye ethic embraced by the ancient Israelites and ignoring the reverberations of an impersonal karmic law, Jesus was shining a light into the dark recesses of the prison, which held human beings hostage to the idea of supernatural judgment and retaliation. Once again he was laying the ax at the root of the tree. Under the Christ covenant whatever so-called debt souls had accumulated through faulty choices in the past—the karma they owed—already was forgiven because those failings counted as nothing when calculated against the magnitude of divine grace. From now on men and women could drop the heavy burden of condemnation and fear of everlasting punishment weighing them down like a millstone around their necks, because no matter how heavy the misdeed on one side of the universal scale, it was counterbalanced by an infinite measure of love and compassion on the other.

Yet despite the explicit message the Master conveyed more than 2,100 years ago, a majority of religious practitioners today still hold fast to the notion that sinners deserve a comeuppance. They keep a close watch for the black clouds of divine reckoning to gather in the skies, signaling the wrath of God ready to rain down on the heads of poor mortals. Yet Jesus' teaching was a reminder that even when the sun is not visible behind the leaden clouds, it has never stopped radiating light and warmth. Limitless mercy and hope meant that whatever happens on this plane was not some massive celestial payback by an egocentric, spiteful deity intent on reprimanding his children. The Master gave no shrift to the idea that any force outside of ourselves—even God—was dealing the cards in a crooked game of chance the universe had forced human beings to play. He placed the onus for the experience on earth squarely on our shoulders. We alone sentenced ourselves to punishing circumstances, because karma is consciousness and we alone are the undisputed sovereigns of that domain.

As You Sow . . .

> And to find that ye only lived, died and were buried under the cherry tree in Grandmother's garden does not make thee one whit better neighbor, citizen, mother or father! But to know that ye spoke unkindly and suffered for it, and in the present may correct it by being righteous—*that* is worthwhile!   5753-2

Infusing more nuance into the general understanding of karma are the Edgar Cayce readings, which refer to it as a kind of memory. And so it is. Karma comprises the sum total of all the mental constructs sewn into the fabric of consciousness during repeated incarnations of the soul. Cayce calls karma " . . . caring for those influences in the experience that satisfy or gratify self without thought of the effect upon that which it has in its own relation to the first cause! . . . " (5753-1) Because each entity is a part of the universal whole, he posits that all knowledge and understanding that have been a part of our consciousness will of necessity be part of our experience. And the manner in which any given situation unfolds in the present is what allows us to become aware of the various experiences through which " . . . either in body or in mind—{we have} passed in a consciousness." (2823-1) Time and space comprise the platform on which these "karmic" scenarios play out.

For instance, concocting the idea of "never enough" and clinging to that thought form lifetime after lifetime puts insatiable greed into the driver's seat of life. And if the overwhelming desire to acquire more leads us to rob or cheat others, then in addition to greed, thievery has permeated our consciousness and dishonesty of one sort or another must accompany us wherever we go. Taking up residence like an unwelcome houseguest, deceit will refuse to leave until we see through the lie that misappropriating property is the method by which to achieve supply—by recognizing our fundamental unity with the Source of the created universe. Similarly if we disdain our brother and pick up a knife to kill him, denying the truth of our Oneness with that divine sibling, hate and murder now belong to us. And in an, as yet, unknown place and future time the bloodshed we have generated and now "own" is bound to reappear by manifesting externally to wake us up to the blind spot. On the other hand, those who reconnect with their Source and use this lifetime to overcome attitudes of cruelty and selfishness, filling consciousness with the fruits of the spirit in everything they say and do, not only gain much spiritually but also realize a peace passing all understanding. So-called karmic debts are paid in full and every jot of recrimination vanishes like a specter evaporating into thin air.

The readings maintain that if we allow our relationships with individuals to " . . . produce a hardening of the heart, or of a determination to get even . . . ," by holding onto discontent, malice, or other pernicious emotions, " . . . these must surely bring the destructive forces . . . " (1234–1) As surely as night follows day, we are building that which we inevitably must meet by whatever we cling to in consciousness. Cayce claims that thoughts are things " . . . as physical as sticking a pin in the hand!" (386–2), and what we construct within the mental forces of the body is as active in our experience as if it were an actual material deed. " . . . For, as was given, 'It hath been said, an eye for an eye, a tooth for a tooth; yet I say unto thee, he that hateth his brother is worse than he that *destroyeth* a body', . . . " (1234–1) the readings assert, harking back to the words of the Master.

And when someone asked Edgar Cayce if we were sentenced by our actions to be punished with fire and brimstone, his response once again placed the burden on us. " . . . For, each soul is a portion of creation—and builds that in a portion of its experience that it, through its physical-mental or spiritual-mental, has builded for itself . . . "(281–16) In other words, heaven or hell is what the soul is choosing to construct for itself. God is not mocked, Cayce reiterates before observing that whatever a soul sows, it must someday, somewhere reap. Then he goes on to express a concept offering endless hope to the human race. Throughout the periods of our many sojourns in the earth, we often have defied the living God, " . . . and yet He hath loved thee and hath again given thee an opportunity, here, now, today, if ye hear His voice . . . " (3660-1)

Keys to Heaven
☞

The rudimentary nature of consciousness is the esoteric principle Jesus was imparting to his disciples when he granted them the keys to the kingdom of heaven. "And I will give unto thee the keys of the kingdom of heaven: and whatsoever thou shalt bind on earth shall be bound in heaven: and whatsoever thou shalt loose on earth shall be loosed in heaven," the Master had pronounced in the Gospel of Matthew. (Matt. 16:18-19) That which lives in consciousness either binds human beings to limitation and pain or sets them free because consciousness is the agent by which the children of God shape what occurs within the sacred realm of this planet. Whatever men and women hold onto—where they place the treasure and attention of their hearts—is ordained to take form in the time-bound sphere we inhabit. Like begets like, and in manifesting the holy energy that lies within in the without, we have the innate capacity to reopen the gates to paradise.

At the same time and notwithstanding the unyielding nature of consciousness, those who walk the spiritual path must never be afraid to utilize free will and take action due to some misplaced concern about making a mistake. Whenever we clear space for the living waters of the Christ to pour through us by giving of ourselves to others—as we open out a way for the imprisoned splendor of our divinity to escape—the floodgates fling wide for everyone. And that mighty current of love washes away the residue of old destructive habits and patterns while expunging any taint of regret. In the divine kingdom the scales of righteousness are perfectly in balance when the inflow of spirit is equal to the outflow of love and compassion one soul bestows upon another. When getting and giving are in parity, the false sense of duality and "otherness" has disappeared and we recognize God as one.

Chapter 20
Mystical Christ

. . . Know, it isn't all of life to live, nor yet all of death to die. Life is creative, and is the manifestation of that Energy, that oneness, which may never be *wholly* discerned or discovered in materiality—and yet is the basis of all motivative forces and influences in the experiences of an individual.   2012-1

One day while Jesus was teaching, some Pharisees and Sadducees approached the rabbi and hoping to tempt him into saying something they could use against him, asked for a sign from heaven. The Master's reply was not what the learned men expected. "When it is evening, ye say, It will be fair weather: for the sky is red. And in the morning, It will be foul weather to day: for the sky is red and lowering," he observed. "O ye hypocrites, ye can discern the face of the sky;

but can ye not discern the signs of the times?" God was present among them and they did not recognize it. The rabbi followed up by noting that only a wicked, adulterous generation seeks a sign. Yet no other sign would be given them but the sign of the prophet Jonah who had emerged from the belly of a fish—the spirit of the Christ released from its entombment in the darkness of a material world. (Matt. 16:1–4)

Jesus had communicated the same message following the miracle of the loaves and fishes after the disciples had gone searching for their teacher and found him on the other side of the sea. Approaching the Master they asked, "Rabbi, when camest thou hither?" and he straight-forwardly replied, "Verily, verily, I say unto you, Ye seek me, not because ye saw the miracles, but because ye did eat of the loaves, and were filled." Then he reminded them not to labor for the meat that perishes but for that meat, which is real and will endure forever. The group persisted, however, probably still hoping to learn the trick of multiplying bread. "What shall we do, that we might work the works of God?" they inquired. Jesus answered, "This is the work of God, that ye believe on him whom he hath sent." (John 6:25–29)

His skeptical apostles must have regarded the whole notion as much too simple, so just like the Pharisees and Sadducees they requested a sign. "What sign shewest thou then, that we may see, and believe thee? what dost thou work?" they asked, before observing that their ancestors had eaten manna in the desert and adding a quote from the holy books: "He gave them bread from heaven to eat." Manna from heaven was something magical and real, actual third-dimensional proof of God's deliverance to his people. But the Master's reaction pointedly moved the issue away from the idea of manifesting a physical substance toward the underlying esoteric truth he was trying to convey. "Moses gave you not that bread from heaven; but my Father giveth you the true bread from heaven. For the bread of God is he which cometh down from heaven, and giveth life unto the world." And when his students beseeched him to supply them with the bread he had described forever, Jesus offered this enigmatic response. "I am the bread of life," he declared. "He that cometh to me shall never hunger; and he that believeth on me shall never thirst." (John 6:30-35) He was speaking of the spirit of the Christ—omnipresent and available to the human race now.

During his tenure on earth, the Master's elevated state of consciousness had been the catalyst for healing, feeding the multitudes, and even raising people from the dead. Yet those miracles were only the means to a greater end: understanding God as Spirit. Since the people Jesus had fed as they sat on the hillsides were bound to become hungry again, and the sick whose afflictions had disappeared would no doubt die someday, passing on from the physical sense of life to a consciousness of other realms and dimensions.

Trying to define what is holy by the performance of signs and wonders or venerating God because of the tangible benefits a deity may bestow is to ascribe a limited material character to the omnipotent, formless being undergirding the universe. Even the most astounding miracles are pale reflections of the true nature of this immanent energetic force, which cannot be perceived with the human eye. Thus when the seventy returned and joyfully announced to their teacher that "even the devils are subject unto us through thy name," the Master's blunt response was, "rejoice not, that the spirits are subject unto you; but rather rejoice, because your names are written in heaven." (Luke 10:17, 20) He had not dispatched his envoys to produce marvels and impress an audience but to carry their God lights into the world.

"For many shall come in my name, saying, I am Christ; and shall deceive many," (Mark 24:5) Jesus had warned his followers, referring to those prone to grandstanding or flamboyantly making a show of their holiness by manipulating matter. This is why when a woman in the crowd cried, "Blessed is the womb that bare thee, and the paps which thou hast sucked," he answered, "Yea rather, blessed are they that hear the word of God, and keep it." (Luke 11:27–28) The Master repeatedly had told the throngs of people who witnessed his work and sought to worship him as a God that he made no claims to divinity for himself. The man called Jesus was only a man. The invisible, Creative Forces alive within and around him—the Christ spirit—was the source of his life and activity.

Infinite Source
೭๏෨

... All force, all power, comes from the same source ...   262-3

Unmanifested, unseen forces pervade this universe, testifying to the
Oneness of all reality. As a fish immersed in a limitless ocean neither ap-
preciates nor understands the water enveloping it, so do we exist within
the all-pervading embrace of infinite Spirit. One cogent reading neatly
summed up the idea with this declaration: "Know, all time is one—as is
space, as is patience . . . " (2012-1) "For in him we live, and move, and
have our being," (Acts 17:28) voiced the biblical text in an attempt to
translate the idea of a divine presence interpenetrating and upholding
the created world. Pondering the truth of omnipresent Oneness, the
prophet Jeremiah had declared, "Can any hide himself in secret places
that I shall not see him? saith the Lord. Do not I fill heaven and earth?
saith the Lord." (Jer. 23:24) In the same way a psalmist reflecting on the
subject in the Old Testament verbalized his understanding in the lyrical
words of a poem. "Whither shall I go from thy spirit? or whither shall
I flee from thy presence? If I ascend up into heaven, thou art there: if I
make my bed in hell, behold, thou art there. If I take the wings of the
morning, and dwell in the uttermost parts of the sea; Even there shall
thy hand lead me, and thy right hand shall hold me." (Psalm 139:7-10)

Edgar Cayce's answer to the question "What *is* Life?" was "a manifestation of the first cause—God!" (5753-1) And as such it is infinite and
continuous. According to the readings, the power sparking the cosmos
is an ever-present, eternal reality—a transcendental energy, which
cannot disappear but merely becomes transformed to assume different shapes and guises. " . . . For, life is of the Creator—and it may only
be changed," states Cayce. "It *cannot* be ended or destroyed. It can *only*
return from whence it came . . . " (497-1) He goes on to explain that " . . .
because an atom, a matter, a form, is changed does not mean that the
essence, the source or the spirit of it has changed—only in its form of
manifestation, and *not* in its relation with the first cause . . . " (5753-1)

The causative principle of the universe, including man's true being,
consists of a single essence: Spirit. And " . . . What is the spirit? . . . "
Cayce asks. " . . . The *manifestation of god*! . . . "(262-83) He calls this " . . .
all-wise, all-inclusive, all-manifesting force in the experience of man
. . . " (262-57) the Creative Force, which at this moment is working in,
with and upon " . . . the awareness, the interconsciousness of the *body*,
the mind, the spirit, as separated in individuals! . . . " (262-83) A kindred
remark mentions that for the most part we tend to look upon Spirit

as just a term, rather than actually allowing ourselves to experience it. " . . . Yet," the readings contend, "we use it, we manifest it, we are a part of it . . . " (262–119) Cayce further suggests that as "one sees the infinite in the *Christ* life, one sees infinity in man's life" (1158–14) since every soul is no less than a hologram of the divine.

Spirit Is the Life
_ↅ

And ye shall know the truth, and the truth shall make you free.
John 8:32

The approach taken by the Cayce readings defines Spirit as the " . . . impelling influence of infinity, or the one creative source, force, that is manifest." (5749–3) Under that rubric we learn that Spirit is life; mind is the builder; and the physical is the result. (349–4) Or to put this radical alteration of our perception of reality another way: Spirit is the motivating force whose expression is in the physical, and it constructs or forms through the activity of thought. " . . . The mind is not the spirit," Cayce explains, "it is a companion to the spirit; it builds a pattern . . . " (2533–6)

One's conscious awareness of this undeviating divine presence infusing the cosmos—the alpha and omega—is the Holy Ghost or Comforter that Jesus promised would teach us and bring all things to our remembrance when he said, "And I will pray the Father, and he shall give you another Comforter, that he may abide with you for ever." (John 14:16) In Cayce's view this statement of the Master's refers to the revival or renewal of the soul's abilities " . . . to take hold upon the witnesses of the life itself! And what is life? God!" (281–33) God as life is the core supposition behind Jesus' proclamation that "whosoever shall speak a word against the Son of man, it shall be forgiven him: but unto him that blasphemeth against the Holy Ghost it shall not be forgiven." (Luke 12:10) Since the Holy Ghost is the illimitable spirit of God out of which we are made and within which we subsist, there exists no "other" to forgive us for defaming the very nature and essence of our own beings. We are born of and reside within an uninterrupted stream of spiritual energy, boundlessly creative and relentlessly advancing toward the light.

The Lord Is One
༼ა

Correlate not the differences, but where all religions meet—*There
is one god!* "Know, O Israel, the Lord thy God is *one!*"   991-1

A brief incident in the Gospel of Mark talks about the time Jesus
was walking along the coast between Tyre and Sidon and a Canaanite
woman approached him, crying out, "Have mercy on me, O Lord, thou
son of David; my daughter is grievously vexed with a devil." For a moment the Master says nothing until his disciples beseech him to send
the woman away presumably because she was not a member of their
group. But Jesus' quick rejoinder challenges their way of thinking. "I
am not sent but unto the lost sheep of the house of Israel," he counters.
Falling down to worship the rabbi, the desperate mother pleads, "Lord,
help me" to which he replies that it is not right to take the children's
bread and cast it to the dogs. The woman's immediate response is to
blare out, "Truth, Lord: yet the dogs eat of the crumbs which fall from
their masters' table." Struck by her great faith, the Master remarks, "Be
it unto thee even as thou wilt. And her daughter was made whole from
that very hour." (Matt. 15: 22–28)

This telling incident from the Master's ministry reveals that the Spirit
or God he preached and demonstrated was not something human
beings should try to partition or cut up into little pieces in a vain attempt to personally possess access to the divine. The God of Abraham,
Isaac, and Jacob did not belong solely to the progeny of those ancient
Hebrew prophets. "God is not the God of the dead, but of the living,"
(Matt. 22:32) Jesus had proclaimed and, as such, is available to all who
will spend their lives wholeheartedly searching for it. " . . . Know, ye
seekers of truth, the Lord thy God is One! He is *not* divided, but *one* . . . ,"
echo the Edgar Cayce readings. (1456–1)

The readings go on to explain that although we may be called " . . . this,
that and the other name . . . ," which can cause confusion, " . . . when
ye say Creative Force, God, Jehovah, Yahweh, Abba . . . ," it means one
and the same thing as carried through " . . . the various phases of thine
own consciousness . . . " (262–86) Cayce once made the comment that the
issue of religious divisions began to arise as early as man's advent into

the world. That was when individuals and personalities found expression by " . . . *subduing* the earth, and man—with his natural bent—not only attempted to subdue the *earth*, but to subdue one another . . . " The result was not only differences of opinion but also the disparate sects, sets, classes, and races. (396-8)

Describing religious differences as swords " . . . brought into man's material understanding . . . ," the readings maintain there have been more wars and blood shed over racial and religious differences than any other issue. Yet these, too, " . . . must go the way of all others; and man must learn . . . that God loveth those who love Him, whether they be called of this or that sect or schism or ism or cult! The Lord is *one!*" (3976-27) A second observation sums up the principle beautifully. "How did thy Master work? In the church, in the synagogue, in the field, in the lakes, upon the sands and the mountains, in the temple! And did He defy those? Did He set up anything different? Did He condemn the law even of the Roman, or the Jews, or the Essenes, or the Sadducees, or any of the cults or isms of the day? All, He gave, are as *one*—under the laws! . . . " The readings put us on notice that " . . . grudges, cisms, isms, cults, must become as naught . . . " so that the Christ as manifested in Jesus of Nazareth " . . . may be made known to thy fellow man!" (254-92) This Christ constitutes the prototype for every soul on earth, " . . . whether he be Gentile or Jew, Parthenian or Greek. For all have the pattern, whether they call on that name or not . . . " (3528-1)

One of Edgar Cayce's dreams used the symbol of a field of corn to highlight the reason for the broad array of churches and denominations in the world. His interpretation began by mentioning that "A man finds in nature that which is an illustration of himself, and the experience we call Life itself." In considering a field of corn, one recognizes life as present in every grain. The farmer plants the kernel in the soil, works it then reaps his harvest. " . . . Not every man selects the same kind of corn. Not every man ploughs it alike. Not every man sows it alike. Not every man reaps it alike. Yet in each case it brings forth the very best that there is . . . " Cayce then proceeds to say it is the God or Life found within each grain the man is seeking both to sustain his body and produce enough seed to raise more. "That's religion. That's the denominations." (1089-3, Report #3)

No two approaches to the divine are exactly alike, even among the vast conglomeration of sects designated as Christian. The readings infer that this hodgepodge of spiritual paths begins to make more sense when viewed from the angle of the soul's panoramic history and unique set of experiences. " . . . For not all peoples walked in the field when the wheat was ripe. Neither did all stand at the tomb when Lazarus was called forth. Neither were they all present when He walked on the water, nor when He fed the five thousand, nor when He hung on the Cross. Yet each experience answered, and does answer to something within each individual soul-entity . . . " From the Cayce perspective each soul comprises a corpuscle in the body of God and when disagreements arise causing those corpuscles to be at variance with the common purpose for that body, sin enters the picture. It surfaces in groups and organizations " . . . stressing differences rather than the coordinating channels through which all may come to the knowledge of God." (3395-2)

For some, the pain they endured at the hands of corrupt and domineering spiritual leaders or the helplessness they felt in being forced to follow the artificial rules and joyless dogma of a heavy-handed denomination has engendered a deep sense of mistrust or even revulsion for religion. "No wonder, then, that these have a peculiar feeling for the entity . . . ," Cayce told one Jewish rabbi who felt there must be " . . . those things mightier than the walls which bespeak of the efforts of man . . . " in building his paltry monuments to God. Because in reality it is as the lowly Nazarene taught, " . . . Not in this mountain, nor in this city; rather in the hearts of men, should the God of Israel be worshipped . . . " The Almighty does not require priests, doctrines, ceremonies, silver, or gold but simply the sacrifice " . . . that ye be just and patient and longsuffering with thy fellow man . . . " The readings define these as the qualities which bespeak the words of Jehovah rather than our submitting to some kind of indoctrination or following this or that rule. " . . . For who is the law? He that loveth mercy and justice, or he that ruleth in the thunder or in the might? *God* is a God of Love!" (991-1)

Later on in the same reading when the man asked if he ought to keep working as a rabbi or go into business, Edgar Cayce counseled him to remain in his spiritual work but as a rabbi in the truest sense of that word. " . . . That is—a teacher, a minister. *Not* as bound by creeds! Not as bound by modes! Not as bound by any law!" (991-1) His recommendation was to work as a teacher and lecturer who could " ... *coordinate* the teachings, the philosophies of the east and the west, the oriental and the occidental, the new truths and the old. For, as the sage of old gave, 'There is nothing new under the sun . . . '" (991-1) The subtext running throughout the Cayce material is first to know oneself, then to associate with those groups and activities, which answer most closely to what cries out from within us, always remembering, " ... Not as a schism, not as a cult, not as an ism; but He is *one* God, and thus He is no respecter of persons . . . " (2787-1)

Full Circle

Q. Where does the soul go when fully developed?
A. To its Maker.   3744-5

The philosophy espoused in the readings insists that life in all its expressions is one and each soul or entity returns, or cycles, just as nature does in its variegated manifestations. " . . . Thus leaving, making or presenting—as it were—those infallible, indelible truths that it—Life—is continuous . . . ," states Cayce. (938-1) He compares the idea to the sun shedding light and heat on the children of God and in the process becoming part of the " . . . composition of which man is made, or of that termed the earth . . . " We easily recognize elements of the sun's influence in a variety of forms: solid matter, liquid and vapor. Yet " . . . all are one in their various stages of consciousness . . . ," (5757-1) affirm the readings. This is the basic tenet underlying the process of reincarnation.

"All souls were created in the beginning," Cayce declares, "and are finding their way back to whence they came." (3744-5) "Each soul was, is, and is to be a companion with that creative influence or force called God. Thus each entity is a child of God, and is a part of that whole." (2533-1) And while there may be a few short years in this or that experience, these, too, are one and serve as the means by which the soul or inner self is purified by being lifted up, " . . . that it may be one with that first cause, that first purpose for its coming into existence." (938-1) The readings urge us to keep in mind that the earth is that speck or portion of creation where souls projected themselves into matter, thus consciously becoming aware of themselves as " . . . entertaining the ability of creating without those forces of the spirit of truth." Moreover, they refer to humanity's original, woeful choice in Eden as an expression of that serpent, Satan, or power manifested by " . . . entities that, created as the cooperative influence, through will separated themselves." (5755-2)

Viewing the days and years spent here on earth through this wider lens upends the predominant theories about the nature of death as men and women typically have characterized the departure from this world. Cayce teaches us that death like birth is a human construct—merely the second half of a parentheses in a continuous stream of life. And the brief season we term "life" that occurs between the two brackets of the soul's entrance into and exit from this planet, affords it lessons until such time it chooses to rise to the heights of divine glory again. "For I have no pleasure in the death of him that dieth, saith the Lord God: wherefore turn yourselves, and live ye," quotes the prophet Ezekiel. (Ezek. 18: 32)

The oppressive image of death that mortals have embraced since the fall of Adam is powerless to affect the uninterrupted, enduring spiritual reality, which eternally was and will continue to be forever. "Man is like to vanity: his days are as a shadow that passeth away," (Psalm 144:4) pronounced the psalmist in an attempt to portray the fleeting nature of the earthbound existence human beings have identified as the one and only reality. In another astounding revelation while speaking directly to the question of death, Edgar Cayce alleges that no one has to die. " . . . For, as may be told by any pathologist, there is no known reason why any individual entity should not live as long as it desires," he told one seeker. "And there is no death, save in thy consciousness. Because all others have died, ye expect to—and you do! These are a part of thy consciousness, in what? In the mental, in the spiritual—and the physical reacts to same." (2533-6)

Reincarnation
ᠵᡅ

> . . . For each soul grows to the awareness, or to heaven—not go to
> heaven but grow to heaven . . .   3605-1

An intriguing episode in the New Testament recounts the day Jesus and his disciples were en route to the city of Caesarea Philippi when the rabbi asked his disciples, "Whom do men say that I am?" They replied, "John the Baptist; but some say, Elias; and others, One of the prophets." (Mark 8:27-28) His students' observation reflected a standard way of thinking during that era, which presupposed that their teacher could be the reincarnated soul of one of those renowned Jewish prophets and leaders. For the most part, people living in the first century did not consider reincarnation an outlandish proposition but like the cycles of nature evident in field and forest, accepted the belief as a working principle of life. The readings subscribe to the same point of view and draw attention to the innate value of the reincarnating soul within the universal scheme of spiritual evolution. *"The earth is only an atom in the universe of worlds!"* (5749-3) Cayce reminds us, but every soul is a living portion of that whole. Thus it is not by chance that we enter this planetary sphere, " . . . but that the entity—as a part of the whole—may fill that place which no other soul may fill so well . . . " (2533-1)

Because souls originally were created to be companions with the Creator—" . . . a little lower than the angels . . . "(1567-2)—the step-by-step process of achieving soul growth is designed to continue lifetime after lifetime until the realization finally dawns that "I and my Father are one." (John 10:30) Further, since all force or power originates from the same source, the ongoing process of physical manifestation and spiritual elevation deems every soul integral to the greater divine purpose and plan. "Is the oak the lord over the vine?" Cayce asks. "Is the Jimson beset before the tomato? Are the grassy roots ashamed of their flower beside the rose?" The human race is in a position to gain a great lesson from the forces of nature, which exist to satisfy the reason God called them into being. " . . . Each fulfilling their purpose, singing their song, filling the air with their perfume, that they—too—may honor and praise their Creator . . . " just as every individual should do in " . . . their particular sphere—*their* concept of their Maker!" (1391-1)

A fundamental tenet of the Cayce school of thought is that the " . . . soul enters each experience for a lesson, a development." (1089-3) And we will regain the state of paradise forfeited in the beginning through the deliberate choice to separate from our Creator by the conscious efforts made lifetime after lifetime to realign our wills with the will of the One. Until—like the lily or the rose—we, too, become luminous reflections of the divine. As the readings so aptly put it, the purpose for being on earth is to know ourselves to be uniquely ourselves yet one with God. " . . . To be one with Him yet to *know* self to *be* self, I *Am*, in and with the *Great I Am*" states reading 262-86. This is why the soul keeps returning, cycling in and out of the material sphere, because successive rounds of departing, then returning to live out an assortment of experiences in this dimension provide the most effective means for such evolution to occur.

Time and again the readings stress that the movement of the soul through physicality is not by chance but for the fulfillment of what was set in motion when Spirit entered into matter. And as each soul progresses by passing through the different spheres just as our elder brother did, " . . . the sun, the planets, the earth—it develops *towards*—taking all, being a portion of all, *manifesting* all . . . " then carries everything encountered back to the Source from which it came. (413-1) The crucial point to remember is that the process affords each soul the chance to grow in awareness and ultimately reach the elevated state our Master-teacher attained and has promised to all: Christ consciousness. When someone inquired of Edgar Cayce whether this consciousness might be described as " . . . the awareness within each soul, imprinted in pattern on the mind and waiting to be awakened by the will, of the soul's oneness with God . . . ," he unequivocally answered, "Correct. That's the idea exactly!" (5749-14)

How Long, Lord?

> But who is the worthy servant? He that has endured unto the
> end!   5749-5

Life on earth is bound to reflect what individuals have built up through recurring cycles of reincarnation until the day they fully attain or have " . . . completely met all that has been error in the experience of the body, mind and soul in the earth experience." (2533-8) This is the state of awareness the Master Jesus achieved and signifies the manner in which we also may reach the throne of God, defined by the readings as leaving " . . . the carnal forces and be{ing} one in spirit with the Father." (262-29) What becomes of the soul if it fails to improve? Cayce reiterated that this is why it reincarnates, " . . . that it may have the opportunity. Can the will of man continue to defy its Maker?" (826-8) The readings consistently portray the choice to evolve as a critical one with potentially colossal repercussions, proclaiming that " . . . though a soul may be as but a speck upon the earth's environs, and the earth in turn much less than a mote in the universe . . . ," (1469-1) when the spirit of man is so attuned to the Infinite, it impacts the whole of creation.

Another person who sought out Cayce's advice raised a question about the need for someone who dies in childhood to reincarnate. The sleeping prophet's response indicated that the sojourn in *each* experience is necessary for a soul to develop the correct attributes and " . . . become again aware of being in the *presence* of the Father . . . " He then added that those who reincarnate and are conscious even for an instant of the material or carnal influences " . . . may be as *greatly* impressed as were a finite mind for a moment in the presence of Infinity . . . " (262-57) How long was Saul's experience on the road to Damascus? When contemplating the birth of a soul into the earth more often than not it is the physical form or body-mind that is foremost in our thinking. Seldom do we consider the soul itself, which was " . . . full-grown in a breath . . . " according to the readings, for it was the Father (or Infinity) that brought the earth and all the worlds into existence. " . . . How much greater is a day in the house of the Lord—or a moment in His presence, than a thousand years in carnal forces?" the readings ask. "Hence a soul even for a flash, or for a breath, has perhaps experienced even as much as Saul in the way." (262-57)

The experience of the "good thief" who hung on the cross next to Jesus and was blessed by the Master comports with this general theory. The gospel account states that when "one of the malefactors which were hanged railed on him [Jesus], saying, If thou be Christ, save thyself and us," the second criminal rebuked his counterpart. "Dost not thou fear God, seeing thou art in the same condemnation?" he chided. "And we indeed justly; for we receive the due reward of our deeds: but this man hath done nothing amiss." In those few short moments the criminal who spoke up in Jesus' defense had grown in awareness. By taking responsibility for his offenses and complicity in evoking that terrible punishment, the man was able to recognize the purity and innocence of the Christ hanging beside him. "And he said unto Jesus, Lord, remember me when thou comest into thy kingdom. And Jesus said unto him, Verily I say unto thee, Today shalt thou be with me in paradise." (Luke 23:39–43) The willingness of the "good thief" to take an honest look at himself and achieve some self-mastery signified his spiritual progress and readiness to move into a higher state of being.

Jesus' brief interchange with the crucified thief was validation that the way back to heaven begins and ends in consciousness because life is continuous and consciousness never dies. It makes no difference whether we live on one side of the grave or the other; the one thing we carry with us into either place is our consciousness. And even in the midst of the most trying circumstances, whenever a soul chooses to rise in awareness and acknowledge the unblemished presence of the Christ near at hand, it unlocks the doors to paradise.

Immanuel

Then Mind, as He, was the Word—and dwelt among men; and
we beheld Him as the face of the Father.   1567-2

The power of a single thought is so immense and pervasive that it cannot be adequately described in words. And we must, each of us, live out every thought we create, for that is the law. " . . . Thoughts are things," warns Cayce, "and may be miracles or crimes in action . . . " (105-2) Each image emerging from the mind manifests as an effect and therein lies the great mystery of Jesus of Nazareth's secret life. He had laid down his life—every thought and desire spawning a personal story rooted in the third dimension—to live as the full and complete expression of his divinity in the earth.

Balance was the hallmark of the Master's tenancy on this planet. The outer form he manifested was that of the male, but by the time of his thirtieth year he had also become the perfect expression of the fully developed "female" principle—a visible representation of the unseen forces out of which all life emanates. He was, indeed, the new Adam. For the first time since Eden a human being had reclaimed the spiritual androgyny surrendered in paradise.

The Son of Man had demonstrated the importance of integration to the soul, which has a foot in two camps: the interior and exterior worlds. His mastery of this principle is what had enabled him to so effectively combine the active and contemplative life, moving easily from the interior world of Spirit to the sensate world: teaching, meditating, healing, and praying. The long days and weeks of working with multitudes of anxious people, ministering to their mental, spiritual, and physical needs, were relieved only momentarily by the retreat to a solitary spot. Yet again and again, Jesus had wrenched himself away from the peace of that inner realm to face the crowds, the noises, the endless demands.[46] The Adam soul had arrived among us to impart the truth about the unseen God whose wisdom and tenderness were embodied in human beings who could choose to give birth to them in this world. But the way to achieve that end was not a passive one. Our teacher's way did not involve losing the crucial equilibrium between the inner and outer by becoming a recluse and withdrawing to dwell in the bliss of Nirvana. Jesus had discovered the kingdom within, yet always returned to manifest it in visible expression in the world without—laying down his life in service to the God who is One.

Be Ye Perfect
ᴄᴀ⌒

Our elder brother taught an active way of life yet one wholly reliant on the power of faith. Not faith in a man named Jesus but unequivocal trust in the presence and power of illimitable Spirit. "It is the spirit that quickeneth; the flesh profiteth nothing," (John 6:63) Jesus had informed his disciples in the Gospel of John. The Master knew, beyond a shadow of a doubt, that the unseen Creative Forces were real and that he was perpetually upheld by this sacred presence, cradled in the loving arms of the divine.

The deliverer had come to earth to teach us the truth about ourselves and had placed the key to liberation squarely in our hands: God is. And this God lives among us for we are all children of the same divine Father/Mother. Still, many refused to believe and rejected his message

---

[46]Janet Highland, "New Testament" (unpublished manuscript, 1979).

or tried to twist it their own ends. Yet, just as he had predicted, his words about the incorruptible unity of God and man have never died, and the instructions he left behind to guide the lost souls home remain as fresh and new today as when he first articulated them in his parables. "Neither do I condemn thee," (John 8:11) he had said to assure his brothers and sisters that love and mercy reign supreme and nothing would ever sever the bond between them and their Creator. Children who do not recognize the priceless treasure they clutch in their hands are not to be blamed for their naiveté.

For some the idea that they were children of God—divine—was perverted by later generations into a belief that they were children, not divine, just children—a self-image that allowed them to wheedle, cajole, pressure, and petition a heavenly father to do good things for them. The call to be co-creators with God of a better world, a world to which the new kingdom could come, was ignored and the truth about humanity's strength and promise repressed. So they put the man Jesus up on a pedestal and worshipped him, conveniently forgetting what this Master had said about our responsibilities to each other. The message to go out and spread the good news of God-with-us became a tale that once a deity had come to earth to redeem the world, and someday he was going to come again to finish his work and save us. But they waited in vain. It was human beings who were to complete the work Jesus had started. He had shown the way, the pattern to be followed, and had lived his life as an example that what he had preached could be practiced. The proof lay in his work, which is still bearing fruit twenty-one centuries after the fact.[47]

But a remnant understood. They had searched and found the holy fire of the burning bush inside themselves, choosing to carry the flame of their God-selves into the world to cast its light and warmth on all who needed comfort. The true believers did not boast or proselytize but placed themselves wholly into the hands of the divine within, " . . . not attempting, not *trying* to be good, to be kind, to be thoughtful—but just {to} be . . . " (5563-1) And in being that light, uplifted everything they touched. These are the faithful few whose lives give testimony to the power, strength, and beauty of other-dimensional realms—and to

---

[47] Janet Highland, "New Testament" (unpublished manuscript, 1979).

the potency of a spiritual ideal. These are ones who in spite of every obstacle patiently place one foot in front of the other and try to live the Christ way.

Slowly, they change the world.

Bibliography

Print Sources

Cayce, Edgar. *A Search for God, Book I*. Compiled by Study Group #1 of the Association for Research and Enlightenment. Virginia Beach, VA: A.R.E. Press, 1942.

Encyclopedia Judaica, (16 volumes). Jerusalem: Keter Publishing House, 1972.

Hall, Manly P. *An Encyclopedic Outline of Masonic, Hermetic, Quabbalistic and Roscicrucian Symbolical Philosophy*. Los Angeles: Philosophical Research Society, Inc., 1957.

Highland, Janet. "New Testament." Unpublished manuscript, 1979.

Puryear, Meredith. *Healing through Meditation and Prayer*. Virginia Beach, VA: A.R.E. Press, 1978.

Read, Anne. *Edgar Cayce on Jesus and His Church*. Edited by Hugh Lynn Cayce. New York: Warner Books, Inc., 1970.

Schonfield, Hugh, ed. *The Authentic New Testament*. New York: New American Library, 1958.

Smith, A. Robert. *The Lost Memoirs of Edgar Cayce*. Virginia Beach, VA: A.R.E. Press, 1997.

Swami Prabhavananda and Christopher Isherwood, trans. *The Song of God: Bhagavad-Gita*. New York: New American Library, Inc., 1951.

Tolle, Eckhart. *The Power of Now*. Novato, CA: New World Library, 1999.

Web Sources

http://www.biblestudytools.com/dictionary/satan/

A.R.E. PRESS

Edgar Cayce (1877–1945) founded the non-profit Association for Research and Enlightenment (A.R.E.) in 1931, to explore spirituality, holistic health, intuition, dream interpretation, psychic development, reincarnation, and ancient mysteries—all subjects that frequently came up in the more than 14,000 documented psychic readings given by Cayce.

Edgar Cayce's A.R.E. provides individuals from all walks of life and a variety of religious backgrounds with tools for personal transformation and healing at all levels—body, mind, and spirit.

A.R.E. Press has been publishing since 1931 as well, with the mission of furthering the work of A.R.E. by publishing books, DVDs, and CDs to support the organization's goal of helping people to change their lives for the better physically, mentally, and spiritually.

In 2009, A.R.E. Press launched its second imprint, 4th Dimension Press. While A.R.E. Press features topics directly related to the work of Edgar Cayce and often includes excerpts from the Cayce readings, 4th Dimension Press allows us to take our publishing efforts further with like-minded and expansive explorations into the mysteries and spirituality of our existence without direct reference to Cayce specific content.

A.R.E. Press/4th Dimension Press
215 67th Street
Virginia Beach, VA 23451

Learn more at EdgarCayce.org. Visit ARECatalog.com to browse and purchase additional titles.

ARE PRESS.COM

Who Was Edgar Cayce?
Twentieth Century Psychic and Medical Clairvoyant

Edgar Cayce (pronounced Kay-Cee, 1877-1945) has been called the "sleeping prophet," the "father of holistic medicine," and the most-documented psychic of the 20th century. For more than 40 years of his adult life, Cayce gave psychic "readings" to thousands of seekers while in an unconscious state, diagnosing illnesses and revealing lives lived in the past and prophecies yet to come. But who, exactly, was Edgar Cayce?

Cayce was born on a farm in Hopkinsville, Kentucky, in 1877, and his psychic abilities began to appear as early as his childhood. He was able to see and talk to his late grandfather's spirit, and often played with "imaginary friends" whom he said were spirits on the other side. He also displayed an uncanny ability to memorize the pages of a book simply by sleeping on it. These gifts labeled the young Cayce as strange, but all Cayce really wanted was to help others, especially children.

Later in life, Cayce would find that he had the ability to put himself into a sleep-like state by lying down on a couch, closing his eyes, and folding his hands over his stomach. In this state of relaxation and meditation, he was able to place his mind in contact with all time and space—the universal consciousness, also known as the super-conscious mind. From there, he could respond to questions as broad as, "What are the secrets of the universe?" and "What is my purpose in life?" to as specific as, "What can I do to help my arthritis?" and "How were the pyramids of Egypt built?" His responses to these questions came to be called "readings," and their insights offer practical help and advice to individuals even today.

The majority of Edgar Cayce's readings deal with holistic health and the treatment of illness. Yet, although best known for this material, the sleeping Cayce did not seem to be limited to concerns about the physical body. In fact, in their entirety, the readings discuss an astonishing 10,000 different topics. This vast array of subject matter can be narrowed down into a smaller group of topics that, when compiled together, deal with the following five categories: (1) Health-Related Information; (2) Philosophy and Reincarnation; (3) Dreams and Dream Interpretation; (4) ESP and Psychic Phenomena; and (5) Spiritual Growth, Meditation, and Prayer.

Learn more at EdgarCayce.org.

What Is A.R.E.?

Edgar Cayce founded the non-profit Association for Research and Enlightenment (A.R.E.) in 1931, to explore spirituality, holistic health, intuition, dream interpretation, psychic development, reincarnation, and ancient mysteries—all subjects that frequently came up in the more than 14,000 documented psychic readings given by Cayce.

The Mission of the A.R.E. is to help people transform their lives for the better, through research, education, and application of core concepts found in the Edgar Cayce readings and kindred materials that seek to manifest the love of God and all people and promote the purposefulness of life, the oneness of God, the spiritual nature of humankind, and the connection of body, mind, and spirit.

With an international headquarters in Virginia Beach, Va., a regional headquarters in Houston, regional representatives throughout the U.S., Edgar Cayce Centers in more than thirty countries, and individual members in more than seventy countries, the A.R.E. community is a global network of individuals.

A.R.E. conferences, international tours, camps for children and adults, regional activities, and study groups allow like-minded people to gather for educational and fellowship opportunities worldwide.

A.R.E. offers membership benefits and services that include a quarterly body-mind-spirit member magazine, Venture Inward, a member newsletter covering the major topics of the readings, and access to the entire set of readings in an exclusive online database.

Learn more at EdgarCayce.org.

EDGARCAYCE.ORG